ALTERNATING CURRENT

ALSO BY OCTAVIO PAZ

Aguila o Sol: Eagle or Sun
Labyrinth of Solitude: Life and Thought in Mexico
Marcel Duchamp or the Castle of Purity
Selected Poems
Anthology of Mexican Poetry (Editor)

Octavio Paz

Alternating Current

Translated from the Spanish by Helen R. Lane

A Richard Seaver Book

THE VIKING PRESS · NEW YORK

© Siglo XXI Editores, S.A. 1967
English-language translation Copyright © 1973 by The Viking Press, Inc.
All rights reserved
A Richard Seaver Book/The Viking Press
First published in 1973 by The Viking Press, Inc.
625 Madison Avenue, New York, N.Y. 10022
Published simultaneously in Canada by
The Macmillan Company of Canada Limited
SBN 670-11526-6
Library of Congress catalog card number: 72-76796
Printed in U.S.A.

ACKNOWLEDGMENT

New Directions Publishing Corp. and Faber and Faber Limited:
"In a Station of the Metro" by Ezra Pound
from *Personae* (New Directions)
and *Collected Shorter Poems* (Faber and Faber),
Copyright 1926 by Ezra Pound.
Reprinted by permission of
New Directions Publishing Corp.
and Faber and Faber Limited.

Second Printing April 1973

Foreword

The majority of the texts in this book were first published in Hispano-American and French periodicals under the general title *Corriente Alterna*. They date from two periods: 1959 to 1961, and 1965 to March 1967. Rather than presenting these reflections on life in our time in the order in which they were written and published, I have decided to group them in three sections: the first deals with literature and art; the second with certain contemporary subjects (drugs, forms of atheism); the third with ethical and political problems. I hope that the contrapuntal unity of these pieces will be apparent despite their fragmentary nature. I believe the fragment to be the form that best reflects the ever-changing reality that we live and are. The fragment is not so much a seed as a stray atom that can be defined only by situating it relative to other atoms: it is nothing more nor less than a *relation*. This book is a tissue of relations.

—O. P.

Contents

1

2

3

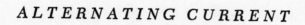

ALTERNATING CURRENT

1

What Does Poetry Name?

Poetry has been likened to mysticism and to eroticism. The similarities between them are obvious; the differences are no less apparent. The first and most important of these differences is the meaning, or rather the object of poetry: what the poet names. The mystical experience—including that of atheist sects such as primitive Buddhism and Tantrism—is a search for contact with a transcendent good. The object of poetic activity is essentially language: whatever his beliefs and convictions, the poet is more concerned with words than with what these words designate. This is not to say that the poetic universe lacks meaning or that its meaning is peripheral. I am simply saying that in poetry meaning is inseparable from words, whereas in ordinary discourse, and even in the discourse of the mystic, the meaning lies in what the words point to, in something *beyond* language. The experience of the poet is above all else a verbal experience; in poetry every experience immediately takes on a verbal quality. This has been true of all poets in every age, but since Romanticism this preoccupation with language has become what we may call a poetic *consciousness*, an attitude that played no part in the classical tradition. The poets of former times were as keenly

3

aware of the value of words as modern poets; but they were less sensitive to meaning. Góngora's hermeticism does not imply a criticism of meaning, whereas that of Mallarmé or Joyce is primarily a criticism, and at times a destruction, of meaning. Modern poetry is inseparable from the criticism of language, which in turn is the most radical and the most virulent form of criticism of reality. Language now occupies the place once occupied by the gods or some other external entity or outward reality. The poem does not refer to anything outside itself; what a word refers to is another word. The meaning does not reside outside the poem but within it, not in what the words say, but in what *they say to each other.*

Góngora and Mallarmé, Donne and Rimbaud cannot be read in the same way. The difficulties in Góngora are external; they are grammatical, linguistic, mythological. Góngora is not obscure: he is complicated. His syntax is unusual, there are veiled mythological and historical allusions, the meaning of each phrase and even each individual word is ambiguous. But once these knotty problems and teasing enigmas have been solved, the meaning is clear. This is also true of Donne, a poet no less difficult than Góngora, who writes in a style that is even more dense. The difficulties presented by Donne's poetry are linguistic, intellectual, and theological. But once the reader has found the key, the poem opens like a tabernacle. Donne's best poems embody an erotic, intellectual, and religious paradox. In both these poets, the references are to something outside the poem: to nature, society, art, mythology, theology. The poet speaks of the eye of Polyphemus, the whiteness of Galatea, the horror of death, the presence of a young girl. In Rimbaud's major works, the attitude is completely different. In the first place, his *œuvre* is a criticism of reality and of the "values" that support it or justify it: Christianity, morality, beauty; in the second place, it is an attempt to lay the foundations of a new reality: a new fraternity, a new eroticism, a new man. All this is to be the mission of poetry, "the alchemy of the Word." Mallarmé is even more rigorous. His *œuvre*—if that is the proper word for a few signs left on a handful of pages, the traces of an unparalleled journey of exploration and a shipwreck—is something more than a criticism and a negation of reality: it is the obverse side of being. The word is the obverse side of reality: not nothingness but the Idea, the pure sign that no longer points to anything and is neither being nor nonbeing. The "theater of the spirit"—the Work or the Word —is not only the "double" of the universe: it is true reality. In Rimbaud and Mallarmé language turns back upon itself, it ceases to designate, it is neither a symbol of, nor does it refer to, external realities, whether physical or suprasensible objects. For Góngora a table is "squared pine," and for Donne the Christian Trinity is "bones to philosophy but milk to faith." Rimbaud does not address the world, but rather the Word on which that world rests:

> Elle est retrouvée!
> Quoi? L'éternité.
> C'est la mer allée
> Avec le soleil.

The difficulty of modern poetry does not stem from its complexity—Rimbaud is far simpler than Góngora or Donne—but rather from the fact that, like mysticism or love, it demands total surrender (and an equally total vigilance). If the word were not ambiguous, I would say that the nature of the difficulty is not intellectual but *moral*. It is an experience that implies a negation of the outer world, if only a provisional one, as in philosophical reflection. In short, modern poetry is an attempt to do away with all conventional meanings because poetry itself becomes the ultimate meaning of life and of man; therefore, it is at once the destruction and the creation of language—the destruction of words and meanings, the realm of silence, but at the same time, words in search of the Word. Those who dismiss this quest as "utter madness" are legion. Nonetheless, for more than a century a few solitary spirits, among them the noblest and most gifted human beings who have ever trod this earth, have unhesitatingly devoted their entire lives to this absurd undertaking.

Form and Meaning

The real ideas of a poem are not those that occur to the poet *before* he writes his poem, but rather those that appear in his work *afterward*, whether by design or by accident. Content stems from form, and not vice versa. Every form produces its own idea, its own vision of the world. Form has meaning; and, what is more, in the realm of art only form possesses meaning. The meaning of a poem does not lie in what the poet wanted to say, but in what the poem actually says. What we think we are saying and what we are really saying are two quite different things.

Homage to Aesop

Everything we name enters the circle of language, and therefore the circle of meaning. The world is a sphere of meanings, a language. But each word has its own particular meaning, which is different from and opposed to that of all other words. Within language, meanings battle among themselves, neutralize each other, annihilate each other. The statement: "Everything is meaningful because it is a part of language" can be reversed: "Nothing is meaningful because everything is language." The world is a sphere, etc. . . .

Language and Abstraction

For many years now, it has been a commonplace that abstract painting has gone as far as it can go: it has reached its absolute limits. This seems to me to be a misstatement of the facts: what is most characteristic of the great movements in art is their radicalism, their continual surpassing of their own limits, their effort to approach the absolute, to go beyond the outermost boundaries of art. When that furthest limit has been reached, another painter arrives on the scene, makes the crucial leap, discovers yet another free space beyond, and once again is stopped short by a wall—a wall that he must leap over in order to reach the open spaces beyond. Retreat is impossible. Has abstraction become a new academism? It does not matter: all movements become formal schools and all styles mere recipes. What is deplorable is to end up being an academic painter; but making academism a steppingstone is not at all to be deplored. The great Baroque and Mannerist painters did not scorn the art of their predecessors; by exaggerating it, they went beyond it. The same thing is true of Symbolist poetry: Symbolist poets did not deny Romanticism; they made it aware of its real nature. After the classicism of the early abstractionists and the romanticism of "abstract expressionism," what we need is a Mannerism, a Baroque-abstract.

The real danger of sterility confronting abstract painting lies in its pretension that it is a language sufficient unto itself. By the very fact that it pretends to be totally subjective—since it is the individual painter and he alone who creates and uses this language—it lacks an element essential to all language: a system of signs and symbols with meanings shared by all those who use it. If each artist speaks in his own private language, the result is lack of communication, the death of language. A dialogue between schizophrenics. The best abstract painters arrived at a sort of universal language when they rediscovered certain archetypal forms that represent man's most ancient and most universal heritage. But was it really a language? It was, rather, a pre-language or a meta-language. Abstract painters waver between stammering and mystical illumination. Though they disdain communication, they occasionally contrive to express communion. The opposite is true of poetry: the only thing at a poet's disposal is words—each of which has a meaning that is the same for everyone—and it is out of these words that he must try to create a new language. The poet's words continue to be a language, but at the same time they are also something else: poetry, something *never before heard, never before expressed*, something that is language and at the same time something that denies language and goes beyond it. Abstract painting seeks to be a pure pictorial language, and thus attempts to escape the essential impurity of all languages: the recourse to signs or forms that have meanings shared by everyone. It either falls short of language or goes beyond it, resulting either in silence or in onomatopoeic interjection: Mondrian or Pollock. It is an attempt at expression that implicitly denies what it affirms. Therein perhaps lies its possibility of renewing itself: only that creative work which does not deny its own inner contradiction and brings it into the full light of day is capable of revealing its true nature, which is always twofold. If it were to take this contradiction as its point of departure and refuse to conjure it away, abstract painting might go beyond the limits imposed upon it and realize itself by affirming the very thing that denies it. That was the secret of Baroque art and poetry.

A Peruvian Painter

After many years, I have had the chance to see once again the works of Fernando de Szyszlo, for some of his latest paintings have recently been shown in Mexico City (1959). Szyszlo is Peru's best painter, or at any rate the Peruvian painter whose works are best known outside his own country. He was one of the first practitioners of abstract painting in Hispano-America, and he has not changed very much. I have a series of engravings entitled *Homage to César Vallejo*, dating from the years Szyszlo and I spent in Paris together, the period in his life when he managed to earn the praise of a severe judge, Hans Hartung. On comparing these works of Szyszlo's with his recent oil painting, I find that he is more the master of his craft, freer and more venturesome, though still the same; his style is still difficult and austere, at once violent and lyrical. It is painting that is not outgoing, that looks inward toward intimate truths, that disdains the complicity of the senses and demands a more ascetic contemplation on the part of the viewer. Among Mexican painters, Soriano would represent the opposite pole, all immediate impulse and effusion, a great fountain of dizzying colors and forms. I do not mean to say that Szyszlo's painting is only an intellectual construction. There is a visible struggle between rigorous discipline and spontaneity; he is not merely an intellectual painter: he has sensitivity. His taut, swooping forms can be aggressive and cruel; at other times, they are such dense concentrations of color that they give off sparks of boundless energy. A flight captured on canvas, an explosion, reserve. Many painters—spurred on by the example of Picasso—change style from one day to the next; but Szyszlo does not change: he matures. He explores more and more remote regions within himself.

Notes on La realidad y el deseo*

In recent months (of the year 1958), a one-volume edition of Luis Cernuda's collected poems has been published. Cernuda has been faithful to himself all his life, and his book, which has grown slowly and steadily, as living things grow, has an internal consistency that is quite unusual in modern poetry. There are so many new poems in this latest edition, and they shed such revealing light on those published in the past, that for the first time we begin to catch a glimpse of the real significance of his œuvre. Like the voyager who sees the real outline of an un-

* [Reality and Desire.]

known land gradually take shape before his eyes as he draws closer and closer to its coast, so in the space of the last twenty-five years our generation has witnessed the gradual revelation of a new poetic continent.

If we except Cernuda's critical essays and a number of his occasional fictional pieces—all written as an offshoot of his poetry—he is the author of a single book. It requires a great faith in one's own powers (or a proud despair) to thus gamble everything on a single card. Despair, faith, pride: contradictory words that nonetheless naturally go together. All of them are related to yet another word that acts as a tenuous support for them: fate or necessity. Cernuda is one of the rare poets of our time marked with the brand of fate. He writes because he *must* write. To the poet fated to be a poet, self-expression is as natural and as involuntary as breathing is to us ordinary mortals. A demon, Cernuda's poetic conscience, refuses to loose its grip on him, demanding that he put into words what he has to say, come what may. Cernuda is fond of citing a phrase from Heraclitus: "Character is destiny."

Examples of different sorts of loyalty to the poetic demon: Éluard, the author of many books of poems, wrote only one poem all his life, and each of his books contains countless versions of this one poem; Cernuda, the author of a single book, is a poet of many poems.

I wrote: a poetic continent. Perhaps the expression is more applicable to Neruda, given the physical immensity, the natural massiveness, the awesome geographical monotony of that Chilean's poetry. Geography is of little concern to Cernuda, and in his poems all of nature, from the sea and nameless rocky cliffs to the Castilian plateau, is steeped in history. Cernuda's *œuvre* is a spiritual biography, that is to say the precise opposite of a geography: a human world, a universe at whose center we find that half comic, half tragic creature, man. Lilting song and probing analysis, soliloquy and supplication, frenzy and irony, confession and circumspection, all governed by a consciousness seeking to transform lived experience into spiritual wisdom.

Critics have either said nothing about Cernuda's book, or they have heaped empty praise upon it—which is another way of saying nothing. As has happened with other great poets in the past, the critics' coolness toward Cernuda's poetry, their uneasiness and insecurity, are due to the unintentionally *moral* nature of his inspiration. His book does not point a moral, to be sure; nonetheless, it puts before us a vision of reality that is a threat to the fragile edifice that goes by the name of Good and Evil. Blake said that every true poet, wittingly or unwittingly, is on the devil's side.

As a love-poet, Cernuda resembles Bécquer. As a poet of poetry, he is Baudelaire's descendant, having inherited his awareness of the loneliness of the poet, his vision of the modern city and its bestial powers, his split personality as lyric poet and critic. The two poets share the same desperate, mad yearning for happiness on earth and the same certainty that they have failed to attain it. The Christian note is missing in Cernuda: the consciousness of original sin, the nostalgia for paradise, a sense of the supernatural. At the same time, there is in Cernuda something almost without precedent in the history of Spanish poetry, which has always been profoundly Christian: a rebirth of the tragic consciousness, that is to say an acceptance of the human condition and the rejection of the possibility of any sort of afterlife, either in history or in eternity. Cernuda's pessimism is not a negation of life; it is, rather, a celebration of its powers: "Love does not die; it is only we who die. . . ." But all this is merely a description of the surface of Cernuda's poetry. Perhaps all we need say about this poet is that he has written some of the most intense and most lucid poems in the history of the Spanish language. They cut into the flesh of reality like a knife.

Cernuda's book brings the Latin poets to mind. They have the reputation of being highly rhetorical and not very original. I believe that reputation to be undeserved; with the exception of Sappho, we would be hard put to name a Greek writer of love-poems as modern in feeling as those of Catullus and Propertius. These two poets were the first to reveal the ambivalent and destructive side of love. The idea of love is said to have been born in Provence. That is quite true, but Greece and Rome (not to mention the Arab world) give us glimpses of it much earlier. In Greece, love takes the form of homosexual passion; in Rome, it appears in the guise of unrequited passion. In the poetry of Catullus and Propertius, love is a sense of need rather than a fulfillment: a somber, raging, broodingly introspective passion. And on being subjected to psychological analysis, this passion proves to be humiliating for a twofold reason: because it is a desire for a despicable creature, and because satisfaction of this desire leaves an aftertaste of ashes. It is an emotion tinged with selfishness, with contempt for the object of one's desire and for oneself. Jealousy and sensuality, rapture and self-analysis, idolatry and hate: the whole endless dialectic of physical pleasure and humiliation that we find in the modern novel, from Benjamin Constant to F. Scott Fitzgerald. Love can only be born in the presence of a free being who graces us with her presence or deprives us of it. In antiquity, a woman might be an object of worship or desire, but never of love. A goddess or a slave, a sacred object or a household utensil, a mother or a courtesan, a daughter or a priestess, not even her body was her own: she was the ambiguous double of the cosmos, the repository of the beneficent or evil powers of the universe. Woman first begins the gradual reconquest of herself in Alexandria, and, even more importantly, in Rome. While denying her physical freedom, Christianity later gives her a soul and free will. This process of liberation, which is still far from ended today, began in Rome: that great city foreshadows the possibility of love, of the physical and spiritual dialogue between two free human beings. Is the freedom of the twentieth century true freedom or only a mask disguising a new form of slavery? I cannot say. In any event, love is not sexual freedom but the freedom to feel passion: not the right to perform a physiological act but the right to freely choose to be intoxicated.

La realidad y el deseo is not a book carefully planned in advance: it is poems allowed to grow naturally, finally becoming a book. If we separate any one part from the whole, we risk tearing a living thing apart, denaturing it. The level of intensity of Cernuda's poems varies, to be sure. Between 1929 and 1934, he discovers, simultaneously, Surrealism and erotic passion. Thanks to the moral influence of André Gide, he accepts his homosexuality. Far from hiding his nature, he uses it as a weapon against Spanish morality. It took great courage to do this in a society infected with *machismo*, as the Spain of those days was. His language later loses its tension and a rhetorical tone gradually creeps into his poems, drowning out his real poetic voice little by little: a poem becomes a dissertation and a condemnation of our time. The reader agrees with the moralist, but he cannot help wondering whether all this might not be better expressed in prose. The stiffness of written prose has won out, rather than the lively prose-rhythms of everyday spoken language, the fountainhead of modern poetry. Listening too intently to his own inner monologue, Cernuda failed to hear the voices of others. I wonder whether young people read Cernuda the way we did. I find it impossible to believe that they do not experience the same sensation—not amazement, but rather something much more rare and much more precious: the discovery of a spirit that knows itself and dares to confront itself, a rigorously disciplined, lucid passion, a freedom that is at once a rebellion against the world and the acceptance of one's own personal fate. No consolation, no preaching of comforting thoughts, no concessions. And above all else: a handful of poems in which the voice of the poet is the voice of poetry itself, timeless poems that will be forever fresh and young. Is that so little? I am inclined to think that it is quite enough. Sheer scope is not what counts: "More time is not more eternity," as Jiménez has reminded us.

Landscape
and the Novel in Mexico*

I do not know whether literary nationalists have noticed that our novels present a rather sketchy and superficial image of the physical setting in Mexico. In a number of the best pages of two novelists writing in English, D. H. Lawrence and Malcolm Lowry, on the other hand, our mountains and our skies appear in all their somber, intoxicating grandeur, and in all their innocence and freshness as well. In *The Plumed Serpent* and various collections of short stories and critical pieces, Lawrence's prose reflects the extremely subtle, nearly imperceptible changes of light, the feeling of panic when torrential rains begin to fall, the terror of darkness descending on the altiplano, the shimmering vibrations of the sky at twilight in harmony with the respiratory rhythms of the great forests and the pulsing heartbeat of women. In *Under the Volcano*, the gardens of Cuernavaca, the flowers and plants, the distant volcanoes and the tangled green vines of the ravine—a true "gate of hell"—loom up before us bathed in the light of the first day of creation. The first day or the last? Perhaps both: the novel takes place on All Souls' Day in 1939, and during the twelve hours of this day the hero wanders about in a hallucinatory landscape that is also a labyrinth and a Purgatory, followed by a dog, the companion of the dead if we are to believe the Egyptians and the Aztecs.

The real theme of *Under the Volcano* is the age-old story of

* This note was written before the works of the new Mexican novelists had been published.

the expulsion from Paradise; and that of *The Plumed Serpent* the construction of a magic space—that is to say, a nature that has regained its innocence—wherein the reconciliation of heaven and earth, of body and soul, of man and woman, is celebrated. For both these novelists, it is not the natural surroundings that give rise to the vision; on the contrary, it is the poetic vision that gives the landscape its concrete form. The spirit sustains the stone, rather than vice versa. The landscape does not function as the background or the physical setting of the narrative; it is something that is alive, something that takes on a thousand different forms; it is a symbol and something more than a symbol: a voice entering into the dialogue, and in the end the principal character in the story. A landscape is not the more or less accurate description of what our eyes see, but rather the revelation of what is behind visible appearances. A landscape never refers only to itself; it always points to something else, to something beyond itself. It is a metaphysic, a religion, an idea of man and the cosmos.

Whereas Malcolm Lowry's theme is the expulsion from Paradise, the theme of Juan Rulfo's novel *Pedro Páramo* is the return to Paradise. Hence the hero is a dead man: it is only after death that we can return to the Eden where we were born. But Rulfo's main character returns to a garden that has burned to a cinder, to a lunar landscape. The theme of return becomes that of an implacable judgment: Pedro Páramo's journey home is a new version of the wanderings of a soul in Purgatory. The title is a (unconscious?) symbol: Pedro, Peter, the founder, the rock, the origin, the father, the guardian, and the keeper of the keys of Paradise, has died; Páramo (the Spanish word for wasteland) is his garden of long ago, now a desert plain, thirst and drought, the parched whispers of shadows and an eternal failure of communication. Our Lord's garden: Pedro's wasteland. Juan Rulfo is the only Mexican novelist to have provided us an image— rather than a mere description—of our physical surroundings. Like Lawrence and Lowry, what he has given us is not photographic documentation or an impressionist painting; he has incarnated his intuitions and his personal obsessions in stone, in dust, in desert sand. His vision of this world is really a vision of *another world*.

Metamorphosis

Apuleius recounts how Lucius was turned into an ass; Kafka tells us how Gregor Samsa was turned into a cockroach. We know what Lucius's sin was: his interest in witchcraft and his concupiscence; we are not told what Samsa's fatal flaw was. Nor do we know who is punishing him: his judge is nameless and faceless. After he is turned into an ass, Lucius wanders all over Greece and a thousand marvelous, terrible, or amusing things happen to him. He lives among bandits, assassins, slaves, vicious landholders, and equally cruel peasants; he is made to transport on his back the altar of an Oriental goddess worshiped by sexually perverted priests, thieves, and devotees of flagellation; on a number of occasions his virility is endangered, though this does not prevent him from having amorous relations with a wealthy and passionate woman; he experiences both times of feast and times of famine. . . . Nothing at all happens to Gregor Samsa: his horizon is bounded by the four dreary walls of a dreary house. Despite the beatings he suffers, the ass's health is never impaired; the cockroach is beyond both sickness and health: abjection is his permanent state. Lucius represents Mediterranean common sense and truculence, gastronomy and a sensuality that has a faint tinge of sadism, Greco-Latin eloquence and Oriental mysticism—the Phallus and the Idea. All of which culminates in the glorious vision of Isis, the universal mother, one night on the seashore. The end for Gregor Samsa is a domestic servant's broom sweeping out his room. Apuleius: the world seen and judged from the point of view of an ass. Kafka: the cockroach does not judge the world; he endures it.

Invention,
Underdevelopment,
Modernity

To us, the value of a work lies in its newness: the invention of new forms, or a novel combination of old forms, the discovery of unknown worlds or the exploration of unfamiliar areas in worlds already discovered—revelations, surprises. Dostoevski digs down into the subsoil of the spirit, Whitman names realities that traditional poetry had disdained, Mallarmé subjects language to more rigorous experiments than those of Góngora and invents the critical poem, Joyce turns the spoken language into an epic and makes a hero of a linguistic happenstance (Tim Finnegan is the death and resurrection of English and every other language), Roussel makes a poem out of a charade. . . . From the Romantic era onward, a work of art has had to be unique and inimitable. The history of art and literature has since assumed the form of a series of antagonistic movements: Romanticism, Realism, Naturalism, Symbolism. Tradition is no longer a continuity but a series of sharp breaks. The modern tradition is the tradition of revolt. The French Revolution is still our model today: history is violent change, and this change goes by the name of progress. I do not know whether these notions really apply to art. We may be convinced that driving a car is much better than riding horseback: but I fail to see how we can say that Egyptian sculpture is inferior to that of Henry Moore, or that Kafka is a greater writer than Cervantes. I believe in the tradition of a sharp break and in no way do I reject modern art: all I am saying is that we employ dubious standards in our attempt to understand it and judge it. Changes in our aesthetic tastes have no value or meaning in and of themselves; what has value and meaning is the idea of *change itself*. Or, better stated: not change in and of itself, but change as an agent or inspiration of modern creations. Imitation of nature and classical models—the idea of imitating, rather than the act of imitating—sustained the artists of the past; and for more than two centuries now, modernity—the notion of original and absolutely personal creation—has sustained us. Had such a notion not existed, the most perfect and most enduring works of our time would not have existed. The characteristic feature of modernity is criticism: what is new is set over and against what is old and it is this constant contrast that constitutes the *continuity* of tradition. In the past, continuity consisted in the prolongation or the persistence of certain archetypal forms or features in works of art; today, this continuity takes the form of negation or opposition. In classical art, novelty meant some sort of variation of the model; in Baroque art, an exaggeration; in modern art, a sharp break. In all three cases tradition was a living relation, even when it was a polemical one, and the dialogue between generations was not broken off.

If imitation becomes mere repetition, the dialogue ceases and tradition petrifies; if modernity is not self-critical, if it is not a sharp break and simply considers itself a prolongation of "what is modern," tradition becomes paralyzed. This is what is taking place in a large sector of the so-called avant-garde. The reason for this is obvious: the idea of modernity is beginning to lose its vitality. It is losing it because modernity is no longer a critical attitude but an accepted, codified convention. Rather than being a heresy, as in the nineteenth century and the first half of the twentieth century, it has become an article of faith that everyone subscribes to. The Institutional Revolutionary Party—that monumental logical and linguistic invention of Mexican politics —is a label that aptly describes a large part of contemporary art. For more than fifteen years now we have been greeted by a rather comical spectacle, in painting and sculpture in particular; although various "schools" follow one upon the other in rapid succession, all this raking of the coals can be reduced to a simple formula: repetition at an ever-accelerating rate. Never before has there been such frenzied, barefaced imitation masquerading as originality, invention, and innovation. For our forebears in the classical age, imitation was not only a legitimate practice but a duty; imitation did not stand in the way of the creation of new and truly original works. The artist is a living contradiction: he tries to imitate and he invents, he tries to invent and he copies. If contemporary artists sincerely seek to be original, unique, and new, they should begin by disregarding the notions of originality, individuality, and innovation: they are the clichés of our time.

A number of Mexican critics use the word "underdevelopment" to describe the present situation in Hispano-American arts and letters: our culture is "underdeveloped," the work of X or Y represents a breaking away from the "underdevelopment of the novel in our country," and so on and so forth. As I see it, the word refers to certain currents that are not to these critics' liking (or to mine): chauvinistic nationalism, academicism, traditionalism, and the like. But the word "underdevelopment" is a United Nations euphemism for backward nations. The notion of "underdevelopment" is an offshoot of the idea of social and economic progress. Aside from the fact that I am very much averse to reducing the plurality of cultures and the very destiny of man to a single model, industrial society, I have serious doubts as to whether the relationship between economic prosperity and artistic excellence is one of cause and effect. Cavafy, Borges, Unamuno, and Reyes cannot be labeled "underdeveloped" writers, despite the marginal economic status of Greece, Spain, and Latin America. Moreover, the rush to "develop" reminds me of nothing so much as a frantic race to arrive at the gates of Hell ahead of everyone else.

Many peoples and many cultures have taken their name from that of a god, a virtue, a destiny, a brotherhood: Islam, the Jews, the Japanese, the Tenochcas, the Aryans. Each one of these names is a sort of cornerstone, a covenant with permanence. Our age is the only one to have chosen a meaningless adjective to describe itself: modern. Since modern times will inevitably cease to be modern, this is tantamount to not having any name at all.

The idea of imitating the classics stems from a view of ongoing time as a falling away from a primordial time that is perfect. This is the exact opposite of the idea of progress: the present is insubstantial and imperfect by comparison with the past, and tomorrow will be the end of time. Implicit in this conception is the belief, first, that the past has restorative powers, and the belief, secondly, in an eternal repetition of the cycle of decadence, extinction, and a new beginning. Time consumes itself, and thereby re-engenders itself. The past is the model of the present: imitating the ancients and nature, the universal model within whose forms all times are contained, is a way of slowing up the process of decline. The idea of modernity is the product of rectilinear time: the present does not repeat the past and each instant is unique, different, and self-sustaining. The aesthetic of modernity, as Baudelaire, one of the first to define it, was well aware, is not synonymous with the idea of progress: it is difficult —or even absurd—to believe that such a thing as progress exists in the realm of art. But modernity and progress resemble each other in that both are the products of a view of time as rectilinear. This view of time is dying today. We are witnessing a twofold phenomenon: a criticism of progress in the countries that are most highly developed, and a degeneration of the avant-garde in the realm of art and literature. What distinguishes modern art from the art of other ages is criticism—and the avant-garde is no longer critical. Its powers of negation are blunted when it enters the circuit of production and consumption of industrial society, either as an *object* or as *news*. In the first case, *price* becomes the one real criterion of the worth of a painting or a piece of sculpture; in the second case, what counts is not what the poem or novel says but what *is said* about them, pointless talk that degenerates into a mere flood of publicity.

Another art is dawning. The relation of art to the idea of recti-linear time is beginning to change, and this change will be even more radical than that of two centuries ago when the idea of modernity undermined the Christian notion of time as a finite process ending in motionless eternity. The future is losing its fascination as the idea of progress begins to decline. The end of our idea of time also means the end of "world centers of art." Today we all speak, if not the same tongue, the same universal language. There is no one center, and time has lost its former coherence: East and West, yesterday and tomorrow exist as a confused jumble in each one of us. Different times and different spaces are combined in a here and now that is everywhere at once. A synchronic vision is replacing the former diachronic vision of art. This movement began when Apollinaire endeavored to juxtapose different spaces within a single poem; Pound and Eliot dealt with history in the same way, incorporating texts from other times and other languages in their works. These poets believed that in so doing they were being modern; their time was a *summa* of all times. But what they were really doing was taking the first step toward destroying modernity. The old frontiers are disappearing and others opening up; we are wit-nessing the end of the idea of art as aesthetic contemplation and returning to something that the West has long forgotten: the re-birth of art as collective action and representation, and the re-birth of their complementary opposite, solitary meditation. If the word had not lost its strict meaning, I would call the new art a *spiritual* art. A mental art, then, which will demand of the reader and the listener the sensitivity and the imagination of a performer who, like the musicians of India, is also a creator. The works of the new time that is aborning will not be based on the idea of linear succession but on the idea of combination: the conjunction, the diffusion, the reunion of languages, spaces, and times. Fiesta and contemplation. *An art of conjugation.*

The Seed

The art of the great historic civilizations, including those of pre-Columbian America, are capable of arousing our admiration and our enthusiasm, and may even enrapture us, but they never impress us as much as an Eskimo harpoon or a mask from the South Pacific. I use the word *impress* not only in the sense of causing us to feel strong emotion, but also in the etymological sense of "leaving a trace or mark by pressure." The contact is physical, and the feeling we experience is very much like acute anxiety. Inner or outer space, the world below or beyond, becomes a great weight pressing down upon us. Each work is a solid block of time, time standing still, time more massive than a mountain, despite the fact that it is as intangible as air or thought. Is it because these works are age-old, because the weight of thousands upon thousands of years has been compressed into a small chunk of matter? I do not believe so. The arts of so-called primitive peoples are not the most ancient arts we know of. Quite aside from the fact that many of these objects were created only yesterday, I would not venture to call the most ancient art we have any knowledge of, that of the Paleolithic era, a primitive art. What the animals painted on walls of caves in France, Spain, and elsewhere most resemble, if any comparison at all is possible, is the great figurative paintings decorating the walls of temples and palaces dating from the urban revolution. They not only have a similar form, but also a similar function. The theory that these figures were magic representations connected with hunting rites is giving way to the theory that they were a form of religious painting, at once naturalistic and symbolic. Specialists such as André Leroi-Gourhan believe these caves to be something like the cathedrals of Paleolithic man. No, the time of which the creations of primitive peoples are a living symbol is not antiquity; or rather, these works reveal another antiquity, a time previous to chronological time. A time before the idea of antiquity: the real original time, the time that is always *before*, no matter when it occurs. A Hopi doll or a Navajo painting are not *older* than the caves at Altamira or Lascaux: they are *before* them.

The handiwork of primitive peoples reveals the "time before time." What is this time like? It is almost impossible to describe it in words and concepts. I would call it the original metaphor. The first seed within which everything that will later be the plant—roots, stem, leaves, fruit, and its final decay—has been quickened with a life that will unfold only in the future yet is also already present. To be more precise: it is the imminence of the unknown—not as a presence but as an expectation and a threat, as an emptiness. It is the breaking through of the *now* into the *here*, the present in all its instantaneous actuality and all its dizzying, hostile potentiality. What is this moment concealing? The present is both revealed and concealed in the handiwork of the primitive, as in the seed or the mask: it is both what it is and what it is not, the presence that both is and is not there before us. This present never occurs in historical or linear time, nor does it occur in religious or cyclical time. In profane and sacred time, the intermediaries—a god or a concept, a mythical date or the little hand of the clock—keep us from being battered by the great paw of the present. There is something or someone standing between us and brute time to defend us: the calendar clears a path through the dense thickets of time, makes its immense expanse navigable. The handiwork of the primitive cannot be dated, or rather, it is before any date on any calendar. It is the time previous to *before* and *after*.

The seed is the original metaphor: it falls on the ground, into a crack in the earth, and is nourished by the earth's substance. The idea of a Fall and that of spatial separation are implicit in our image of the seed. If we think of animal time as a seamless present with all of reality an endless *now*, human time will then appear to be a divided present. Separation, a sharp break: *now* falls into *before* and *after*. This fissure in time announces the advent of the kingdom of man. Its most perfect manifestation is the calendar, whose object is not so much to divide time up as to bridge the yawning gap between the precipice of yesterday and that of tomorrow. The calendar names time, and since it fails utterly to tame the present, it *distances* it. A date on the calendar masks the original instant: that moment when primitive man, suddenly aware that he is outside of natural or animal time, realizes that he is a stranger, a creature who has fallen into a literally fathomless *now*. As man's history unfolds, the fissure becomes broader and broader, deeper and deeper. Calendars, gods, and philosophies fall, one by one, into the great pit. Suspended over the abyss as we are today, our fall seems imminent. Our instruments can measure time, but our minds can no longer conceive it: it has become both too large and too small.

The handiwork of primitive peoples fascinates us because the situation that it reveals is somewhat analogous to the one in which we find ourselves today: time without intermediaries, the abyss of time that cannot be measured. Not so much a vacuum as the presence of the unknown, an immediate brute force. For thousands of years, the unknown had a name, many names: gods, signs, symbols, ideas, systems. Today, it has once again become the abyss that has no name, just as it was nameless before history began. The beginning and the end resemble each other. But primitive man is a creature who is less defenseless spiritually than we are. The moment the seed falls into a crack, it fills it and swells with life. Its fall is a resurrection; the gash is a scar; and separation is reunion. All time lives in the seed.

A pygmy funeral hymn—to my mind possessed of a taut, spare beauty far greater than that of many of our classic poems —expresses, better than any disquisition, this world-view in which fall and resurrection are simultaneous:

> An animal is born, passes this way, dies,
> And the great cold comes,
> The great cold of night, blackness.

A bird passes this way, flies, dies,
And the great cold comes,
The great cold of night, blackness.

A fish darts by, passes this way, dies,
And the great cold comes,
The great cold of night, blackness.

A man is born, eats, sleeps,
And the great cold comes,
The great cold of night, blackness.

The sky bursts into flame, its eyes go out,
The morning star shines,
The cold below, the light above.

A man has passed this way, the prisoner is free,
The shadow has melted away. . . .

Primitives and Barbarians

The poem or sculpture of primitive man is the swollen seed, the superabundance of forms: a focal point of different times, the point of intersection of all spatial trajectories. I wonder whether the famous sculpture of Coatlicue in the Mexican National Museum, an enormous block of stone covered with signs and symbols, might not be described as primitive despite the fact that it belongs to a very definite historical period. On second thought: it is a barbarous work, like many others left us by the Aztecs. It is barbarous because it does not possess the unity of the primitive artifact, which puts the contradictions of reality before us in the form of an instantaneous totality, as in the pygmy poem; and barbarous because it has no notion of the pause, of the empty space, of the transition between one state and another. What distinguishes classic art from primitive art is the intuition of time not as an instant but as succession, symbol-

ized in the line that encloses a form without imprisoning it:
Gupta or Renaissance painting, Egyptian or Huastec statuary,
Greek or Teotihuacán architecture. Coatlicue is more an idea
turned to stone than a palpable form. If we look on it as a discourse in stone, at once a hymn and a theology, its rigor may
seem admirable. It strikes us as a cluster of meanings, its symbolic richness dazzles us, and its sheer geometrical proportions,
which have a certain grandeur all their own, may awe us or
horrify us—a basic function of a sacred presence. As a religious
image, Coatlicue humbles us. But if we really study it, rather
than simply thinking about it, we change our minds. It is not a
creation; it is a construction. Its various elements and attributes
never fuse into a form. This mass is the result of a process of
superposition; more than a powerful accumulation of separate
elements, it is a juxtaposition. Neither a seed nor a plant: neither
primitive nor classical. And not Baroque either. The Baroque is
art reflecting itself, line that caresses itself or tears itself apart, a
sort of narcissism of forms. A volute, a spiral, mirrors reflecting
each other, the Baroque is a temporal art: sensuality and meditation, an art that feeds the illusions of the disillusioned. A dense
jumble of forms, Coatlicue is the work of semicivilized barbarians: it attempts to say everything, and is not aware that the
best way to express certain things is to say nothing about them.
It scorns the expressive value of silence: the smile of archaic
Greek art, the empty spaces of Teotihuacán. As rigid as a concept, it is totally unaware of ambiguity, allusion, indirect
expression.

Coatlicue is a work of bloodthirsty theologians: pedantry and
cruelty. In this sense it is wholly modern. Today, too, we construct hybrid objects which, like Coatlicue, are mere juxtaposi-
tions of elements and forms. This trend, which has carried the
day in New York and is now spreading all over the globe, has a
twofold origin: the collage and the Dada object. But the collage
was meant to be a fusion of heterogeneous materials and forms:
a metaphor, a poetic image; and the Dada object was an attempt

to destroy the idea of physical objects as useful tools and the idea of works of art as valuable things. By regarding the object as something that destroys itself, Dada made the useless the antivalue par excellence and thus attacked not only the object but the market. Today, the successors of Dada deify the object: their art is the consecration of the artifact. The art galleries and the museums of modern art are the chapels of the new cult and their god goes by the name of the product: something that is bought, used, and thrown away. By the workings of the laws of the marketplace, justice is done, and artistic products suffer the same fate as other commercial objects: a wearing out that has no dignity whatsoever. Coatlicue does not wear out. It is not an object but a concept in stone, an awesome idea of an awesome divinity. I realize that it is barbarous; but I also appreciate its power. Its richness strikes me as uneven and almost formless, but it is a genuine richness. It is a goddess, a great goddess.

Can we escape barbarism? There are two sorts of barbarians: the barbarian who knows he is one (a Vandal, an Aztec) and therefore seeks to borrow a civilized life-style; and the civilized man who knows that the "end of a world" is at hand and does his utmost to escape by plunging into the dark waters of savagery. The savage does not know that he is a savage; barbarism is a feeling of shame at being a savage or a nostalgia for a state of savagery. In both cases, its underlying cause is inauthenticity.

A truly modern art would be one that would reveal the hollowness rather than mask it. Not the object-that-is-a-mask, but the frankly truthful work, opening out like a fan. Was not the aim of Cubism and, more radically, the goal of Kandinsky the revelation of essence? For the primitive, the function of the mask is to reveal and conceal a terrible, contradictory reality: the seed that is life and death, fall and resurrection in a fathomless *now*. Today the mask hides nothing. In our time it may well be impossible for the artist to invoke presence. But another way, cleared for him by Mallarmé, is still open to him: manifesting absence, incarnating emptiness.

Nature, Abstraction, Time

"From the imitation of nature to its destruction": this might well be the title of a history of Western art. The most vital of modern artists, Picasso, may also have been the wisest: if we cannot escape nature, as a number of his successors and his contemporaries have vainly endeavored to do, we can at least disfigure it, destroy it. Basically, this is a new homage to nature. Nothing pleases nature more, Sade said, than the crimes whereby we attempt to violate her. In her eyes creation and destruction are one and the same. Wrath, pleasure, sickness, or death wreak changes in the human being no less terrible (or comic) than the mutilations, the deformations, the furious stylizations that Picasso delights in.

Nature has no history, but its forms are the living embodiment of all the styles of the past, present, and future. I have seen the birth, the full flowering, and the decline of the Gothic style in rocks in the valley of Kabul. In a pond covered with green scum —full of little stones, aquatic plants, frogs, tiny monsters—I recognized both the temple sculpture of the Bayon at Angkor and one of the periods of Max Ernst. The form and plan of the buildings of Teotihuacán are a replica of the Valley of Mexico, but this landscape is also a prefiguration of Sung painting. The microscope reveals that the formula of the Tibetan *tankas* is already hidden in certain cells. The telescope shows me that Tamayo is not only a poet but also an astronomer. White clouds are the quarries of the Greeks and the Arabs. I am bemused by *plata encantada*, obsidian covered with a vitreous, opalescent white substance: Monet and his followers. There is no escaping the fact: nature is better at abstract art than at figurative art.

Modern abstract painting has taken one of two forms: a search for essences (Kandinsky, Mondrian), or the naturalism of Anglo-

American abstract expressionists.* The founders of the school wanted to get away from nature, to create a world of pure forms or reduce all forms to their essence. In this sense, the first abstract painters could be called *idealists*. Americans have not taken their inspiration from nature, but they have decided to work in the same way as nature. The act or the gesture of painting is more or less the ritual double of the natural phenomenon. Painting is *like* the action of sun, water, salt, fire, or time on things. To a certain degree abstract painting and natural phenomena are an *accident*: the sudden, unforeseen intersection of two or more series of events. Many times the result is striking: these paintings are fragments of living matter, chunks sliced out of the cosmos or heated to a seething boil. Nonetheless, it is an incomplete art, as can be seen in Pollock, one of the most powerful of these artists. His great canvases have no beginning or end; despite their huge dimensions and the energy with which they are painted, they seem to be giant chunks of matter rather than complete worlds. This kind of painting does not assuage our thirst for totality. Fragments and stammerings: a powerful urge to express, rather than a total expression.

Whether idealist or naturalist, abstract painting is a timeless art. Essence and nature lie outside the flow of human time: natural elements and the Idea have no date. I prefer the other current in modern art that endeavors to capture the meaning of change. Figuration, disfiguration, metamorphosis, a temporal art: Picasso at one end of the scale, Klee at the other, the great Surrealists in the middle. We owe to idealist abstract art some of the purest and most perfect creations of the first half of this century. The naturalist or expressionist tendency has left us great and intense works, tragic and, at times, hybrid art. It is the result of the contradiction between the natural phenomenon (pure objectivity) and human activity (subjectivity, intention-

---

* I don't like the term expressionism applied to abstract painting: there is a contradiction between expressionism and abstraction. The term "abstract painting" is no less misleading. As Benjamin Péret has pointed out, art is always concrete.

ality). A mixture, a conflict, or a fusion of two different orders of reality: the living material of the painting (energy and inertia) and the romantic subjectivism of the painter. A heroic painting, but also a theatrical painting: part daring feat, part dramatic gesture. Temporal art, for its part, is a vision of the instant that envelops presence in its flame and consumes it: an art of presence even though it hacks it to pieces, as in Picasso's work. Presence is not only what we see: André Breton speaks of the "inner model," meaning that ghost that haunts our nights, that secret presence that is proof of the otherness of the world. Giacometti has said that the one thing he wants to do is to *really* paint or sculpture a face some day. Braque does not search for the essence of the object: he spreads it out over the transparent river of time. The empty hours of Chirico with not a single person in sight. Klee's lines, colors, arrows, circles: a poem of movement and metamorphosis. Presence is the cipher of the world, the cipher of being. It is also the scar, the trace of the temporal wound: it is the instant, instants. It is meaning pointing to the object designated, an object desired and never quite attained.

The search for meaning or its destruction (it makes no difference which: there is no way of escaping meaning) is central to both tendencies. The only meaningless art in our time is realism: and not only because its products are so mediocre, but also because it persists in reproducing a natural and social reality that has lost all meaning. Temporal art resolutely confronts this loss of meaning, and therefore it is an art of imagination par excellence. In this respect, the Dadaist movement was an example (and an inimitable one, despite its recent imitations in New York). Dada not only took the absence of meaning and absurdity as its province, but made lack of meaning its most effective instrument of intellectual demolition. Surrealism sought meaning in the magnetic excitement of the instant: love, inspiration. The key word was *encounter*. What is left of all this? A few canvases, a few poems: a branch of living time. That is enough. Meaning lies elsewhere: always just a few steps farther on.

Modern art oscillates between presence and its destruction, between meaning and the meaningless. But we thirst for a *complete art*. Are there any examples?

Figure and Presence

Dada torpedoed the speculative pretensions of Cubist painting and the Surrealists countered the object-idea of Juan Gris, Villon, or Delaunay with an inner vision that destroyed its consistency as a *thing* and its coherence as a *system* of intellectual coordinates. Cubism had been an analysis of the object and an attempt to put it before us in its totality; both as analysis and as synthesis, it was a criticism of *appearance*. Surrealism transmuted the object, and suddenly a canvas became an *apparition*: a new figuration, a real transfiguration. This process is being repeated today. Abstract painting had rejected aesthetic reality along with every other reality—whether in the form of appearances or in the form of apparitions. Pop Art is the unexpected return of figurative art, a hostile and brutal reappearance of reality, such as we see it every day in our cities, before it is passed through the filter of analysis. Both Surrealism and Pop Art represent a reaction against the absolutism of pictorial speculation, in the form of a return to spontaneous, concrete vision. Fantasy, humor, provocation, hallucinatory realism. The differences between the two movements are as great as the similarities, however. We might even say that the resemblance is merely an outward one; it is not so much a fundamental similarity as a historical and formal coincidence: they are one extreme of the modern sensibility, which continually oscillates between love of the general and passion for the individual, between reflection and intuition. But Pop Art is not a total rebellion as Dada was, nor is it a movement of systematic subversion in the manner of Surrealism, with a program and an inner discipline. It is an individual attitude; a response to reality rather than a criticism of it. Its twin and its enemy, Op Art, is not even an attitude: it is literally a point of view, a procedure. It is really a more or less independent branch of the abstractionist tendency, as is clear in the works of one of the best representatives of the school: Vasarely.

The Pop artist accepts the world of things we live in and is accepted by the society that possesses and uses these things. Neither rejection nor separation: integration. Unlike Dada and Surrealism, Pop Art from the beginning was a tributary of the industrial current, a small stream feeding into the system of circulation of objects. Its products are not defiant challenges of the museum or rejections of the consumers' aesthetic that characterizes our time: they are consumer products. Far from being a criticism of the marketplace, this art is one of its manifestations. Its works are often ingenuous sublimations of the show windows and counter displays of the big department stores. Nonetheless Pop Art is a healthy trend because it is a return to an immediate vision of reality, and, in its most intense expressions, a return to a vision of immediate reality. How can we fail to see the poetry of modern life, as defined by Apollinaire, in certain of Rauschenberg's works, for instance? The world of the streets, machines, lights, crowds—a world in which each color is an exclamation and each form a sign pointing to contrary meanings. Pop Art has reinvented the figure, and this figure is that of our cities and our obsessions. At times it has gone further and turned this mythology into a blank space and a question: the art of Jasper Johns is that of the object become a Saint Sebastian. A truly metaphysical art in the great tradition of Chirico, yet deeply American. But Johns is an exception—a more rigorous imagination beyond both the easy charms and the mindless brutality of most of Pop Art. . . . What these artists have restored to us is a figure, not presence itself: a mannequin rather than a true apparition. The modern world is man, or his ghost, wandering among things and gadgets. In the work of these young people, I miss something that Pound saw in a Paris métro station and expressed in two lines:

> The apparition of these faces in the crowd;
> Petals on a wet, black bough.

The New Acolytes

Another similarity between yesterday's European avant-garde and today's American avant-garde: in both cases, poetry anticipated and paved the way for the new pictorial vision. Dada and Surrealism were above all else poetic movements in which poet-painters such as Arp and painter-poets such as Ernst and Miró participated. In the United States, the phenomenon is being repeated in a slightly different form. The change began in the 1950s, and the spark that set it off was the rebellion of poets against intellectual and academic poetry—a rebellion in which Pound and William Carlos Williams fulfilled the same exemplary (and ambiguous) function as Apollinaire and Reverdy within the Surrealist movement in France. A few years later, around 1960, American painters rebelled—independently but in much the same way—against abstract expressionism. It was more or less a repetition of what had happened in Europe, especially in France, between 1920 and 1925. Repetition, of course, is neither absolute similarity nor imitation. The resemblance stems from the fact that the circumstances are analogous, and may be regarded as an illustration of the rhythmic law that I have mentioned above: a swing of the pendulum between periods of reflection and periods of spontaneity.

The same cannot be said, however, of the Hispano-American imitators of the North Americans, at least in the realm of poetry. (Except for Brazil, where there is a genuine avant-garde in the strictest sense of the word: the concrete poets.) Imitating Olson

or Ginsberg in Lima, Caracas, Buenos Aires, Santiago, Mexico
City, or Tegucigalpa is tantamount to ignoring—or, what is
worse, forgetting—the fact that this poetic revolution has already taken place in the Spanish language. This movement began in our countries more than forty years ago; its founders
were Macedonio Fernández, Huidobro, Tablada. It culminates in
two moments that are true zeniths: the first represented primarily by the names Neruda and Vallejo; the second represented by a number of less widely known but equally important
works by various poets of my generation: Lezama Lima, Nicanor
Parra, Enrique Molina, Alberto Girri, Vitier, and a few others.
It is a movement that has not yet come to an end, a living
tradition.

The acolytes repeat and translate what has already been done:
they are outsiders following a rite that they only half understand. Denying one's heritage has always seemed to me to be a
tonic and a stimulant. Nonetheless I believe that it is necessary
to be acquainted first with what one is rejecting before it is possible to really reject it. Breton broke with Valéry's aesthetic
only after many years of intimate contact with this poet's works;
the Argentinian *ultras* rebelled against Lugones, but they were
not unaware of his existence. The acolytes swim in an empty
pool; they explore territories that are shown on all the maps.
Perhaps this attitude is the result of an unconscious extension of
the notion of "underdevelopment" to the area of artistic creation.
Latin America is admittedly a continent of obtuse, grasping
oligarchies, bloody dictatorships, oppressed peoples, and governments that are puppets of Washington, but since the days of
Rubén Darío, this somber world has produced an unbroken
series of good poets. These poets are part of the universal modern tradition, and their works are no less important than those of
Benn, Yeats, Michaux, Ungaretti, Montale. I am not saying that
young people ought to continue, repeat, or imitate their predecessors; I am merely saying that all rejection, if it is not to be an
empty protest against emptiness, implies an adversary relationship with what is being rejected. What worries me is not the

rebellion against tradition but rather the *absence* of a tradition. This is a sign of alienation; even more important, when acolytes cut themselves off from tradition, they mutilate themselves. . . . But all this is perhaps only a holdover from the past, the last twitches of a dying "modernity." Another time is dawning: another art.

On Criticism

On first hearing a parrot speak, the Spanish gentleman recently arrived in the New World bowed deeply and said: "Pardon, Your Excellency, I thought you were a bird."

It is an open secret that criticism is the weak point of Hispano-American literature. This is also true of Spain. There is no lack of good critics, of course. Among Latin American critics, I could readily point to two outstanding ones, Anderson Imbert and Rodríguez Monegal (not to mention a younger one such as the Venezuelan poet Guillermo Sucre). But we lack a "body of doctrine," or rather doctrines, that is to say, a world of ideas that as it develops creates an *intellectual space*: a critical sphere surrounding a work of literature, an echo that prolongs it or contradicts it. Such a space represents the meeting place with other works, the possibility of a dialogue between them. Criticism is responsible for the creation of what we call a literature, which is not so much the sum of individual works as the system of relations between them: a field of affinities and oppositions.

Criticism and creation live in permanent symbiosis. Criticism feeds on poems and novels, but at the same time it is the water, bread, and air of creation. In the past, the "body of doctrine" was made up of closed systems: Dante was nourished by theology and Góngora by mythology. Modernity represents the rule of criticism: not a system, but the negation and the confrontation of all systems. Criticism has been the staple nourishment of all modern artists, from Baudelaire to Kafka, from Leopardi to the Russian Futurists. It has also become a form of creation: the work in the end becomes a celebration of negation (*Un coup de dés*) or a negation of the work itself (*Nadja*). In Spanish and Portuguese literature there are very few examples of this sort of radicalism: there is Pessoa, and Jorge Luis Borges, both authors of a work built upon the dizzying theme of the absence of a work. Criticism as a method of creation, negation as a metaphysic and a rhetoric. Among those who have come after them—aside from Cortázar and Sarduy—I find no evidence of the will to construct a discourse based on the absence of discourse. *No* is a transparent obelisk, but our poets and novelists prefer geometric figures that are less disturbing; we have a number of extraordinary works based on a *yes*, at times a dense, compact affirmation, and at other times fissured with negations and ruptures.

If we turn from criticism as creation to criticism as intellectual sustenance, we encounter even greater poverty. The thinking of our time—ideas, theories, doubts, hypotheses—lies elsewhere, written in other languages. Except in rare moments bearing the names of Miguel de Unamuno and Ortega y Gasset, we are the parasites of Europe. If we turn, finally, to literary criticism per se, poverty becomes abject misery. The space that I have referred to, the space created by critical action, the place where works meet and confront each other, is a no man's land in our countries. The mission of criticism is not to invent works but to establish relations between them: to order them, to lay bare their relative position within the whole on the basis of their biases and tendencies. In this sense, criticism has a creative function: it creates a literature (a perspective, an order) out of individual works. This is precisely what our criticism has failed to do. And that is why there is no Hispano-American literature, even though there exists a whole body of important works. And that is also why there is no point in attempting to solve the much-discussed question of the essential *nature* of Hispano-American literature. What is to the point is the need to ponder the *situation* of our literature: its frontiers, its form, its structure, its movements. To answer this question would be to relate individual works to each other, and show us that they are not isolated monoliths, not steles erected in a desert to commemorate a disaster, but a society: not a chorus but a dialogue of many contradictory voices.

There is little point in condemning sins of omission. But discussing sins of commission is not pointless. For a number of years now our critics, those in particular who have immured themselves within the fortress of daily papers and periodicals, have had nothing but praise for "our great Latin-American literature." (Twenty or so years ago, it was fashionable to decry the poverty of our literature.) This recent, vociferous "critical" activity, which is almost indistinguishable from the more vacuous forms of publicity and consists largely of a string of name-dropping clichés, has now chosen as its warhorse the theme of "the success of our writers, especially novelists, in Europe and the U.S." The word "success" embarrasses me: it belongs not to the vocabulary of literature but rather to that of business and sports. Moreover, the vogue for translations is a universal phenomenon, not restricted to Latin American works. It is a consequence of the increasing importance of publishing as a business enterprise, an epiphenomenon of the prosperity of industrial societies. Literary agents are now scouring the five continents, from the slums of Calcutta to the patios of Montevideo and the bazaars of Damascus, in search of manuscripts of novels. Literature is one thing and publishing quite another. The attitude of these critics is very much like that of the Latin American bourgeois twenty years ago who refused to drink anything but imported whisky or champagne. It would appear that in order to receive any attention in Latin America, a work must first have the blessing of London, New York, or Paris. This situation might be amusing if it did not imply a dereliction of duty. The province of criticism is language, and giving up jurisdiction in that realm means giving up not only the

right to render an opinion but also the use of words. This is
abject surrender: the critic gives up the right to judge what is
written in his own language.

I do not deny the need and even the necessity of criticism
from abroad: I consider modern literatures to be a single literature. And how can we ignore the fact that often foreigners see
what critics on the spot have failed to see? Caillois did not
discover Borges, but he did something that those of us who
admired him failed to do when he was a writer for a small
audience: Caillois read him within a universal context. Instead of
repeating what anonymous reviewers in Chicago or Milan say,
our critics should read our authors as Caillois has read Borges:
from the point of view of the modern tradition and as part of
that tradition. Two complementary tasks: to show that Hispano-
American works are a *single literature*, a field of antagonistic
relations; and to describe the relationships of this literature to
other literatures.

It is frequently said that the weakness of our criticism is due
to the marginal, dependent status of our societies: it is regarded
as one of the effects of "underdevelopment." This opinion is one
of those half-truths that is more dangerous than an outright
falsehood. This famous "underdevelopment" did not prevent
Rodó from writing a fine critical essay on Darío. Literature admittedly has close ties to the society that produces it: though it
is not simply a reflection of social relations, neither is it an entity
that has no connection with history. Literature is a social relation, but at the same time it is a relation that is irreducible to
others. To my mind, our lack of a solid body of criticism is more
readily explainable as a result of our lack of communication.
Latin America has no center comparable to Paris, New York, or
London. In the past, Madrid more or less fulfilled that function
(rather less than more). It was in Madrid that Darío, Reyes,
Neruda, and a few others were first hailed as major writers. And
yet we hypocritically refuse to forgive Spaniards for having
ignored Huidobro and Vallejo (as though we ourselves had been

models of generosity toward them: Vallejo died in exile and one of Huidobro's last books is entitled, significantly enough, *El ciudadano del olvido* [*The Citizen of Oblivion*]). During the Spanish Civil War, Buenos Aires and Mexico City became the successors of Madrid. They had been literary capitals before the Civil War, but in the sense of being focuses of cosmopolitan and anti-Spanish rebellions such as modernism and avant-gardism. A literary center is a nervous system sensitive to any sort of stimulus: neither Buenos Aires nor Mexico City has been very responsive to the rest of Latin America. Argentinian Europeanism and Mexican nationalism are two different forms of the same infirmity: deafness. Things have admittedly changed somewhat in recent years. Other centers are coming into being: Havana, Caracas, Montevideo, Santiago, Lima. Periodicals and groups whose outlook is Latin American are appearing even in self-centered Bogotá and the Managua of Somoza the shark. Despite the fact that the media are almost always in the hands of dictators, government agencies, and large private corporations, communication is being established and gradually becoming a chaotic but vital reality.

Though literature is not communication—and may in fact be its very opposite, the *mise en question* of communication—it nonetheless is one of its products: *a contradictory product*. Criticism shares this ambiguous attitude toward communication: its mission lies not so much in transmitting information as in filtering, transmuting, and classifying it. The tools of criticism are selections and associations: it defines, it isolates, and then it relates. I will even go further: in our time criticism is the cornerstone of literature. As literature comes to be a criticism of words and the world, a self-questioning, criticism comes to look upon literature as a world of words, as a verbal universe. Creation is criticism and criticism creation. Our literature lacks critical rigor and our criticism lacks imagination.

Mask and Transparency

Carlos Fuentes's first book was a thin volume of short stories: *Los días enmascarados* [*Masked Days*] (1954). This title foreshadows the direction that his later work has taken. It refers to the last five days of the Aztec year, the *nemontani*: "five days masked/with maguey leaves" as the poet Tablada puts it. Five nameless days, empty days during which all activity was suspended—a fragile bridge between the end of one year and the beginning of another. In Fuentes's mind, doubtless, the expression also is more or less of a mocking question: "What is there behind these masks?" The vessel full of sacrificial blood in pre-Hispanic times, the taste of dust as a firing squad executes a prisoner at dawn, the black hole of sex, the hairy spiders of fear, the laughter of the basement and the privy. Since this strange book, Fuentes has published five novels, a *novella* that is both macabre and perfect (as the genre demands: geometry as the antechamber of horror), and another collection of short stories.* His first novel, *La región más transparente* (*Where the Air Is Clear*), would appear to be an answer to the short stories written in his youth: transparency versus the mask. The first modern vision of Mexico City as an urban complex, this book was a twofold revelation to Mexicans: it showed them the face of a city that was theirs but completely unknown to them, and it brought to their attention a young writer who would never cease to amaze them, disconcert them, and irritate them. The secret center of the novel is an enigmatic character, Ixca Cienfuegos; though he plays no part in the events of the book, he somehow precipitates them, and thus serves as a sort of consciousness of

---

* The novels are *La región más transparente* (1958), *Las buenas conciencias* (1959), *La muerte de Artemio Cruz* (1962), *Zona sagrada* (1967), and *Cambio de piel* (1967). The novella is *Aura* (1962), and the book of short stories *Cantar de ciegos* (1964).

the city. He is the other half of Mexico City, the pre-Columbian past that is deeply buried yet still alive. He is also a mask of Carlos Fuentes, just as Mexico City is a mask of Ixca. Literature as a mask of the author and the world. Yet the opposite is also true: Ixca is a critical conscience. Literature as a critique of the world and of the author himself. The novel centers on this duality: mask and consciousness, creative language and criticism, Ixca and modern Mexico City, Fuentes and Ixca.

The axis whose two poles are verbal invention and criticism of language is central to Fuentes's entire work, with the exception of *Las buenas conciencias*, an infelicitous attempt to return to traditional realism. Each one of his novels strikes the reader as a hieroglyph: and, at the same time, the invisible action underlying them is a passionate, persistent attempt to decipher this hieroglyph. Each sign leads to another sign: Mexico City leads to Ixca, Ixca to Artemio Cruz (an anti-Ixca, a man of action) and so on, from novel to novel and from character to character. Fuentes questions these signs and these signs question him: the author is yet another sign. Writing is a ceaseless interrogation, an interminable task, and one that the novelist is obliged to embark upon again and again: in order to decipher a hieroglyph a writer's only recourse is signs (words) that immediately form another hieroglyph. Criticism bares the falsehoods of words by means of other words which congeal and become new masks the moment they are uttered. At the most obvious level, the duality takes the form of moral or political criticism and a nostalgia for a heroic age. The description of the contemporary social structure of Mexico is a cruel (and just) criticism of the world that our revolution created, but the very violence of this criticism immediately evokes another reality: the apocalyptic years of armed struggle. Criticism becomes the creation of a myth, and this myth in turn is constantly undermined by criticism.

The rise in society of the revolutionary and the moral degradation that results have been a persistent theme in the modern novel, ever since Balzac. *The Death of Artemio Cruz* is the story of a revolutionary who becomes corrupted. Cruz's fall gradually takes on a mythical tone. Fuentes is not so much consciously concerned with providing yet another example of the revolutionary origins of the conservative bourgeoisie as he is fascinated by the character he is attempting to portray, as he was in his earlier book by Ixca, the survivor of the pre-Hispanic era. If he can decipher the mystery of Cruz, he will be able to exorcise him. Cruz's death-throes are the deciphering of the mystery. The dying man relives his entire life: as a lover, as a guerrilla, as a political adventurer, as a businessman. . . . Cruz as a young boy and Cruz as an adolescent spy upon his last moments, believing that his death will reveal what lies behind and beyond reality; as he breathes his last, the old man seeks in his past life the sign of what he really is, the pure moment that will allow him to gaze upon death face to face. These shifts in time do not occur one after the other, but simultaneously. Fuentes does away with *before* and *after*, a life-story as linear time: events do not follow one upon the other; all times and spaces coincide, conjoin in this final moment in which Artemio Cruz ponders his life. Cruz dies an undeciphered enigma. Or rather: his death traces another hieroglyph, the sum of everything Cruz the man was, and its negation. The whole process must be begun all over again.

The world is not presented as a reality to be described, but as a language to be decoded. Fuentes's motto might well be: *Tell me how you speak and I will tell you who you are.* Individuals, social classes, historical periods, cities, deserts are languages: all the languages that go to make up the Hispano-Mexican language, and several other tongues as well. An enormous, joyous, painful, hallucinatory verbal material which may remind the reader of the Baroque style of José Lezama Lima's *Paradiso*—if the word Baroque is a proper description of two modern writers. But the vertigo we experience when we confront the constructions of the great Cuban poet is that caused by perfect, frozen immobility; his verbal world is that of the stalactite; Fuentes's reality, by contrast, is all movement, a continual explosion. Lezama Lima's universe is an accumulation, a petrification, an immense verbal geology; Fuentes's is a continual uprooting, an exodus of languages, tongues meeting and scattering to the four winds. The one solid earth, the other a great gale. Because of his cosmopolitanism, Fuentes may also appear to resemble Cortázar, paradoxically the writer furthest from and closest to his national roots: even when Cortázar writes in the dialect of Buenos Aires, there is an irony that separates the writer from the language he uses. The Hispano-American cosmopolitanism of Cortázar is the end product of a process of abstraction and purification, a crystallization, whereas Fuentes's cosmopolitanism consists of a juxtaposition and a combination of different idioms within the Spanish language and outside of it. Because it is turned in upon itself, Cortázar's language is a process of reflection that obliges the reader to venture out onto a thinner and thinner and sharper and sharper edge until he is confronted by an empty space: a destruction of language, a leap in the direction of silence. In Fuentes, on the other hand, there is verbal eroticism, violence and pleasure, an encounter and an explosion. A chemical retort and a fireworks display.

The body occupies a central place in Fuentes's universe. Cold, heat, thirst, the sexual urge, fatigue, the most immediate and direct sensations; and the most refined and complex sensations: combinations of desire and imagination, the derangements and the hallucinations of the senses, their errors and their divinations. Erotic passion has a privileged place, and therefore imagination, its implacable double, also is uniquely privileged. In two other important Hispano-American novelists, one belonging to his own generation and another belonging to the preceding generation, Gabriel García Márquez and Adolfo Bioy Casares, love is also a sovereign passion. In García Márquez's world, love is the primordial power that reigns as an obscure, impersonal, and all-powerful presence: the world of the first day of creation, or, more precisely, the primordial night. Bioy Casares's theme is not cosmic but metaphysical: the body is imaginary, and we bow to the tyranny of a phantom. Love is a privileged perception, the most complete and total perception not only of the unreality of the world but of our own unreality: not only do we traverse a realm of shadows; we ourselves are shadows.* Unlike García Márquez, Fuentes does not regard men and women as mere projections of desire: they are his accomplices and his enemies. Like Bioy Casares, he regards phantoms as no less real than physical bodies, except for the fact that these phantoms are incarnations: we can touch them, and they can touch us; they can rend our flesh. The body is a very real thing, and the revelation that it offers us, whether animal or divine, is inhuman: it tears us away from ourselves and projects us into another, more total, life or death.

Bodies are visible hieroglyphs. Every body is an erotic metaphor and the meaning of all these metaphors is always the same: death. Love for Fuentes is a way of looking upon death, and through death he has a glimpse of that territory that was once called sacred or poetic, but lacks a name in our day. The modern world has not yet invented words to designate the other side of reality. Fuentes's obsession with the wrinkled, toothless countenance of a tyrannical, mad, passionate old woman should not surprise us. She is the age-old vampire, the witch, the white serpent of Chinese tales: the lady of dark passions, the outcast. Eroticism is inseparable from horror, and Fuentes is a past master of the horrible. In many passages in his novels and in almost every one of his short stories he delights in displaying a sort of fierce joy. If what he is pleased to put before us is not the sacred, it is something no less violent: profanation. A humor in which three heritages—the American, Spanish, and Mexican traditions —are conjoined, a humor that is not intellectual but physical, sexual, visceral. A humor that goes beyond irony, the absurd, and satire, whose parodic exaggeration borders on the sublime —a humor that can only be described as bloodthirsty. A humor

---

* Despite (or perhaps because of?) the fact that Bioy Casares has written two novels, *La invención de Morel* (*The Invention of Morel*) and *El sueño de los héroes* [*The Dream of Heroes*], which may be described, without exaggeration, as *perfect* novels, our critics have ignored them, or what is worse, have misinterpreted them by regarding them as two successful instances of fantastic literature.

that is carnal, corporeal, and ritual, as incongruous as an Aztec sacrifice in Times Square.

A number of European critics have said that the second half of our century will be marked by the emergence of Latin American literature as its first half and the end of the nineteenth were marked by the rise of American and Russian literature. I do not place much faith in this sort of prophecy; what is more, I believe that these three literatures are intelligible only within the context of European literature. Moreover, contemporary literature tends to be world-wide in scope. We may deplore it, but it is a fact that the old historical oppositions between nation and nation, or between various cultures, are evaporating little by little. The new antagonisms are different in nature and are manifested *within* our societies: conflicts between industrial society and the Third World, the quarrel between generations and ethnic minorities within industrial society. Whether or not the prophecy concerning the future of literature in Latin America will come true does not worry me, but I am fascinated and excited by the works of a handful of Latin-American poets and novelists: they are not a promise but a presence. Among these works are those of Carlos Fuentes. He is now at the peak of his powers and has not yet said all he has to say. I am certain that the mask will become a transparent one, not rock crystal but water.

Remedios Varo's Appearances and Disappearances[*]

With the invisible violence of wind scattering clouds, but with greater delicacy, as if she painted with her eyes rather than with her hands, Remedios sweeps the canvas clean and heaps up clarities on its transparent surface.

[*] Remedios Varo was a little-known Spanish Surrealist painter. The wife of the French poet Benjamin Péret, she went to Mexico during World War II and remained there until her death in the early 1960s.

In their struggle with reality, some painters violate it or cover it with signs, explode it or bury it, flay it. Remedios volatilizes it: it is not blood but light that flows through its body.

She slowly paints lightning-quick apparitions.

Appearances are the shadows of archetypes. Remedios does not invent: she remembers. Except that these appearances resemble nothing and no one.

Sea voyages within a precious stone.

A speculative painting, a mirror-image painting: not the world in reverse, but the reverse of the world.

The art of levitation: the loss of gravity, the loss of seriousness. Remedios laughs, but her laughter echoes in another world.

Space is not an expanse but a magnet attracting Appearances. A woman's hair—the strings of a harp—the sun's rays streaming down—the strings of a guitar. The world seen as music: listen to Remedios's lines.

The secret theme of her work: harmony—lost equality.

In Appearance she paints Disappearance.

Roots, fronds, rays, locks of hair, flowing beards, spirals of sound: threads of death, of life, of time. The weft is woven and un-woven: the unreality that we call life, the unreality that we call death—only the canvas is real. Remedios the anti-Moira.

She does not paint time, but the moments when time is resting.

In her world of stopped clocks, we hear the flow of substances, the circulation of shadow and light: time ripening.

Forms seek their own form, form seeks its own dissolution.

André Breton or the Quest
of the Beginning

It is impossible to write about André Breton in any other language than that of passion. To him the powers of the word were no different from the powers of passion, and passion, in its highest and most intense form, was nothing less than language in its wildest, purest state: poetry. Breton: the language of passion—the passion of language. Perhaps even more than an exploration of unknown psychic territories, his lifelong quest represented the regaining of a lost kingdom: the original Word, man before men and civilizations. Surrealism was his order of chivalry and his entire life was a Quest of the Holy Grail. The surprising evolution of the Spanish word *querer* reflects very well the nature of this quest; *querer* comes from the Latin *quaerere* (to search, to inquire), but in Spanish the meaning soon changed, and the word came to mean *to desire, to love. Querer*: a passionate, amorous quest. A quest whose goal lies neither in the future nor in the past, but at that point of convergence that is simultaneously the beginning and the end of all time: the day before the beginning and after the end.

Breton's indignation at the "infamous Christian idea of sin" is something more than a violent rejection of the traditional values of the West: it is an affirmation of the original innocence of man. This distinguishes him from almost all of his contemporaries and successors. For Georges Bataille, eroticism, death, and sin are interchangeable signs whose combinations repeat the same meaning again and again, with terrifying monotony: the nothingness of man, his irremediable abjection. For Sartre, too, man is an accursed creature, ontologically or historically, the victim of a malediction that may be labeled either anguish or working for a daily wage. Both are rebel sons of Christianity. Breton belongs to another tradition. His life and his work are proof that he was not so much the heir of Sade and Freud as of Rousseau and Meister Eckhart. He was not a philosopher but a great poet, and, even more important, a man of honor in the old sense of the word. His stubborn refusal to entertain the idea of sin was a point of honor: the notion struck him as being in effect a *stain*, a blot not on man's life but on man's dignity. Belief in sin was incompatible with his conception of man. This conviction, which made him a violent opponent of many modern philosophies and all religions, was itself basically religious: it was an act of faith. What is most amazing—or I should say most admirable—is that this faith never failed him. He denounced other people's weaknesses, their shortcomings, their betrayals, but he never believed that our guilt was congenital. He was a sectarian spirit, but one without the slightest trace of Manichaeism. For Breton, sinning and being born were not synonymous.

Man, even man debased by the neocapitalism and pseudo-socialism of our time, is a marvelous being because he sometimes *speaks*. Language is the mark, the sign, not of his fall but of his original innocence. Through the Word we may regain the lost kingdom and recover powers we possessed in the far-distant past. These powers are not ours. The man inspired, the man who really speaks, does not say anything personal: language speaks through his mouth. Dreaming favors the explosion of the Word because it is an affective state: its passivity permits desire to be active. Dreaming is by nature passionate. Here, too, Breton's opposition to Christianity had religious roots: in order to express itself, language destroys the conscious self. Poetry does not redeem the poet's personal self: it dissolves it in the vaster, more powerful reality of language. The practice of poetry demands the surrender, the renunciation of the ego. It is regrettable that Buddhism did not interest him: that tradition also destroys the illusion of the self, though its aim is not to foster language but to foster silence. (I must add that this silence is one that for more than two thousand years has never ceased emitting meanings.) I mention Buddhism because I believe that "automatic writing" is something of a modern equivalent of Buddhist meditation; I do not think it is a method for writing poems, nor is it a rhetorical recipe: it is a psychic exercise, a convocation and an invocation meant to open the floodgates of the verbal stream. Poetic automatism, as Breton himself often emphasized, is very close to asceticism: a state of passivity must be reached, a very difficult task, for it requires the suspension of all criticism and self-criticism. It is a radical criticism of criticism, an interdiction of consciousness. In its way, it is a *via purgativa*, a method of negation aimed at calling forth the appearance of true reality: the primordial language.

The basis of "automatic writing" is the belief that speaking and thinking are one and the same thing. Man does not speak because he thinks; he thinks because he speaks. Or rather, speaking is no different from thinking: to speak is to think. Breton justifies this idea on the following grounds: *"Nous ne disposons spontanément pour nous exprimer que d'une seule structure verbale excluant de manière la plus catégorique toute autre structure apparemment chargée du même sens."** One immediate objection to this trenchant formula that we might raise is the fact that both in everyday speech and in written prose we come across phrases that might be expressed in different words or by the same words in a different order. Breton would rightly reply that not only the syntactical structure but also the idea itself would change from one version to another, even though the change might be imperceptible. Any change in the verbal structure results in a change of meaning. Strictly speaking, what we call synonyms are merely translations or equivalents within a language; and what we call translation is really only an approximation in another language or an interpretation. Words such as *nirvana, dharma, tao,* or *jen* are really untranslatable; the same is true of *physics, nature, democracy, revolution,* and other Western terms that have no exact equiva-

* "In spontaneous expression, we have at our disposal *only one* verbal structure, which categorically excludes any other structure supposedly possessing the same meaning."

lent in languages outside of our tradition. As the relation between the verbal structure and the meaning becomes more
intimate—in mathematics and poetry, for instance, not to mention nonverbal languages such as music and painting—translation becomes more and more difficult. At either extreme of language—the exclamation and the equation—the two halves of
the semantic sign become impossible to separate: the signifier
and the signified are one and the same. Perhaps unwittingly,
Breton thus opposes Saussure's view: language is not simply an
arbitrary convention linking sound and meaning, as linguists are
beginning to realize today.

There is a strong magical element in Breton's view of language. He not only made no distinction between magic and
poetry; he also was convinced all his life that poetry was a force,
a substance, an energy truly capable of changing reality. At the
same time his ideas were so precise and penetrating that I
would not hesitate to call them scientific. On one hand, he saw
language as an autonomous current possessed of a power all its
own, a sort of universal magnetism; on the other hand, he conceived of this erotic substance as a system of signs governed by
the twofold law of affinity and opposition, similarity and difference. This view is quite close to that held by modern linguists:
words and their constituent elements are fields of energy, like
atoms and their particles. The old notion of analogy is coming
to the fore once again: nature is a language, and language in
turn is a double of nature. To rediscover man's natural language
is to return to nature, before the Fall and History: poetry is the
proof of man's original innocence. *The Social Contract* becomes
for Breton the verbal, poetic accord between man and nature,
word and thought. Considered from this point of view, the oft-
repeated statement that Surrealism is not a school of poetry but
a movement of liberation becomes more understandable. A way
of rediscovering the language of innocence, a renewal of the
primordial pact, poetry is the basic text, the foundation of the
human order. Surrealism is revolutionary because it is a return to
the beginning of all beginnings.

Breton's earliest poems bear the traces of a passionate reading of Mallarmé. Not even in his moments of greatest violence and verbal freedom did he ever abandon this predilection for words that are at once precise and precious. Words with iridescent colors, a language of echoing reverberations. He was a "Mannerist" poet, in the proper sense of the word: within the European tradition, he belongs to the family of poets descended from Góngora, Marino, Donne—poets I cannot be certain he read, poets whose poetic ethic I fear he would have disapproved of. Verbal splendor, and intellectual and emotional violence. A curious but not infrequent combination of prophecy and aestheticism that makes his best poems both objects of beauty and spiritual testaments. That is perhaps the reason why he worshiped Lautréamont, the poet who discovered the *form* in which to express psychic explosion. That may also be the reason for Breton's instinctive and openly avowed repugnance for the simplistic, brutal destructiveness of Dada, even though he considered it a "revolutionary necessity" that was both inevitable and healthy. There were different reasons underlying his reservations concerning other poets. His admiration for Apollinaire is somewhat hesitant because to Breton poetry was the creation of realities through the Word, and not simply verbal invention. Novelty and surprise in art pleased him, but the term *invention* was not to his liking; on the other hand, the word *revelation* shines in many of his texts. Speaking is the noblest activity of all: revealing what is hidden, bringing the buried word back to life, calling forth our double, that Other which is us but which we never allow to exist—our suppressed half.

Revelation is resurrection, exposure, initiation. It is a word that calls for rites and ceremonies. Except as a means of provocation, of insulting the public, or rousing it to rebellion, Breton detested open-air spectacles: fiestas should be held in catacombs. Each of the Surrealist expositions revolved around two opposite poles: exhibitionism and secrecy, consecration and profanation. Consecration and conspiracy are consanguineous terms: revelation is also rebellion. The Other, our double, is a denial of the illusory solidity and security of our consciousness, that pillar of smoke on which we build our arrogant philosophical and religious constructs. The Others, proletarians and colonial slaves, women and poets, primitive myths and revolutionary utopias, are equally violent threats to the beliefs and institutions of the West. Breton reaches his hand out to all of them, to Fourier and the Papuan of New Guinea alike. Rebellion and revelation, language and passion are manifestations of a single reality. The true name of this reality is also a double one: innocence and marvels. Man is the creator of marvels; he is a poet because he is an innocent being. Children, women, lovers, the inspired, and even the insane are the incarnation of the marvelous. Everything they do is uncanny and they do not realize it. They know not what they do: they are not responsible, they are innocents. Magnets, lightning rods, high-tension wires: their words and their acts are senseless and yet they have a meaning. They are the scattered signs of a language in perpetual motion that opens out before our eyes a fan of contradictory meanings that in the end becomes a single, ultimate meaning. The universe speaks to us and to itself in and through them.

I have mentioned a number of Breton's words: revelation and rebellion, innocence and marvels, passion and language. There is another one: magnetism. He was one of the centers of gravity of our time. He not only believed that we humans are governed by laws of attraction and repulsion; he himself was the personal incarnation of these forces. I confess that for a long time the thought that I would say or do something that might provoke his reprobation kept me awake nights. I believe that many of his friends felt much the same way. A few years ago, Buñuel invited me to a private showing of one of his films. When it was over, he asked me: "Would Breton think it within the Surrealist tradition?" I mention Buñuel not only because he is a great artist, but also because he is a man possessed of great moral integrity and freedom of spirit. These feelings have nothing to do with fear or respect for a superior (although I believe that if there is such a thing as superior men, Breton was one of them). I never considered him a leader, much less a Pope, to repeat the ignoble epithet popularized by certain swine. Despite the fact that we were personal friends, my activities within the Surrealist group were quite tangential. Nonetheless, his affection and generosity always amazed me, from the beginning of our relationship till the very end of his life. I have never known why he was so kind to me. Was it perhaps because I was from Mexico, a country he loved all his life? Apart from these personal reasons, I must confess that many times I write as though I were having a silent conversation with Breton: objections, answers, agreement, disagreement, homage, all these things at once. I am experiencing that sensation at this very moment.

In my adolescence, in a period of isolation and great elation, I happened to read a few pages which I found out later are Chapter V of *L'Amour fou*. In them he tells of climbing the volcanic peak of Teide, on Tenerife, in the Canary Islands. This text, which I read at almost the same time as *The Marriage of Heaven and Hell*, opened the doors of modern poetry to me. It was an "art of loving," not in the trivial manner of Ovid's *Ars Amatoria*, but an initiation to something that my later life and the East have given me further proof of: the analogy, or, rather, the identity between woman and nature. Is water feminine, or is a woman a succession of waves, a river at night, a beach at dawn tattooed by the wind? If we are a metaphor of the universe, the human couple is the metaphor par excellence, the point of intersection of all forces and the seed of all forms. The couple is time recaptured, the return to the time before time. Against wind and tide, I have endeavored to be faithful to that revelation: the powers the word *love* has over me have remained intact. Or as Breton says: *"On n'en sera plus jamais quitte avec ces frondaisons de l'âge d'or."** This stubborn belief in a paradisiac age, coupled with the vision of the primordial couple, can be seen in all his writings, from the first to the last. The woman is a bridge, a place where the natural world and the

* "We will never again escape from these leafy fronds of the golden age."

human are reconciled. She is language made palpable, revelation incarnate: *"La femme n'est plus qu'un calice débordant de voyelles."**

Some years later I met Benjamin Péret, Leonora Carrington, Wolfgang Paalen, Remedios Varo, and other Surrealists who had sought refuge in Mexico during World War II. Then the war ended, and I saw Benjamin again in Paris. He took me to the Café de la Place Blanche. I saw Breton frequently over a long period of time. Although spending a great deal of time together sometimes interferes with the interchange of ideas and feelings, I was often aware of that sort of free-flowing current that really unites two people talking together, even if their views are not identical. Among all these conversations, I shall never forget one we had in the summer of 1964, just before I returned to India. I remember it not because it was the last one we ever had but because of the atmosphere surrounding it. This is not the proper place to tell about this meeting. (I have promised myself that someday I will write about it.) To me, it was an *encounter*, in Breton's meaning of the word: predestination and election. That night, as the two of us strolled through Les Halles together, the conversation turned to a subject that was worrying him: the future of the Surrealist movement. I remember what I told him, more or less: that to me Surrealism was the sacred malady of our world, like leprosy in the Middle Ages or the state of possession of the Spanish Illuminati in the sixteenth century; since it was a necessary negation in the West, it would remain alive as long as modern civilization remained alive, whatever political systems and ideologies might prevail in the future. My elation moved him, but he answered: "Negation is a function of affirmation and vice versa; I doubt very much whether the world that is now dawning can be defined in terms of affirmation or negation: we are entering a neutral zone, and the Surrealist rebellion will be obliged to express itself in forms that are neither negation nor affirmation. We have gone beyond approval or

---

* "Woman is nothing more than a flower-cup overflowing with vowels."

disapproval. . . ." I would venture the guess that this was the idea behind the group's last exposition: total separation. This was not the first time that Breton had urged the Surrealists to "go underground," but he seldom had done so that frankly and openly. Perhaps he thought that the movement would become fertile again only if it proved capable of turning itself into a clandestine force. A return to the catacombs? I don't know. I wonder whether what Mallarmé called "limited action" ("*l'action restreinte*") still makes sense in a society such as ours, a society in which the old contradictions have disappeared—not because they have been resolved in a higher synthesis, but because all values have so deteriorated that they cancel each other out. Is publishing still a form of action, or has it dissolved into an anonymous flood of publicity?

It is frequently said that the ambiguity of Surrealism stems from the fact that it is a movement of poets and painters who refuse to be judged on the basis of aesthetic criteria. Hasn't the same thing been true of all artistic schools in the past and all the works of the great poets and painters? "Art" is an invention of aesthetics, which in turn is an invention of philosophers. Nietzsche buried both and danced on their graves: what we call art is a game. The Surrealists' determination to abolish the boundaries separating art from life is nothing new; what is new are the terms Surrealists use to express themselves and the meaning of their activities. Neither "an artistic life" nor a "vital art": a return to the original source of language, to the moment when speaking is synonymous with creating. I have no idea what the future of the Surrealist group will be; I am certain, however, that the current that has flowed from German Romanticism and Blake to Surrealism will not disappear. It will live a life apart; it will be the *other* voice.

Surrealism is no longer in the vanguard, according to the critics. Quite apart from the fact that I thoroughly dislike that military term, I do not believe that novelty, that being in the vanguard of history, is the essential characteristic of Surrealism.

Nor were the Dadaists as frantic worshipers of the new as the Futurists, for instance. Neither Dada nor Surrealism adored machines. Surrealism desecrated them: it built machines that produced nothing, "dust-raisers," melting watches. The machine as a method of criticism—of the cult of machines, of men who worship progress and their buffoonery. Is Duchamp the beginning or the end of painting? Through his *œuvre*, and even more importantly through his negation of "the work of art," Duchamp closes a period of Western art (that of painting properly speaking) and opens another which is no longer "artistic": the dissolving of art in life, of language in the circle of word games, of reason in its philosophical antidote, laughter. Duchamp undermines modernity with the same wave of the hand with which he dismisses tradition. In Breton's case, there is also his vision of time as an invisible, innocent present hidden beneath the flow of hours and days. The future fascinated him because it seemed to him to be the realm of the unexpected; not what *will be* according to the calculations of reason, but what *might be* according to the imagination. The destruction of today's world would permit the appearance of real time, not historical time but natural time, governed not by progress but by desire. This was what a Communist-libertarian society meant to him. In his eyes there was no essential contradiction between myths and utopias, poetry and revolutionary programs. He read Fourier as we might read the Vedas or the Popul Vuh, and he regarded Eskimo poems as revolutionary prophecies. The dawn of history and the most remote future were naturally conjoined in his mind. His materialism was not a vulgar "scientism" and his irrationalism was not a hatred of reason.

The determination to embrace every sort of opposite—Sade and Rousseau, Novalis and Roussel, Juliette and Héloïse, Marx and Chateaubriand—is constantly in evidence, in his writings and in his acts. This attitude is at the furthest possible remove from the complacent tolerance of the skeptic. He detested eclecticism in the realm of thought and promiscuity in the realm of eroticism. His best pages, both in his prose works and in his poetry, are those inspired by the idea of free choice and its correlative, fidelity to what one has freely chosen, whether in art or in politics, in friendships or in love. This idea was the axis of his life and of his conception of love: a passion whose many facets have been polished by freedom. Our age has delivered love from the prison bars of the past century only to convert it into a pastime, one more consumer item in a society of busy consumers. Breton's vision is the exact opposite of almost everything that in our day passes for love and even for eroticism (another word in wide circulation, like a coin of very little value). I have the greatest difficulty understanding his boundless admiration for Sade's works. I can see why Sade's spirit of absolute negation moved him and excited him, but how can this total negation be reconciled with a belief in love as the radiant center of the golden age?

Sade denounces love: it is a hypocritical lie, or, worse still, an illusion. His system is hallucinatory, not incoherent: his negation is no less total than Saint Augustine's affirmation. Augustine and Sade are equally violent opponents of any sort of Manichaeism; for the Christian theologian, Evil has no ontological reality; for the atheist philosopher, what lacks reality is what we call Good: his version of *The Social Contract* is the statutes of the Society of the Friends of Crime. Bataille has endeavored to transform Sade's monologue into a dialogue, bringing absolute eroticism face to face with a no less absolute adversary: Christian divinity. The result is silence and laughter: "atheology." The unthinkable and the unnamable. Breton reintroduces love into eroticism, or, more exactly, consecrates eroticism through love. We find again, underlying his opposition to any and every religion, a passionate wish to consecrate. And even a passionate wish to reconcile. Commenting on a passage in the *New Justine*—the episode in which one of the characters mingles his sperm with the lava of Etna—Breton observes that the act is one of loving homage to nature, "*une façon, des plus folles, des plus indis-*

*cutables de l'aimer."** Breton's admiration for Sade was almost boundless, and all his life he believed that *"tant qu'on ne sera pas quitte avec l'idée de la transcendance d'un bien quelconque . . . la représentation exaltée du mal inné gardera la plus grande valeur révolutionnaire."†* But with this one reservation, in the dialogue between Sade and Rousseau, Breton is irresistibly inclined to side with the latter: with Rousseau the friend of primitive man, the lover of nature, as with Fourier the utopian. Love is not an illusion: it is the intermediary between man and nature, the place where terrestrial and spiritual magnetism intersect.

Each one of the facets of Breton's works reflects all the others. It is not the passive reflection of the mirror, however: it is not a repetition but a reply. A play of contrary beams of light, a dialogue of glimmers. Magnetism, revelation, a thirst for innocence, and also disdain. Is there hauteur here? Yes, in the etymological sense of the word: Breton is a winged creature whose kingdom is the upper air, a bird whose realm is lofty heights. All the words of this family apply to him. He was a soaring spirit, a man exalted; his poetry uplifts us. Above all, he maintained that the body of the woman and the man are our only altars. And as for death? Every man is born several times and dies several times. This is not the first time that Breton has died. He knew, better than anyone, that we die more than once: each one of his central books is the story of a resurrection. I know that this time it is different, that we will never see him again. His latest death is not an illusion. Nonetheless, Breton lived certain instants, saw with his own eyes certain evidences that are the negation of time and what we call an everyday outlook on life. I call such moments poetic instants, even though they are experiences common to all men: the only difference is that the poet remembers them and endeavors to reincarnate them in words, sounds, colors.

---

* "One of the most insane, one of the most unquestionable ways of loving it."
† "So long as we have not freed ourselves of the idea of the transcendence of some sort of good . . . the impassioned representation of innate evil will continue to have the greatest revolutionary value."

The man who has lived these instants and is capable of pondering their meaning knows that the self cannot be redeemed because it does not exist. He also knows that, as Breton repeatedly insisted, the boundaries between waking and dreaming, life and death, time and a timeless present are fluid and vague. We do not know what it is really like to die, except that it is the end of the individual self—the end of the prison. Breton broke out of this prison many times; he expanded time or denied it, and for a measureless instant coincided with the *other* time. This experience, the central core of his life and his thought, is invulnerable and untouchable: it is beyond time, beyond death—beyond us. Knowing that this is so reconciles me to his latest death and to all dying.

The Verbal Pact and Correspondence

The affinities between Rousseau and André Breton are both numerous and obvious. What is more, they are not only intellectual but also (and much more importantly) temperamental. Breton was aware of them, but to my knowledge critics have as yet written almost nothing about them. An excellent essay by the poet Ernesto Mejía Sánchez,* which I read shortly after writing the above pages in memory of Breton, has made the relationship between Rousseau and the founder of Surrealism even clearer. In this solid and scholarly work, Mejía Sánchez analyzes a little-known text of Rousseau's, the *Essai sur l'origine des langues* (*On the Origin of Languages*), which may quite legitimately be regarded as a sort of anticipation of the Surrealist conception of language. I confess that I was not familiar with this work and have no idea whether Breton ever read it. I

* "El pensamiento literario de Rousseau," in the volume *Presencia de Rousseau* (1962).

am inclined to believe he did not know it; if he had, he would have mentioned it in one or another of his writings. But whether due to sheer coincidence or a demonstrable influence, the similarity is immediately obvious. Breton, for example, believed that society is based on language, rather than vice versa; Mejía Sánchez points out that for Rousseau "there is a linguistic pact that antedates the social pact." I shall cite other striking similarities: the idea of language as a nonutilitarian mechanism aimed at satisfying our emotional needs (*"On prétend que les hommes inventèrent la parole pour exprimer leurs besoins; cette opinion me paraît insoutenable . . . [elle vient] des besoins moraux, des passions"*);* metaphor as the primordial form of speech (*"le premier langage dut être figuré"*);† and the connection between verbal image and passion (*"l'image illusoire offerte par la passion se montrant la première, le langage qui lui répondait fut aussi le premier inventé; il devint ensuite métaphorique. . . ."*).†† Passion, primordial language, metaphor: Breton's ideas and preoccupations were already implicit in the *Essai sur l'origine des langues.*

Despite these similarities, of all the writers of the eighteenth century it was not Rousseau but Sade whom Breton admired first and respected most. But did he love him, did he feel that he belonged to the same spiritual family as Sade? I doubt it. I have already said that what fascinated Breton was Sade's thoroughgoing negation. A free spirit such as André Breton could not help but be moved by the persecution Sade suffered and the moral integrity with which he confronted his many tribulations, never once abjuring his ideas. Sade is an example of moral rectitude; Rousseau is not. Although Breton too was an incorruptible man of absolute integrity, his passions were not those of

* "It is commonly said that men invented speech to express their needs; this opinion seems to me to be untenable . . . [language stems from] moral needs, from the passions."
† ". . . language in the beginning was no doubt figurative."
†† ". . . the illusory image offered by passion appearing first, the language that was its expression was also the first to be invented; it then became metaphorical."

Sade but those of Rousseau, and the same holds true of his ideas. Both are centered upon a reality that Sade blindly and stubbornly refused to recognize: the human heart.

According to Rousseau, speech is born "of a mutual pact between men." But as Mejía Sánchez comments: "This unanimous and enduring pact is implicit in language itself, however. Speech does not exist in and for itself; it is speech with others. Rousseau failed to see, however, that a contradiction is involved here. . . ." There is indeed a contradiction: language cannot antedate society because it implies the existence of social intercourse —it is *with and for others* by its very nature.

At the same time, it is not human society that creates language, but language that creates human society. Language lies outside of society because it is its foundation; but it also lies within society because that is the only place where it exists and the only place where it develops. Language lies on the borderline between nature and culture: it does not appear in the former and is the condition of the latter. How and when did men begin to speak? And above all, *why* did they speak? Whatever the cause or causes that led man to utter the first onomatopoeic syllables, the real mystery lies in the fact that of all living creatures man is the only one possessed of the faculty of speech. Since I do not believe that the riddle of the origin of language can be solved by historical methods, we are forced to rely on theology and philosophy or their modern successors, biology and anthropology. Among the hypotheses that have been advanced, two seem quite attractive to me. One of them is Rousseau's: the origin of speech is to be explained by the intervention of a nonhuman, *divine* power. The other is Lévi-Strauss's, even though he has never formulated it:* language is the result of the intervention of a nonhuman, *natural* power. By "nonhuman," I mean that language is not a product of society but rather its condition or foundation; by "natural" I mean that the structure of human brain cells, which may be taken to be the ultimate source

* I have deduced it from the ideas expressed in his writings.

of the language faculty, can be described in terms of chemistry, and these in turn can be explained by physics. Animal language cannot explain human language: both are part of the system of relations constituting nature, but they are different answers to different problems of communication.

These two hypotheses are not as contradictory as they may initially appear to be. In both, there enters into play an element that is foreign to man and irreducible to human society: God or nature. This element is an agent that transcends the dichotomy between culture and nature and does away with the distinction between matter and thought. This latter fact is surprising. Thought, which science has expelled from its place at the top of the spiral of evolution, reappears at the bottom of it: the physical structure of atoms and their particles is a mathematical structure, a relation. What is equally extraordinary is that this structure can be reduced to a system of signs—and is therefore a language. The power of speech is a particular manifestation of natural communication; human language is one more dialect in the linguistic system of the universe. We might add: the cosmos is a language of languages. The new materialism is to nineteenth-century materialism what Marx and Darwin were to eighteenth-century materialism. Our materialism is not dialectical or biological but mathematical, linguistic, mental. Strictly speaking, it is neither idealism nor materialism. It is not idealism because it reduces the Idea to a combination of physicochemical stimuli and responses; it is not materialism because it regards matter as a system of communication: the phenomenon is a message or a relation between factors that continue to be called material only because of our lazy verbal habits. The basic structure of these factors is no different from that of mathematical and verbal symbols: it is a system of relations. Before our era a Providence or a Logos reigned, a matter or a history perpetually tending toward more perfect forms; now an unconscious thought, a mental mechanism guides us and thinks us. A mathematical structure determines us—*signifies* us.

The idea that language does not stem from physical necessity may seem strange, but it is not absurd. If we think about it, Rousseau was right. Whether it comes from God or from nature, language is not intended to satisfy biological needs, since animals survive as individuals and as species without articulate language. There is a gap between animal language and human language because the latter is intended to satisfy nonanimal necessities, the passions, and entities no less powerful and no less illusory than the passions: the tribe, the family, labor, the State, religion, myth, the awareness of death, rites, etc. These necessities are artificial ones since they are not found among animals, but the artifice that satisfies them is *natural*: a system of signs found in nature, from the stars to atomic particles. Rousseau's great merit was to have seen that the boundary lines between culture and nature are very tenuous. This is an idea that is equally repugnant to the Christian and the Marxist: both believe that man is historical, unique, singular. Returning to Rousseau is salutary: he is like one of those fountains we find at a crossroads at the entrance to a town. On drinking from it, we find the water delightfully cool and refreshing, and before losing ourselves in the dusty little streets of the town we turn around one last time to listen to the wind in the trees. The wind may be saying the same thing as the water falling on the stone. For an instant we glimpse the meaning of the word *reconciliation*.

Mejía Sánchez comments that Rousseau, "as though foreseeing the epidemic of *correspondences*, points out the false analogy between colors and sounds." Here I do not agree. If colors and sounds are languages (and they are), it is clear that there is a correspondence between them. It is not an explicit correspondence because each language is in a different key: what colors say, for instance, must be transposed into the language of sounds or words. But we transpose the olfactory "key" into the verbal key and the verbal key into the auditory or tactile every day. This is what Lévi-Strauss has done in a most admirable way in *Le cru et le cuit* (*The Raw and the Cooked*): he has deciphered the mythological code of the Brazilian Indians and translated it into the terms of contemporary logic and science. We live our lives immersed in a language that is not only verbal but also musical and visual, tactile and olfactory, sensory and mental. There are those who will maintain that these correspondences are illusory or subjective: the relation between the sign and what it signifies is arbitrary, the product of a convention. That is true —but only up to a certain point: this is a problem that has not been satisfactorily dealt with as yet. The objection carries little weight for another reason: if we accept Saussure's view that the connection between signifier and signified is an arbitrary one, we must also concede that, once the signs are constituted, we live in a universe of symbols governed by the correspondences between them. We enter the world of symbols the day we are born; once we are given a name, we are a symbol among other symbols, a word related to other words.

What in the past appeared to be fuzzy philosophizing by poets is today a scientifically recognized fact. A linguistic area is a system of symbols that vary from one subarea to another and even within the same language (Hispano-American linguistic symbolism, for example, is not the same throughout the continent). Each linguistic area in turn is related to all the others, and therefore there is a correspondence between the various symbolic systems that go to make up the whole of human societies. These systems are what we call civilizations, and all these systems, taken together, in turn form another universe of symbols. The verbal pact is both something more and something less than a historical fact: it is the symbol of symbols. It refers to the totality of facts, and each and every fact fulfills it, embodies it.

Recapitulations

The poem is unexplainable, not unintelligible.

A poem is rhythmic language—not language with a rhythm (song) or mere verbal rhythm (a property common to all language, including prose).

Rhythm is a relation of difference and similarity: this sound is *not* that one, this sound is *like* that one.

Rhythm is the original metaphor and encompasses all the others. It says: succession is repetition, time is nontime.

Whether lyric, epic, or dramatic, the poem is succession and repetition, a date on the calendar and a rite. The "happening" is also a poem (theater) and a rite (fiesta), but it lacks one essential emenent: rhythm, the reincarnation of the instant. We repeat Góngora's hendecasyllables and the final monosyllables of Huidobro's *Altazor* again and again; Swann listens to the Vinteuil sonata, Agamemnon sacrifices Iphigenia, Segismundo discovers he is dreaming with his eyes open, again and again. But the "happening" occurs only once.

The instant dissolves in the succession of other nameless instants. In order to *save it* we must *convert it* into a rhythm. The "happening" opens up another possibility: the instant that is never repeated. By definition, this instant is the final one: the "happening" is an allegory of death.

The Roman circus is a "happening" *avant la lettre*—and its negation. If the participants in a "happening" were really faithful to their principles, all would die. Moreover, the true representation of the final instant would require the extermination of the human race. The one unrepeatable event: the end of the world.

Somewhere between the Roman circus and the "happening": the bullfight. Risk, but also style.

A poem consisting of a single syllable is no less complex than the *Divine Comedy* or *Paradise Lost*. The Satasahasrika sutra sets forth the basic teachings in a hundred thousand strophes; the Eksaksari in one syllable: *a*. All language, all meaning, and at the same time the ultimate absence of meaning of language and the world, is condensed in the sound of this one vowel.

Understanding a poem means, first of all, *hearing it*.

Words enter through our ears, appear before our eyes, disappear in contemplation. Every reading of a poem tends to call forth silence.

To read a poem is to hear it with our eyes; to hear it is to see it with our ears.

In the United States, it has become the fashion for poets to read their poems in public. This is a dubious practice, because the ability to really listen to poetry is a lost art; what is more, modern poets are writers and therefore "poor actors of their own emotions." But poetry of the future will be oral. A collaboration between speaking machines, and an audience of poets, it will be the art of *listening to messages and combining them*. Isn't that what we do today every time we read a book of poems?

When we read a poem or listen to one, we do not smell, taste, or touch the words. All these sensations are mental images.

In order to experience a poem, we must understand it; in order to understand it we must hear it, see it, contemplate it—convert it into an echo, a shadow, nothingness. Comprehension is a spiritual exercise.

Duchamp said: since a three-dimensional object casts a two-dimensional shadow, we should be able to imagine the unknown four-dimensional object whose shadow we are. I for my part am fascinated by the search for a one-dimensional object that casts no shadow at all.

Each reader is another poet; each poem another poem.

Though it perpetually changes, poetry does not advance.

In ordinary discourse one phrase lays the groundwork for the next; it is a chain with a beginning and an end. In a poem the first phrase contains the last one and the last one evokes the first. Poetry is our only recourse against rectilinear time—against progress.

The writer's morality does not lie in the subjects he deals with or the arguments he sets forth, but in his behavior toward language.

In poetry, technique is another name for morality: it is not a manipulation of words but a passion and an asceticism.

The false poet speaks of himself, almost invariably in the name of others. The true poet speaks with others when he talks to himself.

The difference between a "closed" work and an "open" work is not an absolute one. To be complete, the hermetic poem requires the intervention of a reader to decipher it. The open poem, in turn, implies at least a minimal structure: a starting point, or as the Buddhists put it, a "prop" for meditation. In the first case, the reader *opens* the poem; in the second, he completes it, he *closes* it.

The blank page or the page covered with nothing but punctuation marks is like a cage without a bird inside. The real open work is the one that *closes* the door: the reader, on opening it, lets the bird, the poem, out.

Opening the poem in search of *this* and discovering *that*—always something different from what we expected.

Whether open or closed, the poem demands the demise of the poet who writes it and the birth of the poet who reads it.

Poetry is a perpetual struggle against meaning. Two extremes: the poem encompasses all meanings, it is the meaning of all meanings; or the poem denies language any sort of meaning. In the modern era, Mallarmé represents the attempt to write the first sort of poem; Dada the second. A language beyond language or the destruction of language by means of language.

Dada failed because it believed that the defeat of language would be the triumph of the poet. Surrealism proclaimed the supreme rule of language over the poet. It is up to young poets to abolish the distinction between creator and reader: to discover the meeting point between speaker and listener. This point is the heart of language.

Completing the work of Nietzsche, taking negation as far as it will go. At the end of the road, play awaits us: fiesta, the consummation of the work, its momentary incarnation and its dissolution.

Taking negation as far as it will go. Contemplation awaits us there: the disincarnation of language, transparency.

What Buddhism offers us is the end of relations, the abolition of dialectics—a silence that is not the dissolution but the *resolution* of language.

The poem must provoke the reader: force him to hear—to hear himself.

To hear oneself or to hie oneself: *oírse o irse.* To what place?

Poetic activity is born of desperation in the face of the impotence of the word and ends in the recognition of the omnipotence of silence.

No one is a poet unless he has felt the temptation to destroy language or create another one, unless he has experienced the fascination of nonmeaning and the no less terrifying fascination of meaning that is inexpressible.

Between the cry and silence, between the meaning that is all meanings and the absence of meaning, the poem arises. What does this thin stream of words say? It says that it says nothing not already said by silence and shouting. And once this is said, the tumult and the silence cease. A precarious victory, ever threatened by words that say nothing, by the silence that says: nothing.

To believe in the immortality of a poem would be to believe in the immortality of language. We must bow to the evidence: languages are born and die; any meaning will one day cease to have meaning. And isn't this ceasing to have meaning the meaning of meaning? We must bow to the evidence. . . .

Triumph of the Word: the poem is like those female nudes of German painting that symbolize the victory of death. Glorious living monuments of the corruption of the flesh.

Poetry and mathematics are the two extreme poles of language. Beyond them there is nothing—the realm of the inexpressible; between them the immense but finite realm of speech.

Enamored of silence, the poet's only recourse is to speak.

The Word has its roots in a silence *previous* to speech—a presentiment of language. Silence, *after* the Word, is based on a language—it is an encoded silence. The poem is the trajectory between these two silences—between the wish to speak and the silence that fuses the wishing and the speaking.

Beyond surprise and repetition: ——————————————————

Knowledge, Drugs, Inspiration

There is more than one similiarity between modern poetry and science. Both are experiments, in the sense of "testing in a laboratory": an attempt is made to produce a certain phenomenon through the separation or combination of certain elements which the experimenter has either subjected to the pressure of some outward force or left to develop according to the laws of their own nature. This operation takes place in a closed space, in the most complete isolation possible. The poet deals with words as the scientist deals with cells, atoms, and other material particles: he extracts them from their natural medium, everyday language, isolates them in a sort of vacuum chamber, combines them or separates them; he observes and uses the properties of language as the scientific researcher observes and uses the properties of matter. The analogy might be carried further, but it is pointless to do so because the similarity lies not so much in the outward resemblances between verbal manipulations and laboratory testing as in the attitude toward the object.

As he writes, as he tests his ideas and his words, the poet does not know precisely what is going to happen. His attitude toward the poem is empirical. Unlike the religious believer, he is not

73

attempting to confirm a revealed truth; unlike the mystic, he is not endeavoring to become one with a transcendent reality; unlike the ideologue, he is not trying to demonstrate a theory. The poet does not postulate or affirm anything a priori; he knows that what counts is not ideas but results, not intentions but works. Isn't this the same attitude as that of the scientist? Poetry and science do not imply a total rejection of prior conceptions and intuitions. But theories ("working hypotheses") are not what justify experiments; rather, the converse is true. Sometimes the "testing" produces results that are different from or entirely contrary to our expectations. The poet and the scientist do not find this difficult to accept; both are resigned to the fact that reality often acts quite independently of our philosophy. Poets and scientists are not doctrinaires; they do not offer us a priori systems but proven facts, results rather than hypotheses, works rather than ideas. The truths they seek are different but they employ similar methods to ascertain them. The rigorous procedures they follow are accompanied by the strictest objectivity, that is to say, a respect for the autonomy of the phenomenon being investigated. A poem and a scientific truth are something more than a theory or a belief: they have withstood the acid of proof and the fire of criticism. Poems and scientific truths are something quite different from the ideas of poets and scientists. Artistic styles and the philosophy of science are transient things; works of art and the real truths of science are not.

Yet the similarities between science and poetry must not blind us to a crucial difference between them, one having to do with the subject of the experiment. The scientist is an observer, and plays no part, at least voluntarily, in the experiment. I say "voluntarily" because at times the observer inevitably becomes part of the phenomenon being observed. In the case of modern poetry, the subject of the experiment is the poet himself: he is both the observer and the phenomenon observed. His body and his psyche, his entire being, are the "field" in which all sorts of transformations take place. Modern poetry is an experimental process whereby the knowing subject is the object of knowledge.

To see with our ears, to feel with our minds, to combine our powers and use them to the limit, to know a little more about ourselves and discover within us unknown realities: is that not the aim assigned poetry by spirits as different as Coleridge, Baudelaire, and Apollinaire? I mention only a few names because I believe that there is little doubt in anyone's mind that this is one of the cardinal directions that has consistently been taken by poets and poetry from the beginning of the nineteenth century to our own time. And I might even add that the real modernity of poetry lies in its having won its autonomy. Poetry has ceased to be the handmaiden of religion or philosophy; like science, it explores the universe on its own. And in this respect also there is a great similarity between certain poets and the scientists: they too have not hesitated to engage in dangerous experiments, at the risk of their lives or their spiritual wholeness, in order to explore forbidden zones. Poetry is a form of knowledge, of experimental knowledge.

Modern poetry claims to be a vision, that is to say, a knowledge of hidden, invisible realities. It is true that the poets of all times and all places have said as much. But Homer, Virgil, or Dante insist that their poetry has to do with a revelation that comes from outside themselves: a god or a demon speaks through their mouths. Even Góngora pretends to believe in this supernatural power: *"Cuántas me dictó versas dulce Musa."** The modern poet declares that he is speaking in his own name: he extracts his visions from within himself. The disturbing disappearance of divine powers has coincided with the appearance of drugs as the bestowers of the gift of poetic vision. The familiar demon, the muse, or the divine spirit have been supplanted by laudanum, opium, hashish, and, more recently, Mexican drugs: peyote (mescaline) and hallucinogenic mushrooms. Many drugs were known and used in the ancient world to further contemplation, revelation, ecstasy. The original name of the Mexican

---

* "How many verses the sweet Muse dictated to me."

sacred mushroom was *teononáncatl,* which means "the flesh of of God, the divine mushroom." American Indians and many African and Eastern peoples still use drugs for religious purposes. I myself had the opportunity to try a variety of hashish called bhang during a religious festival in India; all those present, even the children, ate or drank it. But the difference is that for believers these practices constitute a rite; for a number of modern poets, they are an experiment.

Baudelaire is one of the first to have pondered "in a philosophic spirit," as he put it, the spiritual phenomena engendered by the use of drugs. It is quite true that many of his observations are borrowed from Thomas De Quincey and that Coleridge before him had confessed that the composition of one of his most celebrated poems stemmed from a vision produced by laudanum, during which "all the images rose up as things, with a parallel production of the correspondent expressions, without any sensation or consciousness of effort." But neither De Quincey nor Coleridge endeavored to extract an aesthetic and a philosophy from his experience. Baudelaire, on the other hand, stated that certain drugs intensify our sensations to such a degree and combine them in such a way that that they enable us to see life whole. Drugs provoke the vision of the universal correspondence of all things, arouse the powers of analogy, set objects in motion, make the world a vast poem shaped by rhymes and rhythms. Drugs snatch us out of everyday reality, blur our perception, alter our sensations, and, in a word, put the entire universe in a state of suspension. This break with the outside world is only a preliminary phase; with the same implacable gentleness, drugs take us to the very heart of another reality: the world has not changed, but it is now seen to be governed by a secret harmony. Baudelaire's vision is a poet's vision. Hashish did not reveal to him the philosophy of universal correspondence or that of language as a living organism and a sort of archetype of reality: drugs served him as a way of reaching deeper levels within himself. Like other really crucial experiences, drugs turn everyday reality topsy-turvy and force us to contemplate our inner selves. They do not open the doors of another world nor do they free our fantasy: rather, they open the doors of *our world* and bring us face to face with *our phantoms*.

The temptation of drugs, Baudelaire said, is a sign of our love for the infinite. Drugs take us back to the center of the universe, the point of intersection of all the world's paths, and the place where all contradictions are reconciled. Man returns, so to speak, to his original state of innocence. Time stands still, though paradoxically it continues to flow, like a fountain whose waters continually circulate, so that ascent and fall become fused in a single movement. Space becomes a system of flashing signals, and the four cardinal points of the compass submit to our rule. All this is achieved by means of a chemical communion. A pharmaceutical compound, the poet pointed out, can open the gates of paradise to us. This idea shocks or irritates many people. It seems dangerous and antisocial: the use of drugs diverts man from his productive activities, it weakens his will, and makes him a parasite. Could we not say the same thing of mysticism and of all meditation in general? The condemnation of drugs on the grounds of their uselessness might be extended (and is in fact being extended) to mysticism, love, and art. All these activities are antisocial; since it is impossible to do away with them altogether, society continually attempts to limit them. Religious believers—and those who are upholders of conventional morality—are repelled by the idea of drugs as the key to divine vision, or at least to a certain spiritual peace. Those who react in this way may have failed to realize that drugs are not a substitute for the old supernatural powers. The disappearance of the idea of God in the modern world is not due to the appearance of drugs (for drugs have after all been known and used for thousands of years). We might, in fact, say the exact opposite: the use of drugs betrays the fact that man is not a *natural* being; he experiences not only thirst, hunger, dreams, and sexual pleasure, but also a nostalgia for the infinite. The supernatural—to use a convenient but inaccurate term—is part of his nature. Everything he does, including his simplest physical acts, is tinged with a yearning for the absolute. Imagination—the power to produce images and the temptation to incarnate these images— is part of his nature. Imagination: a faculty of our nature to change itself.

Henri Michaux

Henri Michaux has published three books in recent years dealing with his experience with mescaline.* He has also confronted us with a disturbing series of sketches—most of them in black and white, and a few in color—executed shortly after each of his experiences. His prose, his poems, and his sketches are intimately related, for each medium of expression reinforces and illuminates the others. The sketches are not simply illustrations of the texts. Michaux's painting has never been a mere adjunct to his poetry: the two are at once autonomous and complementary worlds. In the case of the "mescaline experience," lines and words form a whole almost impossible to break down into its component elements. Forms, ideas, and sensations intertwine as though they were a single, dizzyingly proliferating entity. In a certain sense the sketches, far from being *illustrations* of the written word, are a sort of *commentary*. The rhythm and the movement of the lines are mindful of a kind of curious musical notation, except that we are confronted not with a method of recording sounds but with vortexes, gashes, interweavings of being. Incisions in the bark of time, halfway between the ideograph and the magical sign, characters and forms "more palpable than legible," these sketches are a criticism of poetic and

* *Misérable miracle* (1956); *L'infini turbulent* (1957); and *Paix dans les brisements* (1959). In *Les lettres nouvelles* (num. 35), there appeared a brief text of Michaux's on hallucinogenic mushrooms: "La Psilocybine (Expérience et autocritique)." See on this latter subject the book by Roger Heim and Gordon Wasson, *Les champignons hallucinogènes du Mexique* (1958).

pictorial writing, that is to say, a step beyond the sign and the image, something transcending words and lines.

Painting and poetry are languages that Michaux has used to try to express something that is truly inexpressible. A poet first, he began to paint when he realized that this new medium might enable him to say what he had found it impossible to say in his poetry. But is it a question of expression? Perhaps Michaux has never tried to express anything. All his efforts have been directed at reaching that zone, by definition indescribable and incommunicable, in which meanings disappear. A center at once completely empty and completely full, a total vacuum and a total plenitude. The sign and the signified—the distance between the object and the conscience that contemplates it—melt away in the face of the overwhelming presence, the only thing that really exists. Michaux's *œuvre*—his poems, his real and imaginary travels, his painting—is an expedition winding its way toward some of our infinities—the most secret, the most fearful, and at times the most derisive ones—in a never-ending search for the *other* infinite.

Michaux travels via his languages: lines, words, colors, silences, rhythms. And he does not hesitate to break the back of a word, the way a horseman does not hesitate to wind his mount. In order to arrive: where? At that nowhere that is here, there, and everywhere. Language as a vehicle, but also language as a knife and a miner's lamp. Language as cautery and as bandage, language as fog and a siren amid the fog. A pick striking rock and a spark in the blackness. Words once again become tools, prolongations of the hand, of the eye, of thought. A nonartistic language. Slashing, cutting words, reduced to their most immediate and most forthright function: clearing a path. Their utility is paradoxical, however, since they are not employed to foster communication, but rather pressed into the service of the incommunicable. The extraordinary tension of Michaux's language stems from the fact that it is an undoubtedly effective tool, but its sole use is to bare something that is completely ineffective by its very nature: the state of nonknowledge that is beyond knowledge, the thought that no longer thinks because it has been united with itself, total transparency, a motionless whirlwind.

Misérable miracle opens with this phrase: "This is an exploration. Through the word, the sign, the sketch. Mescaline is what is explored." When I had read the last page, I asked myself whether the result of the experiment had not been precisely the opposite: the poet Michaux explored by mescaline. An exploration or an encounter? The latter, most probably. A physical encounter with the drug, with the earthquake, with the cataclysm of being, shaken to its very foundations by its inner enemy—an enemy that is one with our own intimate being, an enemy that is indistinguishable and inseparable from ourselves. An encounter with mescaline: an encounter with our own selves, with the known-unknown. The double that wears our own face as its mask. The face that is gradually obliterated and transformed into an immense mocking grimace. The devil. The clown. This thing that I am not. This thing that I am. A martyrisible apparition. And when my own face reappears, there is nobody there. I too have left myself. Space, space, pure vibration. A great gift of the gods, mescaline is a window through which we look out upon endless distances where nothing ever meets our eye but our own gaze. There is no *I*: there is space, vibration, perpetual animation. Battles, terrors, elation, panic, delight: is it Michaux or mescaline? It was all already there in Michaux, in his previous books. Mescaline was a *confirmation*. Mescaline: a testimony. The poet saw his inner space in outer space. The shift from the inside to the outside—an outside that is interiority itself, the heart of reality. A horrible, ineffable spectacle. Michaux can say: I left my life behind to catch a glimpse of life.

It all begins with a vibration. An imperceptible movement that accelerates minute by minute. Wind, a long screeching whistle, a lashing hurricane, a torrent of faces, forms, lines. Everything falling, rushing forward, ascending, disappearing, reappearing. A dizzying evaporation and condensation. Bubbles, more bubbles, pebbles, little stones. Rocky cliffs of gas. Lines that cross, rivers meeting, endless bifurcations, meanders, deltas, deserts that walk, deserts that fly. Disintegrations, agglutinations, fragmentations, reconstitutions. Shattered words, the copulation of syllables, the fornication of meanings. Destruction of language. Mescaline reigns through silence—and it screams, screams without a mouth, and we fall into its silence! A return to vibrations, a plunge into undulations. Repetitions: mescaline is an "infinity-machine." Heterogeneity, a continuous eruption of fragments, particles, pieces. Furious series. Nothing is fixed. Avalanches, the kingdom of uncountable numbers, accursed proliferation. Gangrenous space, cancerous time. Is there no center? Battered by the gale of mescaline, sucked up by the abstract whirlwind, the modern Westerner finds absolutely nothing to hold on to. He has forgotten the names, God is no longer called God. The Aztec or the Tarahumara had only to pronounce the name, and immediately the presence would descend, in all its infinite manifestations. Unity and plurality for the ancients. For us who lack gods: Pullulation and Time. We have lost the names. All we have left is "causes and effects, antecedents and consequences." Space teeming with trivialities. Heterogeneity is repetition, an amorphous mass. Miserable miracle.

Michaux's first encounter with mescaline ends with the discovery of an "infinity-machine." The endless production of colors, rhythms, and forms turns out in the end to be an awesome, absurd flood of cheap trinkets. We are millionaires with vast hoards of fairgrounds junk. The second series of experiments (*L'infini turbulent*) provoked unexpected reactions and visions. Subject to continuous physiological discharges and a pitiless psychic tension. Being split apart. The exploration of mescaline, like a great fire or an earthquake, was devastating; all that remained intact was the essential, that which, being infinitely weak, is infinitely strong. What name can we give this faculty? Is it in fact a faculty, a power, or is it an absence of power, the total helplessness of man? I am inclined to believe it is the latter. This helplessness is our strength. At the last moment, when there is nothing left in us—when self is lost, when identity is lost—a fusion takes place, a fusion with something alien to us that nonetheless is ours, the only thing that is truly ours. The empty pit, the hole that we are fills to overflowing, and becomes a wellspring once again. When the drought is most severe, water gushes forth. Perhaps there is a point where the being of man and the being of the universe meet. Apart from this, nothing positive: a hole, an abyss, a turbulent infinite. A forsakenness, alienation, but not insanity. Madmen are imprisoned within their madness, which is an ontological error, so to speak: taking the part for the whole. Equidistant from sanity and insanity, the vision Michaux describes is total: contemplation of the demoniacal and the divine—there is no way around these words —as an indivisible reality, as the ultimate reality. Of man or of the universe? I do not know. Perhaps of the man-universe. Man penetrated, conquered by the universe.

The demoniacal stage of the experiment was above all the revelation of a transhuman eroticism—and therefore infinitely perverted. A psychic rape, an insidious opening and extending and exhibiting of the most secret parts of being. Not at all sexual. An infinitely sensual universe, from which the human body and the human face had disappeared. Not the "triumph of matter" or that of the flesh, but the vision of the reverse side of the spirit. An abstract lasciviousness: "Dissolution—an apt word that I understood instantly. Delight in deliquescence." Temptation, in the literal sense of the word, as all the mystics (Christian, Buddhist, Arab) have reported. I nonetheless confess that I do not understand this passage at all. Perhaps the cause of Michaux's sense of repulsion was not so much the contact with Eros as the vision of the confusion of the cosmos, that is to say, the revelation of pure chaos. The visible entrails, the reverse side of presence, chaos is the primordial stuff, the original disorder, and also the universal womb. I felt a similar sensation, though a much less intense one, in the great summer of India, during my first visit in 1952. Once I had fallen into that panting maw, the universe seemed to me to be an immense, multiple fornication. I suddenly had a glimpse of the meaning of the architecture of Konarak and erotic asceticism. The vision of chaos is a sort of ritual bath, a regeneration through immersion in the original fountain, a return to the "life before." Primitive tribes, the early Greeks, the Chinese, Taoists, and other peoples have had no fear of this awesome contact. The Western attitude is unwholesome. It is moral. Morality, the great isolator, the great separator, divides man in half. To return to the unity of the vision is to reconcile body, soul, and the world. At the end of the experiment, Michaux recalls a fragment of a Tantric poem:

> Inaccessible to impregnations,
> Enjoying all joys,
> Touching everything like the wind,
> Everything penetrating it like ether,
> The ever-pure yogi
> Bathes in the ever-flowing river.
> He enjoys all joys and nothing defiles him.

The divine vision—inseparable from the demoniacal vision, since both are revelations of *unity*—began with "the appearance of the gods." Thousands, hundreds of thousands, one after the other, in an endless file, an infinity of august countenances, a horizon of beneficent presences. Amazement and gratitude. But before that: surges of whiteness. Whiteness everywhere, sonorous, resplendent. And light, seas of light. Afterward, the divine images disappeared though the tranquil, delightful cascade of being did not cease. Admiration: "I cling to the divine perfection of the continuation of Being through time, a continuation that is so beautiful—so beautiful that I lose consciousness—so beautiful that, as the Mahabharata says, the gods themselves grow jealous and come to admire it." Trust, faith (in what? simply faith), the sensation of being carried along by perfection that flows ceaselessly (and yet does not flow), ever identical with itself. An instant is born, ascends, opens out, disappears, just as another instant is born and ascends. One felicity after another. An inexpressible feeling of abandon and security. The vision of the gods is followed by nonvision: we are at the very heart of time. This journey is a return: a letting go, an unlearning, a traveling homeward to birth. On reading these pages of Michaux, I remembered a pre-Columbian object that the painter Paalen showed me some years ago: a block of quartz with the image of the old and wrinkled god Tlaloc engraved on it. He went over to a window and held it up to the light:

> Touched by light
> The quartz is suddenly a cascade.
> The infant god floats on the waters.

Nonvision: outside of actuality, history, purposes, calculations, hate, love, "beyond resolution and want of resolution, *beyond preferences*," the poet journeys back to a perpetual birth and listens to "the endless poem, without rhymes, without music, without words, that the Universe ceaselessly recites." The experience is participation in an infinite that is measure and rhythm. The words *water, music, light, great open space*, echoing and re-echoing, inevitably come to our lips. The self disappears, but no other self appears to occupy the empty space it has left. No god but rather the divine. No faith but rather the primordial feeling that sustains all faith, all hope. No face but rather faceless being, the being that is all faces. Peace in the crater of the volcano, the reconciliation of man—what remains of man—with total presence.

On embarking on his experiment, Michaux wrote: "I propose to explore the mediocre human condition." The second part of this sentence—a sentence which applies, I might add, to Michaux's entire *œuvre* and to that of any great artist—turned out to be strikingly false. The exploration showed that man is not a mediocre creature. A part of oneself—a part walled in, obscured from the very beginning of the beginning—is open to the infinite. The so-called human condition is a point of intersection with other forces. Perhaps our condition is not merely human.

Grace, Asceticism, Merits*

Confronted by experiences such as those described by Michaux, we may again ask the question: is pharmacy a substitute for grace, is poetic vision a biochemical reaction? Coleridge attributed the composition of his extraordinary "Kubla Khan" to laudanum; Michaux believes that the combination of a state of physiological debility—a slight fever, tonsillitis—and an overdose is enough to unleash the torrent. There is unquestionably a relationship between physiological and psychic states. Fasting, breathing exercises, flagellation, prolonged immobility, solitary confinement in cells or caverns, exposure to the elements atop columns or mountains, songs, dances, perfumes, the repetition of a single word for hours at a time are practices that disturb our physical functions and provoke visions. What we call *mind* would appear to be a product of chemical and biological processes; and what we call *matter* has also turned out to be energy, time, a hole, a fall, in short, something that is no longer "matter." Though the age-old quarrel between materialism and spiritualism scarcely concerns me, I find the fragility of our moral conceptions in the face of the onslaught of drugs disturbing. Among Michaux's many observations, there is one that has long preyed on my mind: the demoniacal vision came *after* the divine vision. This is a dualistic, moral conception, as I have suggested above: mescaline itself is singularly contemptuous of the deas of good and evil. Or rather it is both contemptuous and generous, for it offers revelation without regard to the "merits" of the person who experiences it. Michaux speaks several times of an "undeserved infinite." It is worth our while to ponder this phrase that has echoed and re-echoed throughout

* Everything I have said above and am about to say in the following pages refers exclusively to hallucinogenic substances which have been recognized as being generally nonaddictive physiologically.

man's history. Many mystics and visionaries have said precisely the same thing.

Radical physiological changes do not produce visions automatically; nor are all visions the same. To choose a convenient example, we need only compare the images that sacred Mexican mushrooms provoked in Wasson with those of the professors and students subjected to a similar experiment by Dr. Heim.* The role played by the individual psyche is crucial. Baudelaire had noted earlier, as had De Quincey before him, that the dreams induced by opium in a poet and in a butcher were quite different. Now, the most disturbing effect of drugs is their power in the sphere of morality: a murderer may have angelic visions, the upright man infernal dreams. The visions depend on a certain psychic sensibility that varies from individual to individual, independently of merit or personal conduct. Drugs are nihilistic: they undermine all values and radically overturn all our ideas about good and evil, what is just and what is unjust, what is permitted and what is forbidden. Their action is a mockery of our morality based on reward and punishment. I am both delighted and terrified by the realization that drugs introduce another brand of justice, based on chance or on circumstances that we are unable to determine. They carelessly offer anyone and everyone what has always been looked upon as the recompense of saints, wise men, and the just—the *summum bonum* that man can attain here on this earth: a vision, a glimpse of perfect harmony. And at the same time that they grant spiritual peace to the undeserving, they reward the innocent with the sufferings of Hell. If pharmacy has replaced God, we cannot help but feel that it is a perverse chemistry.

We might cease to be confused if, instead of thinking of a god that acts like a drug, we thought of a drug that acts like a god. What I mean is: if we use the notions of grace and freedom instead of those of chance and fatality. Drugs open the doors of "another world" to us. If this expression means anything

* See Heim and Wasson, *Les champignons hallucinogènes du Mexique.*

at all, it means that we actually enter a kingdom ruled by different laws than those governing our world. Neither physical nor moral laws are the same in this kingdom. Isn't this precisely what happens in the mystical experience? All mystical texts stress the paradoxical nature of the vision. The total change in logical principles (*here* is *there*, *today* is *yesterday* or *tomorrow*, *movement* is *immobility*, etc.) is paralleled by a no less profound overturning of the customary moral laws: sinners are saved; those who are ignorant are the true wise men; innocence is not to be found among virgins but in bordellos; "the good thief" ascends with Christ to Paradise; the village idiot confounds the arrogant theologian; Che the highwayman is purer than the virtuous Confucius; Krishna incites Arjuna to murder. . . . The Spanish theater, nourished by the Catholic doctrines of free will and grace, offers constant examples of this surprising dialectic in which evil is suddenly transformed into good, perdition into salvation, and the Fall into Assumption. How can these paradoxes be explained?

The mystical experience culminates in the vision of being or of nothingness, but in either case, whether it is in the end a plenitude or an emptiness, it begins as a criticism of this world and a negation of its values. The *other* reality requires the destruction of *this* reality. The vision is sustained not only by intellectual criticism but by a *bodily discipline* that rules one's entire being: mysticism of any sort implies an asceticism. Whatever his religion, the ascetic believes that there is a relation between the reality of the body and the reality of the psyche. The Christian humiliates his body, the yogi masters his; both believe implicitly in the connection between body and spirit. This is not surprising: ascetic practices are thousands of years old and antedate the appearance of the idea of the soul as an entity separate from the body. Like so many other techniques that we have inherited from prehistory, asceticism anticipates contemporary science. The analogy with drugs is striking: the action of the latter would be impossible if there were not in fact an intimate relation between physiological and psychological functions.

Ascetic practices and the use of hallucinogenic substances were undoubtedly part of the same ritual, as can be seen in the hymns of the Rig-Veda in praise of soma and the rites of the early Mexicans, still alive today among the Huichols and the Tarahumaras. There is a great deal of anthropological information on the subject. The drug user is admittedly unlike the ascetic in that he does not subject himself to any discipline. The absence of any ritual or discipline explains the destructive effects of drugs among their modern users. Though this is a crucial difference, it is not applicable to those who explore the universe of drugs with the aim of acquiring knowledge about it: scientists, poets. The similarity between drugs and asceticism extends to the sphere of morals and thought. The ascetic scorns worldly conventions, he takes no stock whatsoever in the ideas of progress and profit, he considers material gains to be losses, he looks upon the normality of the ordinary man as a real spiritual anomaly; in short, he wants nothing to do with either the duties or the pleasures of this world. The person who takes a drug implicitly doubts the solidity of reality—he is not sure that it is what it appears to be and what our instruments define it as being, or he suspects that another reality exists. Drugs and asceticism are alike in that both are a criticism and a negation of the world.

With this in mind, we may find it less difficult to understand the "injustice" of drugs. Aren't the infernal visions that Michaux describes the equivalent of the trials and temptations that all ascetics of all religions have undergone? If the drug brings on the appearance of horrifying images, might it not be because it is a mirror that reflects not what we pretend to be for others, but what we really are? The most immediate effect of the drug is to free us of the weight of external reality. It is therefore impossible to judge its action by the weights and measures of the everyday world. The drug does not bring us face to face with another world: Michaux's visions do not contradict his poems, they confirm them. Except that the "true self" that drugs confront us with—like the one we glimpse through poetry and eroticism—

is a stranger, and its appearance is like the resurrection of someone whom we have long since buried. The person dead and buried is alive and his return terrifies us. Drugs transport us to an outside that is an inside: we inhabit a self that has no identity and no name, we live in a *there* that is a *here*, within something that we are and are not. Our acts have another consistency, another logic, and another gravity. The "merits" and the "faults" are different, and the balance in which they are weighed is different. A change of sign: more is less, cold is hot, exaltation is beatitude, rest and movement are the same. Moral values do not escape this metamorphosis. The notions of virtue, goodness, rectitude, and other similar concepts acquire a different and even a contrary meaning from the one they have in the pitiless world of human relations. The words *merit, reward, advantage, honor, profit, interest,* and others like them are mortally wounded; the blood drains from them and they literally become volatilized. A loss of gravity: true virtues weigh little and go by the name of *abandon, indifference, trust, surrender, nakedness.* What counts is not one's value but one's valor: the courage to explore the unknown. Being forsaken, forsaking. Lightness: disinterestedness, letting go. Once freed from "having to be," man may contemplate his true being. In this constellation, the central word is perhaps *innocence*: the "pureness of heart" of the early Christians, the "piece of unpolished wood" of the Taoists. A disappearance of one's ego and one's name, not a loss of being. The appearance of another reality, the reappearance of being. A moral lesson: the experience brings us face to face with the mystery that each of us is and reveals the vanity of our judgments. The world of judges is the world of injustice. Yes, a murderer may have angelic dreams. Each of us has the infinite he deserves. But this merit cannot be weighed with our scales.

Paradises

In Aldous Huxley's essays on mescaline, he emphasizes that one's personal visions almost always correspond to certain archetypes. The world described by Wasson in his book on Mexican hallucinogenic mushrooms immediately evokes the images of myths, poems, and paintings: great river landscapes, trees, thick green and russet foliage, amber-colored earth, all bathed in an otherworldly light. The sensation of movement—the great rivers, the wind, the earth's heartbeat—fuses with that of immobility and repose. Sometimes a woman appears on the bank of the sparkling river, lost in thought—an apparition reminiscent of early Greek sculpture and certain grave steles. A dawning age, a world of paradisiac meanings: how can we fail to be reminded of the images of Genesis, or Arab tales, of the myths of the South Pacific or Central Asia, of the Teotihuacán paradise of Tlaloc? But there is also another sort of vision: deserts, rocks, thirst, panting, the dagger-eye of the sun: the landscape of damnation, the "wasteland" of the Grail legend. Transparent infernos, a geometry of crystals; circular hells; hells of garish, clashing colors, a pullulation of forms and monsters, temptations of Saint Anthony, Goya's Sabbaths, Hindu copulations, Munch's frozen scream, Polynesian masks. . . . Though the images are innumerable, all of them—whether blinding light or mineral blackness, solitude or promiscuity—reveal a universe with no way out. Weight, oppression, asphyxia: hells. We are trapped within ourselves, there is no way out, we cannot cease to be what we are, we cannot change. Hell: *petrification*. The image of heaven is a vision of freedom: *levitation, dissolution of the self*. Light versus stone.

The images of paradise can be reduced, Huxley tells us, to certain elements common to the "mescaline experience" and universal myth: earth and water, fertility, verdure. The idea of abundance (as opposed to the world of toil); the idea of an enchanted garden: "everything is palpable" and birds, beasts, and plants speak the same language. In the center: the couple. Huxley points out that the light in this paradise has a very special quality; it is a light that has no visible source, or to use an old expression, it is an *uncreated* light. And also a creative light (the landscape is born and grows in the rain of light) and a sheltering one (the garden, the visible, nestles within its invisible bosom). I would also mention another no less meaningful presence: water, the image of the return to the primeval age, the symbol of the woman and her powers. Water: calm, fertility, self-knowledge, but also loss, a fall into treacherous transparency. In a number of passages, Baudelaire ponders this vision: "Fugitive waters, frolicking waters, harmonious waterfalls, the immense azure sea, rocking itself, singing, falling asleep. . . . The contemplation of this limpid abyss is perilous for a spirit enamored of space and crystal. . . ." Water: Diana at her bath, the element that brings death to Actaeon and Siegfried.

Light is fixed, immaterial, central. At once fire and ice, it is the symbol of both objectivity and eternity. It is heaven's gaze itself. Clear and serene, it traces outlines, delimits, distributes space into symmetrical areas. It is justice, but it is also the Idea, the archetype engraved upon a cloudless sky. The sixteenth-century poet Herrera calls his beloved light his Idea. Light: the essence, the realm of the intemporal. Water is diffuse, elusive, formless. It evokes time, carnal love; it is the tide itself—death and resurrection—and the gateway to the elemental world. Everything is reflected in water, everything founders in it, everything is reborn in it. It is change, the ebb and flow of the universe. Light separates, water unites. Paradise would appear to be ruled by two warring sisters. In the center, the precious stone. Huxley reminds us that the gates of paradise are studded with diamonds, rubies, emeralds. As light passes through it, the humid landscape of the first day becomes an immense jewel: a golden sun, a silver moon, trees of jade. Light makes water a precious stone. It turns time into a mineral, makes it eternal. It congeals it into an impartial, uniform splendor and thus kills the life in it: it freezes its pulse. At the same time light transmutes stone. Thanks to light, the opaque stone—a symbol of gravity: a heavy fallen weight—takes on the transparency and dancing swiftness of water. The stone sparkles, twinkles, quivers, like a drop of water or blood: it is alive. A moment later, mesmerized by the celestial flash of lightning, it becomes motionless: it is light now, time arrested, a fixed gaze.

The precious stone is an instant of equilibrium between water and light. Left to itself, in its natural state, it is opacity, inertia, brute existence. The dreamless slumber of stone. But the moment it becomes luminous and translucid, its moral nature changes. Its limpidity is as treacherously deceiving as that of water. The opal is an unlucky stone; there are emeralds that bring health; there are stones with a curse on them. This ambiguity should not surprise us. Life per se is neither good nor bad: it is sheer vitality, an appetite for being. In life at the most elementary level, we discover the *same unity* as in spiritual meditation. Diana and her bow, Coatlicue and her skulls, goddesses covered with blood, are life itself, the perpetual rebirth and death of the seasons, time unfolding and turning back upon itself. The paradise of the Douanier Rousseau is a magic jungle, inhabited by wild beasts and ruled by a sorceress. The intruder is the *armed* man, who divides and separates: morality destroying the magic pact between nature and its creatures. The precious stone shares this indifference of life. A nexus of contrary meanings, it oscillates between water and light.

The Metamorphoses of Stone

André Pieyre de Mandiargues is one of the truly original writers to have appeared in France since World War II. His work is an apt, though unintentional, illustration of what we might call "the metamorphoses of stone." What he describes is a "Way of Perfection," fraught with arduous trials and sacrifices, which brute matter must follow if it is to become a precious stone, a solar stone. In one of Mandiargues's books, *Feu de braise*, there are three stories that describe the nature of stone, by turns baleful and beneficent. In the first story ("Les pierreuses"), a schoolteacher taking a walk on the outskirts of the city picks up a stone of the sort that geologists call geodes (rocks or stones, usually of a crystallized substance, with a hollow in the center). Impelled by curiosity—Pandora and her box reappear in many of this author's texts—the teacher opens the stone as though it were an oyster shell, and discovers three minuscule girls inside. The eldest tells him, in vulgar Latin, that she and her two sisters emerged naked from the womb of the Great Mother and will return to it naked. They have been cast into the geode by a "black sun." Their being set free presages their death and that of their liberator, because, she adds, "the emanations of stone are deadly." There would be no point in pondering the meaning of each individual element of this fantasy: all the details fit the conception of stone as a crystallization of water and its awesome powers.

In "Le diamant," Sara, the daughter of a Jewish jeweler, faints after having long contemplated a perfect diamond, an "ice palace." When she comes to her senses again, she finds herself inside the stone. The coldness of the jewel threatens to freeze her instantly, but the morning sun pours through the window and lights on the diamond, transforming it into a fiery furnace. "Like a fish in water," Sara has no difficulty withstanding the great heat. A moment later, she gives herself to a ruddy-faced man with a leonine head. Strange nuptials uniting a Jewish virgin and a solar deity: the fecundation of water by light. The beam of sunlight moves away, it turns freezing cold inside the diamond once again, the young girl loses consciousness a second time, and on coming to her senses realizes that she has left the nuptial stone "as mysteriously, as naturally as she had entered it."

Sara examines the diamond and notices that a tiny reddish flaw mars its perfection, the only trace of her marvelous encounter. A material "defect" that is also a mystic stigma.

In "Le diamant" the metamorphosis is the opposite of that in "Les pierreuses." The "ice palace" is opened like the geode; the teacher finds three naked girls inside the stone and Sara too is naked inside the diamond. Water—a naked woman—inhabits stone like an unpredictable substance that may impart either life or death. The geode is a mineral womb; when a ray of light falls upon it, it becomes a tomb; the diamond, on being subjected to a similar influence, is turned into an alchemical furnace. Fire and water symbolize transmutation. (There is a Nahuatl expression that has the same meaning: "burning water.") Sara's metamorphoses are a parallel of the transformations of the diamond, a stone for sale that becomes a jewel representing mystic union. In "Les pierreuses," the schoolteacher's idle curiosity is rewarded only by the revelation of death; in "Le diamant," trust in the unknown—a spirit of true disinterestedness—leads to union with the solar principle. The schoolteacher is a man of reason and a skeptic who is not at all surprised to discover three lovely little creatures inside the geode. (The one thought that crosses his mind is that his grasp of vulgar Latin is faulty.) Sara "trusts in the power of the absurd," calmly accepts the mystery, and allows herself to be guided by the unexpected. There is nothing at all arbitrary about the professor's death or Sara's marvelous fecundation. But it is a matter of spiritual rather than logical consistency.

"L'enfantillage" deals with the experience we might call "the capital vision," to use Mandiargues's own language. A man goes to bed with a strange woman. While one part of himself anticipates the moment of physical discharge, the other part of himself regresses to his earliest childhood memory: a cart full of Italian peasants plunging over a cliff and his nursemaid's gnarled hand covering his eyes. This frightful image fuses with his rapt contemplation of a gilded knob of the bedstead, gleaming in the light of the noonday sun in the warm shadow. The wanderings of his mind become a delirium: held by the hand by the old woman, he draws closer and closer to the abyss, until the gilded sphere and the old woman's face become one. For a truly glorious instant, the double vision is transformed into a single literally blinding insight: "Is this finally love? Father Sun . . ." Matter has pursued the path of initiation to its end, and now gleams like a naked star. The brass knob is a central sun. "Purity regained," Mandiargues says of this revelation. Is it death or life? The stone, by turns opacity and transparency, water and light, finally becomes incandescent, a state of fusion, the disappearance of contraries.

In the foreword to a book published shortly after World War II,* Mandiargues says that "the hour of total emptiness is also the hour of idiocy, the two ultimate faces of what is sometimes called mysticism. . . ." This phrase is proof that those poets who yield to delirium with the greatest abandon are also the poets who are most lucid. The schoolteacher of "Les pierreuses" is doomed because his knowledge is nothing but a series of "known facts"; Sara is saved because she has no "fund of knowledge," only a trust in life. In both cases the vision is dualist. The "capital vision" evokes that instant in which the blood of the victim spurts from his body with amazing energy and abundance, a symbol of both life and death. "L'enfantillage" is not the vision of the triumph of life over intellect, nor of the coexistence of contradictory forces, but that of their mutual destruction in the fire of a blinding truth. The hour, the instant, of he emptying out of self: the reconquest of nonknowledge.

The Symposium and the Hermit

My commentaries on the experiences of Huxley and Michaux were written and published many years before the use of hal-

* *Le musée noir* (1946

lucinogenic drugs had become a popular subject and the occasion of public debate. A rite or a mystery from antiquity till only yesterday, the use of drugs is now a more or less widespread practice and a subject of discussion in the press and on television and radio. Speaking of certain things only at certain moments was a sign of wisdom as well as politeness among the ancients: words had weight, they were something real. By diminishing the value of silence, publicity has also diminished that of language. The two are inseparable: knowing how to speak has always meant knowing how to keep silent, knowing that there are times when one should say nothing. In the case of drugs, everybody talks about them, but there are few people who listen to those who really have something to say: scientists and poets. The number of young people who have taken LSD and other drugs has admittedly reached such proportions, especially in the United States, that the public's excitement and the authorities' alarm are readily understandable. It is equally obvious that legal measures and police enforcement are neither a solution nor a step toward understanding the problem. On the contrary, they aggravate it and make it an even more inflammatory issue.

We do not have to be sociologists or anthropologists to realize that drug addiction is merely one of the results of the changes industrial society has undergone since World War II. Nor is it surprising that this development is most serious and most widespread in the country where these changes have been greatest: the United States. It would be absurd to maintain that drugs have the power to subvert and undermine American society: youngsters have not ceased to believe in "the American way of life" because they take drugs—they take drugs because they have ceased to believe in these ideas and are fumblingly searching for new ones. The attitude of young people is intelligible only within the general context of rebellion against the society of abundance and its moral and political presuppositions. The increasingly widespread use of drugs is yet another indication of a change in contemporary sensibilities. This change may well be more profound than the material transformations and the ideological struggles of the first half of the century.

It has not been proved that hallucinogenic substances are more harmful than alcohol. Although the reaction in both cases depends on the individual's constitution, it is a well-known fact that alcohol brings our aggressive tendencies to the fore, whereas hallucinogenic substances foster introversion. Sahagún reports that at the end of the sacred-mushroom ceremony a number of the celebrants went off alone and were silent for a long time; others talked to themselves or laughed and wept in a corner. Travelers and anthropologists who have lived with the Huichol Indians confirm Sahagún's observation: peyote may lead in rare instances to suicide, but never to murder. Alcohol draws us out: hallucinogens make us retreat within ourselves. Many psychiatrists share Huxley's belief: these substances are less dangerous than alcohol. We need not necessarily agree entirely with this opinion—though it seems to me that it is not very far from the truth—and still grant that the reasons that the authorities prohibit these substances have more to do with public morality than with public health. They are a threat to the ideas of enterprise, usefulness, progress, work, and other notions that justify our daily comings and goings.

Alcoholism is an infraction of social rules; everyone tolerates this breaking of the rules because it is a violation that confirms them. Prostitution is a similar case: neither the drunk nor the whore and her client question the rules that they break. Their acts are a disturbance of law and order, a departure from the rules of society, not a criticism of them. The recourse to hallucinogens implies a negation of social values, and it is an attempt —though doubtless an illusory one—to escape from this world and drop out from society. We are now in a position to understand the real reason for the condemnation of hallucinogens and why their use is punished: the authorities do not behave as though they were trying to stamp out a harmful practice or a vice, but as though they were attempting to stamp out dissidence. Since this is a form of dissidence that is becoming more widespread, the prohibition takes on the proportions of a campaign against a spiritual contagion, against an *opinion.* What the authorities are displaying is *ideological* zeal: they are punishing a heresy, not a crime. They are thus taking the same attitude as that taken in other centuries toward leprosy and insanity, which were not regarded as diseases but as incarnations of evil. There is even the same superstitious, ambivalent awe involved: like the leper in the Middle Ages, the drug-taker is the victim of a sacred evil; like the utterances of a madman, his words are revelations of another world. Those who hound the users of hallucinatory drugs are no less credulous than those who worship these drugs. There is little use reminding both sides that all the experiments and studies on the subject agree on at least one point: no known substance can make a genius of someone who is not one.

Alcohol and the hallucinogenic drugs are opposites. The drunk is loquacious and expansive; the drug-taker silent and withdrawn. When a person starts drinking, he first gets very sociable and wants everybody to be his pal, drapes his arm around people, and tells them his secrets. Then gradually he gets more and more boisterous, bursting into song or loud laughter, and finally the whole scene ends in angry shouts and racking sobs or some hostile act of violence. In each of these stages of inebriation, there is one common note: the desire to speak and interact with others, to address them as an audience or fight them as opponents. The solitary drinker has always been regarded as a peculiar creature, worse off than a cripple or an onanist. He is lacking something: another person, other people. In Mexico, conversation becomes more of a pleasure if people are drinking, and there is a saying that aptly describes our attitude toward alcohol: "letting the cup have its say." Heavy drinking in the Protestant countries is a way of leaping over the wall that separates one person from another. Protestant society is a community of introverts in which each person mutters a secret monologue under his breath: the morality of personal responsibility is an invisible gag. Alcohol loosens people's tongues, their senses, and their consciences. Drunkenness in other parts of the world is orgiastic. Among the Russians and the Poles it takes the form of an explosion, public confession, and a universal embrace: we are all one, and each one is all.

Alcoholism has been a social problem in two periods of modern history: in Europe during the first industrial revolution, and in the United States in the years immediately following World War I. Dickens and Zola have left us terrifying descriptions of the life of the working class in the large cities; among other terrible consequences the sudden transition from rural life to urban life was responsible for a traumatic rupture of traditional ties, and therefore a breakdown of communication. Zola's novels show that alcoholism was the result. In the United States, the phenomenon may have had different causes but its meaning was the same: it was a reaction to the alienation and the tensions and conflicts engendered when strangers, peoples belonging to different ethnic groups, with different traditions and languages, were forced to live together. In both cases—peasants from the countryside lost in the industrial suburbs and immigrants uprooted from a continent boiling over—alcoholism was a substitute for the old social bonds that had been broken or had disappeared, a desperate attempt to establish communication. Alcoholism is a search for a common language, or at least, it is a compensation for a language that has been lost. The use of drugs does not imply the overestimation of the value of language but of silence. Drunkenness exaggerates communication; drugs destroy it. Young people's preference for drugs reveals a change in the contemporary attitude toward language and communication.

The first to see the differences between drugs and wine was Baudelaire: "Wine exalts the will; hashish destroys it. Wine is a physical stimulant; hashish a suicide weapon. Wine mellows us and makes us sociable; hashish isolates us." Wine is social, drugs solitary; the one inflames the senses, the other rouses the imagination. It is unfortunate that Baudelaire did not venture to draw the conclusions that logically follow from his distinction. He might have added that it is not the merits or the defects of alcohol and drugs that are most important, but their relation to communication. Drinking stimulates communication at first, and then turns it into stammering and fuzzy-headedness. The toper drinks to drown his sorrows and ends up drowning himself. Drunkenness is contradictory: it overvalues communication and destroys it. It is a failure of communication: it first exaggerates it and then degrades it. A caricature of communication, it is a parody of two forms of intercourse that our civilization, from its very beginning, has venerated above all others: religious communion and philosophical dialogue. It is not mere happenstance that distilled alcohol has replaced grape wine in the modern world; this change parallels the gradual disfavor into which conversation, banquets, and religious rites have fallen.

Wine always occupied a central place in the rites, festivals, and ceremonies of pagan antiquity and the Christian West. Without wine, no meal is worth eating. When we say that "wine flowed abundantly" or that a banquet was *washed down* by choice vintages, we are referring to a magic quality of wine: a homologue of water, semen, and the "spiritual fluid" of the ancients, it is fertility, resurrection, and the animation of matter. A circulation of the vital essence, its effect on men is similar to that of irrigation in agriculture. It is the agent that transmits fellow feeling: it exalts us, binds us together, reunites us. It is brotherhood. Communication is also communion: in Christian worship wine is the godhead incarnate. The eucharist is a mystery that is present in all our rituals, whether religious or erotic. The two most beautiful and meaningful images that tradition has passed down to us are the Platonic symposium and Christ's Last Supper. In both, wine is a cardinal symbol whereby our civilization defines its dual vocation; it is the archetype of communication—with others and with the Other.

Isolation and seclusion play a certain role in antiquity and Christianity, but the hermit is not a central figure in our mythology. The philosopher, the wise man, and the savior live among other men; they break the bread of truth together. Wisdom and illumination are common property, like language. To us the anchorite is a venerable figure, not a model or an example. The Oriental attitude is precisely the opposite. India has worshiped the hermit as the supreme figure since the very beginning. To Western peoples, the *summum bonum* is synonymous with communion; to Eastern peoples the key word is liberation. The superior life involves a double liberation: first from social bonds, whether those of caste, family, or community, and second from the chain of transmigration. This is the opposite of the etymological meaning of the word *religion*; it is not a reuniting, a reforging of bonds, but a loosening, a letting go, an escape. Both in Brahmanism and in Buddhism, the image of the saint and the wise man shown us in iconography, art, and poetry is the figure of the hermit in his cave or beneath a tree. Nothing could be further from the banquet table or the open communion of Christians.

India creates extremes: the caste system exaggerates the social bond; asceticism exalts the isolation of the individual. The Hindu continually oscillates between these two poles. There is no meeting point, no point of convergence: there is no symposium, no communion. A large part of the Buddhist canon is in the form of dialogues of the Illuminated with his disciples, but the object of these conversations is not communion: they are sermons extolling solitary meditation. The Platonic philosopher's goal is the contemplation of the Idea, the Buddhist's goal the dissolution of the Idea in emptiness (sunyata). The great Christian mystery is that of divine incarnation; the aim of all the religions and doctrines of India is liberation, disincarnation (moksha, nirvana). In the hymns of the Rig-Veda and the Atharva-Veda, there are many references to a mysterious substance, soma, which many modern Orientalists are convinced was a form of hashish. It is quite likely soma is the same thing as bhang, a drug commonly used in modern India, especially among the sadhus and sannyasis. According to the Vedic hymns, soma brings illumination and knowledge: it is the food of seers and poets, the rishis. Wine, dialogue, communion, incarnation;

drugs, introspection, liberation, disincarnation. The Word and the Silence.

All this gives us good reason to believe that the popularity of hallucinogenic substances is a symptom of a shift in modern sensibilities. Does this shift represent a change of goals or an absence of goals? Both things. The traditional symbols have lost their meaning. They are empty signs. In a world ruled by the communications media no one has anything to say or anything to hear. If words have lost their meaning, why not look for meaning in silence? The popular interest in Buddhism and other Oriental religions and doctrines betrays the same sense of deprivation and the same appetite. It would be a mistake to believe that we are looking to Buddhism for a truth that is foreign to our tradition: what we are seeking is a confirmation of a truth we already know. The new attitude is not a result of a new knowledge of Eastern doctrines, but a result of our own history. No one ever learns a truth from outside: each person must think it through and experience it for himself. It would not be difficult to prove that three contemporary thinkers—Wittgenstein, Heidegger, and Lévi-Strauss—give evidence in their works of a surprising unconscious affinity with Buddhism. Their philosophies have not been influenced in any way by Eastern thought, and their respective philosophical positions are so different that they would appear to be irreconcilable. Yet the preoccupation with language is central in all three, and each of them has been led to a similar conclusion: all speech ends in silence. I might mention other examples in the sphere of literature and art, but there are so many of them and they are so well known that I prefer not to do so. I shall merely limit myself to pointing out once again that if any poet of the recent past is our precursor, our master, and our contemporary, it is Mallarmé. And the fact is that all his poetry is an attempt to realize what may well be an impossible ambition, one mindful of the paradoxes of the Prajnaparamita sutras: incarnating absence, naming emptiness, speaking of silence. Modern art is a destruction of meaning—or of communication—but it is also a search for meaning. Perhaps this exploration will result in the discovery that nonmeaning is identical with meaning.

Now that we have examined the general context in which this change has occurred, we can better understand the meaning of the more and more widespread use of hallucinogenic substances. Like alcoholism, it is a revolt; like alcoholism, it is a revolt that is self-defeating: drugs can give us blissful or terrifying visions, but they cannot give us either silence or wisdom. Unlike alcoholism, drugs are not an exaggeration of a traditional value (communication) but of something foreign to our tradition. Alcoholism is a caricature of the Platonic symposium and of communion; drugs are its negation.

Drugs have always been used in conjunction with a ritual of some sort. Since antiquity they have been an adjunct either of ascetic practices or of initiation ceremonies and other rites. Each year the Huichol Indians go on an arduous expedition in search of peyote and during the entire time they forgo bathing, abstain from any sort of sexual contact, and undergo endless privations. When they find the cactus they do not consume it immediately; they wait until a ceremony can be held, in the course of which, among other rites, public confession takes place. Once purified, they eat the peyote. According to the Huichol Indians, horrible visions are a sort of punishment visited upon those who have lied during the confession or committed other deceitful and mendacious acts. The entire rite and all of its attendant sufferings center around the ideas of trust, unselfishness, pureness of heart, generosity. The beliefs of the Huichols confirm what I have pointed out above with regard to the "morality" of hallucinogenic drugs and their surprising justice. There is little point in listing other examples: in all periods of history and in all cultures the use of drugs is associated with a ritual and some form of asceticism.*

* The brahmin who engages in the soma sacrifice "must abstain from all contact with men of impure castes and with women; he must not answer anyone who asks him a question, and no one must touch him." Louis Renou, *L'Inde classique.*

The same is true of sexual practices and ritual meals within the tradition of Tantrism. It is not surprising, therefore, that in the United States many semireligious and semiartistic groups are attempting to surround the use of drugs with a sort of ritual. It is the only way of taking advantage of the unquestionable power of drugs as hallucinatory agents and instruments of self-knowledge. But such experiments are doomed to failure. Rites cannot be invented: they develop little by little, through the creation of myths, beliefs, and religious practices. Modern society has emptied traditional rites of all their content and has not yet succeeded in creating others to take their place. The prime ritual gathering of the century—political meetings—served for a time as a replacement for traditional rites. But today they have turned into dull official ceremonies and have preserved their vitality only in China and other underdeveloped countries. The reason for this is obvious: rites are based on the idea of time as repetition: they are a date that recurs again and again, representing a present that is also a past and a future.

Modern, historical time is linear and inevitably proves fatal to the rite; the past is irreversible and will never return. The ultimate meaning of the use of drugs in our time is thus clearer now: it is a criticism of linear time and a nostalgia for (or a presentiment of) another sort of time. These remarks on drugs lead to a subject that I shall discuss in the third part of this book: the end of linear time.

Buñuel's Philosophical Cinema

Some years ago, I wrote a few pages about Buñuel. This is what I said: "Even though the common and ultimate aim of all the arts, including those that are most abstract, is the expression and re-creation of man and his conflicts, each one of them has its own particular means for casting its spell over us, and thus each is a separate domain. Music is one thing, poetry another, cinema yet another. But occasionally an artist succeeds in going beyond the limits of his art; we then come face to face with a work whose equivalents lie outside its own world. A number of Buñuel's films—*L'Age d'or, Los olvidados*—belong to the realm of cinema but at the same time they bring us closer to other regions of the human spirit: certain of Goya's engravings, poems by Quevedo or Péret, a passage by Sade, one or another of Valle Inclán's *esperpentos*, a page by Gómez de la Serna. . . . These films can be enjoyed and judged as cinema and at the same time as something belonging to the wider and freer universe of these works of surpassing value whose object is both to reveal human reality to us and to show us a way to go beyond it. Despite the obstacles which our contemporary world places in the way of such endeavors, Buñuel's work continues to pass through the double arch of beauty and rebellion.

"In *Nazarín*, in a style that rejects any sort of suspect lyricism, Buñuel tells us the story of a priest akin to Don Quixote, whose conception of Christianity soon earns him the enmity of the Church, society, and the police. Like so many of Pérez Galdós's characters, Nazarín belongs to the great tradition of Spanish madmen. His madness consists of taking Christianity seriously and attempting to live according to its gospel. He is a madman who refuses to admit that what we call reality is *really* reality and not just a horrible caricature of true reality. Like Don Quixote, who saw his Dulcinea in a farm girl, Nazarín can make out the image of fallen man in the monstrous features of the prostitute, Andra, and the hunchback, Ujo, and recognize the face of divine love in the erotic delirium of a hysterical woman, Beatriz. In the course of the film—in which there are many scenes where Buñuel is at his greatest and most awesome, for here his fury is more concentrated than ever and thus more explosive—we are witness to the attempt to 'cure' the madman. He is rejected by one and all: by those who are powerful because they look on him as a nuisance and ultimately a dangerous troublemaker; by the insulted and injured because they need another, more effective kind of consolation. He is not only persecuted by the authorities; he is constantly a victim of misunderstandings. If he seeks alms he is accused of being a social parasite; if he seeks work, he is accused of taking the bread from the mouths of other laborers. Even his women disciples, reincarnations of Mary Magdalene, have ambivalent feelings about him in the end. Thrown into jail as a result of his good works, the ultimate revelation comes to him there behind bars: his own 'goodness' and the 'evil' of one of his fellow prisoners, a murderer and a robber of churches, are equally useless in a world that worships efficiency as the supreme value.

"Faithful to the tradition of the Spanish madman, from Cervantes to Pérez Galdós, Buñuel's film recounts a loss of illusions. For Don Quixote the illusion was the spirit of chivalry, for Nazarín Christianity. But there is something else besides. As the image of Christ pales in Nazarín's consciousness, another image begins to take its place: that of man. By putting before us a series of exemplary episodes, in the true sense of the word, Buñuel makes us witnesses of a twofold process: the gradual fading away of the illusion of divinity and the discovery of the reality of man. The supernatural yields its place to the marvelous: human nature and its powers. This revelation is embodied in two unforgettable moments: the scene where Nazarín offers the consolations of the beyond to the dying woman in love, who clutches the photograph of her lover and answers: *'Heaven no, Juan yes'*; and the scene at the end when Nazarín first refuses the alms of a poor woman and then accepts them after a moment's hesitation—not as a charitable offering but as a sign of fraternity. Nazarín the solitary man is no longer alone: he has lost God but he has found men."

This short text appeared in the printed program given out at the showing of *Nazarín* at the Cannes Film Festival. It was feared—and doubtless for good reason—that the meaning of the film might be misunderstood. The risk of confusion that threatens every work of art was even greater in this case because of the nature of the novel that inspired the film. Pérez Galdós's theme is the age-old conflict between evangelical Christianity and its ecclesiastical and historical deformations. The hero of his book is a rebellious *illuminato*, a true protestant: he leaves the church but keeps his faith in God. Buñuel's film is meant to demonstrate the exact opposite: the disappearance of the figure of Christ in the conscience of a sincere and pure-hearted believer. In the scene with the dying girl, which is a transposition of Sade's *Dialogue Between a Priest and a Dying Man*, the woman's words are an affirmation of the irreplaceable value of terrestrial love: if there is a heaven, it is here and now, at the moment of carnal embrace, not in a beyond where there is no time, where there are no bodies. In the prison scene, the sacrilegious thief is shown to be a creature no less absurd than the priest. The crimes of the thief are as illusory as the sanctity of Nazarín: if there is no God, there is also no sacrilege and no salvation.

Nazarín is not Buñuel's best film, but it is typical of the duality that governs his entire work. On one hand, ferocity and lyricism, a world of dreams and blood that immediately calls to mind two other great Spaniards, Quevedo and Goya. On the other hand, a bare, spare style that is not at all Baroque and results in a sort of exaggerated sobriety. The straight line, not the Surrealist arabesque. The rigor of rational thought: each one of his films, from *L'Age d'or* to *Viridiana*, unfolds like a *logical proof*. The most violent and most freely soaring imagination in the service of a syllogism as sharp as a knife, as irrefutable as a boulder: Buñuel's logic is the implacable reason of the Marquis de Sade. This name sheds light on the relation between Buñuel and Surrealism: without this movement Buñuel would still have been a poet and a rebel, but thanks to it, he was able to hone his weapons to a keener edge. Surrealism, which revealed Sade's thought to him, was not a school where he learned the uses of delirium, but rather the uses of reason: without ceasing to be poetry, his cinematic poems became criticism. Within the closed arena of criticism, delirium spread its wings and clawed its own chest with its sharp talons. A Surrealism of the bull ring, but also a critical Surrealism: the bullfight as philosophical argument.

In a major text of modern letters, *De la littérature considérée comme une tauromachie* [*Literature as Tauromachy*], Michel Leiris says that he was fascinated by the bullfight because it is a perfect blend of danger and style: the *diestro* (one of the Spanish words for the bullfighter, meaning "the man of skill") must meet the bull's attack without losing his composure. This is true: when we die and when we kill, impeccable manners are absolutely necessary, at least if one believes, as I do, that these two biological acts are also rites, ceremonies. In the bullfight, danger takes on the dignity of form and form the truthfulness of death. The bullfighter strictly complies with a form at the risk of his life. It is what we call *temple* in Spanish: a cool boldness, a well-tempered musical harmony, stubborn courage and flexibility. The bullfighter, like the photographer, must calculate his exposures, and Buñuel's style, by deliberate aesthetic and philosophical choice, is one of exposure. Exposing oneself, taking risks. To expose is also to exhibit, to bare, to demonstrate. Buñuel's films are a process of exposure: they reveal human realities by subjecting them to the light of criticism, as though they were photographic plates. Buñuel's bullfighting is a philosophical discourse and his films are the modern equivalent of the philosophical novels of the Marquis de Sade. But Sade, while an original philosopher, was only an average artist: he failed to realize that art, which takes rhythm and litany to its bosom, refuses to tolerate mechanical repetition and reiteration. Buñuel is an artist, and if his films are open to criticism, it is on philosophical rather than aesthetic grounds.

The argument underlying Sade's entire *œuvre* can be reduced to a single idea: man is his instincts, and the real name of what we call God is fear and frustrated desire. Our morality is a codification of aggression and humiliation: reason itself is only an instinct that knows it is an instinct and therefore fears itself. Sade did not endeavor to demonstrate that God does not exist: he took it for granted. He tried to show what human relations would be like in a truly atheist society. This is what constitutes his real originality, and what explains the absolute consistency of all his writings. The archetypes of a republic of truly free men is the "Society of the Friends of Crime"; and the archetype of the true philosopher is this libertine ascetic who managed to reach a state of perfect insensibility, moved neither to laughter nor to tears. Sade's logic is unassailable and circular: it destroys God but it does not respect man. His system is open to criticism on many grounds, but we cannot possibly accuse him of inconsistency. His negation embraces everything: if he affirms anything at all, it is the right to destroy and be destroyed. Buñuel's criticism has a limit: man. All our crimes are the crimes of a ghost: God. Buñuel's theme is not man's guilt but God's. This idea, present in all his films, is most explicit and most frankly expressed in *L'Age d'or* and *Viridiana*, which, with *Los olvidados*, seem to me to be his most fully developed and most perfect creations. If Buñuel's *œuvre* is a criticism of the illusion of God, that deforming mirror which does not allow us to see man as he is, what are men *really* like, and what meaning will the words love and brotherhood have in a *truly* atheist society?

Sade's answer doubtless does not satisfy Buñuel. Nor do I believe that he is content at this point with the descriptions to be found in philosophical and political utopias. Apart from the fact that these prophecies cannot be proved to be either true or false, at least for the present, it is obvious that they are not consonant with what we know about man, his history, and his nature. To believe in an atheist society governed by natural harmony—a dream we have all had—would today be tantamount to repeating Pascal's wager, though this time the bet would be precisely the opposite. It would be more of an act of desperation than a paradox: it would earn our admiration, but not our approval. I do not know how Buñuel would answer such questions. Surrealism, which denied so many things, was propelled along by a great gust of generosity and faith. Among its ancestors we find not only Sade and Lautréamont but also Fourier and Rousseau. And at least for André Breton, it was perhaps the two latter who were the real source of the movement: the celebration of man's passions, the limitless trust in man's natural powers. I do not know whether Buñuel feels more of an affinity with Sade or with Rousseau; most probably the two of them are at war within him. Whatever his beliefs in this regard, it is certain that we will not find a reply to either Sade or Rousseau in his films. Whether due to reticence, timidity, or disdain, his silence is disturbing, not only because he is one of the great artists of our time, but also because it is the silence of all the art of the first half of this century. Since Sade, no one to my knowledge has dared describe an atheist society. Something is missing in the works of our contemporaries: not God but men without God.

Forms of Atheism

It is almost impossible to write about the *death of God*. It is not a suitable subject for a dissertation, even though for more than a half century it has occasioned hymns of rejoicing and hallelujahs. This vast and sometimes unreadable literature does not exhaust the subject: everything we say and do today bears the mark of this event. Whether implicit or explicit, atheism is universal. But we must make a distinction between various brands of atheists: those who believe they believe in a living God and who really think and live as though he had never existed: these are the real atheists and most of our fellow citizens are of this persuasion; the pseudoatheists, for whom God has not died because he never existed, though they nonetheless believe in one or another of his successors (reason, progress, history); and finally those who accept his death and try to live their lives within this unprecedented perspective. These latter are a minority that can be divided in turn into two groups: those who do not resign themselves, and like Nietzsche's Madman, intone their *Requiem aeternam deo* in empty churches; and those for whom atheism is an *act of faith*. Both groups live the death of God religiously, lightheartedly, and gravely. Lightheartedly, because they live as though a great weight had been removed from their shoulders;

gravely, because with the disappearance of the divine power, the support of all creation, the very ground beneath their feet is shaky. Without God the world has become lighter and man heavier.

The death of God is a chapter in the history of the world's religions, like the death of the Great Pan or the sudden disappearance of Quetzalcoatl. It is also a phase of the modern consciousness. This phase is a religious one. It is religious in a very special way, however, and living through this particular moment calls for a frame of mind that is a combination, in varying proportions, of rigorous thought and passionate faith. Like any other moment, it is transitory; like every religious moment, it is crucial. Bathed in the light of the divine, the religious moment shines brightly and says: forever. It is human time suspended from eternity by a thread, the thread of supernatural presence; if this thread breaks, man falls. The moment that the atheist lives is crucial for the opposite reason: his horizon is the total absence of supernatural presence. As in the religious moment, in the moment of the atheist, too, human time is accepted as fragility and contingency in the face of an extratemporal dimension: the absence of God, like His presence, is eternal. The positive religious moment is the end of profane time and the beginning of sacred time: this end is a resurrection. The negative religious moment is the end of eternity and the beginning of profane time: this beginning is a fall. There is no resurrection because the beginning is an end: the atheist falls into an eternity of successive time in which each minute repeats some other minute. What he has been condemned to is not the pains of hell but repetition. The positive religious moment is a conversion; the negative moment is a reversion. For the believer this moment is an appeal and a response; for the atheist, a silence without appeal.

The atheist's reaction to the silence that results from the death of God is incredulous surprise. Suddenly, literally beside himself, dumped into the world outside himself, he shouts: "I am trying to find God!" A cry that makes no sense because he knows that "we all killed him together: you killed him and I killed him. We are all his murderers." The Madman knows that God is dead because he killed him. Perhaps that is why he cannot resign himself to his death and literally cannot believe what he says. So he shouts and sings, tortures himself and rejoices. He is beside himself. The death of God has exiled him from his own being and made him deny his human essence. The Madman wants to be a god because he is searching for God. The other sort of atheist faces up to what has happened in an equally religious and no less contradictory frame of mind: he knows that the death of God is not a fact but a belief. And he believes. But what can he base his belief on, how can he manifest his faith, in what form can he embody it? It is an empty belief. Both cases involve something that scarcely satisfies the demands of human reason. The incredulity of the Madman is a fit of delirium that cannot answer one major argument: if God is still alive, it means that the moment of his death was also that of his resurrection. The credulity of the other sort of atheist also defies logical proof: if it is a belief, who and what is there to prove that it is true? There is no one who can testify to it or confirm it. It is an anonymous truth since no one embodies it or accepts it save the atheist, and he embodies it as a negation. The atheist's certainty is a very odd sort of thing: he is a believer only if he believes in nothing.

Nietzsche saw the difficulties of atheism with blinding clarity. They seemed to him to be insuperable, at least so long as man continued to be merely man. For that reason, in order to really fulfill itself, to "surpass itself," his "nihilism" required the advent of the superman. Only the superman can be an atheist because only he knows how to play the game. In the famous passage in *The Gay Science*, the Madman, after having announced the murder of God in public squares and marketplaces, says that this is an act that is *excessive* by human standards: "Never has a more magnificent act been committed, and because of it those who are born after us will be part of a more illustrious history than any other. . . ." Though the magnitude of this crime overwhelms us, has another breed of men capable of bearing this terrible burden already been born? And if not, are there signs that such a breed will appear in the future? Nietzsche announced the death of God in 1882; it is not presuming too much to say that the superman has not yet been born. . . . The Madman knows that once God is dead, man must live like a god: man must go beyond the limits of his own being, leave his own nature behind and assume the burden, the risk, and the pleasure of divinity. The death of God forces him to change his nature, to stake his own life in the gamble for divine life. From now on, man must look on all of life, his own life and that of the cosmos, from the viewpoint of a god: as a game. All of creation is a game, a representation. Nietzsche says again and again: in our time what counts is art, not truth. Man works and learns; the gods play and create. Whole worlds rested in the hand of God; now it is man who must support them. They weigh no more than they did yesterday, nor is it their weight that flings man into the precipice of time without end. Our abyss is not the cosmic infinite but death. Man bears the mark of contingency— and knows it. He thus cannot play like a god. Gravity, his original ponderousness, rivets him to the earth. He does not dance on the heights; he dances over a bottomless pit. Man remembers his fall and his dance is a dance of terror.

Nietzsche's subject is not the death of God but his murder. Even though the philosophical name of the murderers is *will to power*, the real guilty parties are each and every one of us. The death of God can be viewed as a historical fact, that is to say, we may believe that he died a natural death, from old age or some illness. In this case, we must look not to philosophy or theology for a diagnosis, but to the history of the ideas and beliefs of the West. It is a familiar one. The idea of a single god may have appeared first in Egypt. This solar divinity of a great empire then underwent a series of metamorphoses: a tribal god who supplants a volcanic deity, the lord of a chosen people, the redeemer of mankind, the creator and king of this world and the other world. Although the Greeks and Romans had philosophized about Being and conceived of the Idea and the Unmoved Mover, the notion of a single Creator was foreign to them. There is an insuperable contradiction between the Judeo-Christian God and the Being of pagan metaphysics: the attributes of Being are not applicable to a personal god who is a creator and a savior. Being is not God. And, what is more: Being is incompatible with any sort of monotheism. Being is necessarily either atheistic or polytheistic. God, our God, was a victim of philosophical infection: the Logos was the virus, the cause of death. Thus the history of philosophy purges us of guilt for the death of God: we were not the murderers; it was time and its accidents. Perhaps this explanation is merely a subterfuge. On close examination, this argument does not hold . water: God died within a Christian society, and died precisely because that society was not Christian enough. Our conversion from paganism was so far from total that we Christians have used pagan philosophy to kill our God. Philosophy was the weapon, but the hand that wielded it was our hand. We are obliged to go back to Nietzsche's idea: within the perspective of the death of God, atheism can only be experienced as a personal act—even though this thought is unbearable and intolerable. Only Christians can really kill God.

I am barely acquainted with the world's other great monotheism. But I suspect that Islam has experienced difficulties similar to those Christianity has undergone. Finding it impossible to discover any rational or philosophical ground for belief in a single God, Abu Hamid Ghazali writes his *Incoherence of Philosophy*; a century later, Averroes answers with his *Incoherence of Incoherence.** For Moslems, too, the battle between God and philosophy was a fight to the death. In this instance God won, and a Moslem Nietzsche might have written: "Philosophy is dead; we all killed it together; you killed it and I killed it." In India there is no one divinity that has created the world and will

---

* Henri Corbin prefers to translate the titles of these two works as *The Self-Destruction of the Philosophers* and *The Self-Destruction of Self-Destruction*, respectively (*Histoire de la philosophie islamique*, 1964).

destroy it—these functions are the responsibility of specialized gods. Indians saved God from the twofold imperfection of creating and of creating imperfect worlds and creatures. In reality they did away with God: if God is not a creator, what kind of god is He? (And if he is a creator . . .) The Hindu divinity is immersed in an abstract, infinite self-contemplation. It is not interested in human events, nor does it intervene in the march of time: it knows that everything is illusion. Its inactivity does not affect believers: myriad minor gods look after their everyday needs. Not satisfied with the existence of many heavens and many hells, each one populated by innumerable gods and demons, the Buddhists conceived the idea of Bodhisattvas, beings (or rather nonbeings) who share both the impassible perfection of the Buddha and the active compassion of the minor divinities: they are not gods but metaphysical entities endowed with redeeming passion. India could dispense with the idea of a Creator because it had already critically examined the notion of time. If true reality is motionless Being—or its contrary, the equally motionless Nothingness of Buddhism—time is unreal and illusory. There would have been no point in inventing a God who is the creator of an illusion.

The difficulties of atheism in the West stem from the notion of time: if time is real, the God who creates it must exist before time. He is its origin and its support. Nietzsche attempted to resolve this mind-boggling puzzle by means of the Eternal Return: the death of God is a moment in circular time, an end that is a beginning. But this cyclical time results in another contradiction: the time of the death of God will be followed by that of his resurrection. As Nerval put it: *"Ils reviendront, ces Dieux que tu pleures toujours!"** The Eternal Return converts God into a manifestation of time, but it does not abolish him. In order to be done with God, time must be done away with: this is the lesson of Buddhism. If we were to venture to formulate a criticism of time as radical as that of Buddhism, it would have to be on en-

---

* "Those Gods whose deaths you still mourn will return!"

tirely different grounds. Whereas the Buddha confronted a time that was cyclical, our time is linear, successive, and unrepeatable. For us, God is not in time but *before* time. . . . Perhaps atheism is a problem of *position*: not our position vis-à-vis God but of God vis-à-vis time. A problem of conceiving of God *after* time. Of thinking of time as having an end—and a purpose: not the creation of a superman but the creation of a real God. Such a God could be thought of without anguish and inner conflict, because he would be not the Creator but the Creature. Not a child of ours but the Child of time who is born when time dies. A problem of conceiving of time not as succession and an infinite fall, but as a finite creative principle: a God developing in the once-empty womb of the instant. If the atheist could conceive of a God that awaits him at the end of time, would this resolve the contradiction and put an end to his rage and remorse? God has not died and no one has killed him: he has not been born yet. This notion is no less terrifying than Nietzsche's since it leads to a conclusion that the West has rejected with horror from the very beginning of its history: the end of time. Will those of us who have killed God dare to kill time?

Nihilism and Dialectics

God and philosophy could not live together peacefully: can philosophy survive without God? Once its adversary has disappeared, metaphysics ceases to be the science of sciences and becomes logic, psychology, anthropology, history, economics, linguistics. What was once the great realm of philosophy has today become the ever-shrinking territory not yet explored by the experimental sciences. If we are to believe the logicians, all that remains of metaphysics is no more than the nonscientific residuum of thought—a few errors of language. Perhaps tomorrow's metaphysics, should man feel a need to think metaphysically, will begin as a critique of science, just as in classical antiquity it began as a critique of the gods. This metaphysics would ask it-self the same questions as classical philosophy, but the start-ing point of the interrogation would not be the traditional one *before* all science but one *after* the sciences. It is difficult to imagine man returning to metaphysics. Having been so deeply disappointed by science and technology, he will seek a poetics. Not the secret of immortality or the key to eternal life: the source of movement and change itself, the stream that fuses life and death in a single image.

The death of God implies the disappearance of metaphysics, even if we do not accept Heidegger's interpretation of Nietzsche's phrase. In his remarkable study—perhaps the best ever written on the subject—Heidegger tells us that the word God designates not only the Christian God but the suprasensible world in general: "God is the name Nietzsche gives to the sphere of Ideas and Ideals." If this were true, the death of God would be merely one episode in a vaster drama: a chapter, the last one, in the history of metaphysics. I do not believe this to be the case. Nietzsche's Madman does not say that God has died a natural or historical death; he says that we have murdered him. This is a personal act, and we may understand the grandeur of our era only if we think of it as a crime committed by each and all of us. But even if God is regarded as having died a natural or philo-sophical death, his disappearance will inevitably lead to the death of metaphysics: thought has now lost its object, its *obsta-cle*. The philosophy of the West fed on God's flesh; once divinity has disappeared, thought perishes. Without sacred food, there is no metaphysics.

Once having devoured the pagan gods, classical metaphysics erected its beautiful systems. When all its enemies had been annihilated, it disintegrated into sects and schools (Stoicism, Epicureanism) or dwindled away in the attempt to found reli-gions (Neoplatonism). This last undertaking proved to be fruit-less: metaphysics receives its sustenance from religion but it is not a creator of religions. Philosophical schools, on the other hand, gave the ancients something that our modern philosophies have failed to give us: *wisdom*. None of our philosophies has produced a Hadrian or a Marcus Aurelius. Or even a Seneca. Our Marxist philosophers prefer "self-criticism" to hemlock. Modern philosophy has admittedly given us a politics, and our revered philosophers go by the names of Lenin, Trotsky, Stalin, and Mao Tse-tung. The descent from these first two names to the last two is a dizzying one. In less than fifty years, Marxism, which Marx defined as a critical system of thought, has turned into a scholastic philosophy of executioners (Stalinism) and the elementary catechism of seven hundred million human beings (Maoism). The source of modern "wisdom" is not philosophy but art. And it is not "wisdom" but madness, a poetics. In the last century it went by the name of Romanticism, and in the first half of our century by the name of Surrealism. Neither philosophy nor religion nor politics has been able to withstand the attack of science and technology. But art has borne up under the onslaught. Dadaists—above all Duchamp and Picabia—exploited technology to make a mockery of it: they turned it into something *useless*. Modern art is a passion, a critique, and a cult. It is also a game and a form of wisdom—the wisdom of madness.

Pagan philosophy created no religion of its own, but it killed the new religion. Christianity brought Plato and Aristotle back to life, and from that point on, God and Being, the One and the Only, were locked in mortal embrace. Reason absorbed God and crowned itself queen: if it was no longer possible to adore a rational God, divine reason at least might be worshiped. Kant dethroned reason. Undermined by his criticism as it had itself undermined the idea of God, reason became dialectics. The transition from the dialectics of spirit to dialectical materialism was the last chapter. The relation between Marx and philosophy is analogous to that between Nietzsche and Christianity. In both cases the crucial factor is a personal act that lays claim to being a universal method; there is no such thing as a history of philosophy: there are philosophers within history. Nietzsche destroyed the principles or the foundations of metaphysics by turning them upside down, a process that resulted in the subversion of all values. Marx's method was similar. As he himself says, his one aim was to put dialectics back in its *natural* position: feet down and head up. The sensible, the material world, was the foundation of the universe, and the old foundation, the idea, was its expression. To Marx the word *natural* means something beyond the usual meaning of the word. It is more than a return to the old materialism. Marx's nature is historical. His great originality lies in his humanization of matter: human action, praxis, makes the opaque natural world intelligible. He attempted thereby to escape the contradiction of traditional materialism, but in so doing he created another pair of opposites that none of his followers has been able to reconcile: the nature/spirit dichotomy reappears as a nature/history duality. If nature is dialectical, history is part of nature and the entire theory of praxis—human action that converts matter into history—turns out to be superfluous; the distinction between dialectical materialism and the old materialism of the eighteenth century turns out to be illusory: Marxism is not a historicism but a naturalism. The other possibility is equally contradictory: if nature is *not* dialectical, a dichotomy appears and there is again a dualism.

According to Heidegger, the method of "total nihilism" involves not so much the change of values or their devaluation as the reversal of the value of values. Denying that the suprasensible—the Idea, God, the Categorical Imperative, Progress—is the supreme value does not necessarily imply the total destruction of values but rather the appearance of a new principle as the source and basis of all values. This principle is life. And life in its most direct and aggressive form: the will to power. The essence of life is will, and will expresses itself as power. I am not at all certain that the essence of life is the will to power. In any event, it does not seem to me to be the source or the origin of value, its underlying cause; nor do I believe that it is its foundation. The essence of the will to power can be summed up in the word *more*. It is an appetite: not more being, but being more. Not *being*, but a passionate *wish to be*. This passionate wish to be is the wound through which the will to power is drained of its blood. Just as movement cannot be the cause or the principle of movement (*who* moves it, *what* supports it?), the will to power is not being but an urge to be and therefore incapable of becoming its own foundation or the foundation of values. It is by nature a going-beyond-itself; in order to discover its reason for being, its prime cause, its *principle*, its impetus must be totally expended, it must go on to the very end: a return to the beginning. Implicit within the Eternal Return of the Same is a new subversion of values: the restoration of the Idea, of the suprasensible, as the foundation of value. Neither the will to power nor the Idea are principles: they are only moments of the Eternal Return, recurring phases of the Same.

Reason encounters similar difficulties when it confronts dialectical materialism. Dialectics is the manner of being, the form in which matter, the only true reality, manifests itself; matter in motion is the foundation of all values. But there is a contradiction between matter and dialectics: the so-called laws of dialectics are not observable in the processes and transformations of matter. If they were, matter would cease to be matter: it would be history, thought, or Idea. On the other hand, dialectics cannot be its own foundation because by its very nature it denies itself the moment it affirms itself. It is perpetual rebirth and perpetual death. If the will to power is continually threatened by the return of the Same, dialectics is similarly threatened by its own movement: every time it affirms itself, it denies itself. In order not to cancel itself out, it needs some sort of ground, some principle *prior* to movement. If Marxism rejects Spirit or the Idea as its foundation, and if matter also cannot be its foundation, the Marxist is trapped in a vicious circle. In the case of both the will to power and the dialectics of matter, the sensible is "an implicit denial of its essence." This essence is precisely what both Nietzsche's doctrine of the will to power and Marxist dialectics do away with: the suprasensible as the foundation of reality, the original principle and the reality of all realities. Both tendencies lead in the end to nihilism. Nietzsche's nihilism is aware of its own nature, and therefore is "total": it looks forward to nothing but the return of the Same and at this particular point in history it is in essence a game: a tragedy being staged, art. Marx's nihilism is not aware of its own nature. Although it is Promethean, critical, and philanthropic in spirit, it is nonetheless nihilistic.

Dialectical materialism and the Nietzschean doctrine of the will to power succeeded in bringing about a subversion of values that both lightened our burden and tempered our souls. But they have now lost their power of contagion.* Both tendencies are essentially a drive for *more*, but as this awesome energy accelerates, its force decreases. Today the best expression of this drive for *more* is not thought (art or politics) but technology. The inversion of values wrought by technology leads to a devaluation of all values, not excluding those of Marxism and those of Nietzsche. Life ceases to be an art or a game and becomes "a technique for living." The same thing happens in the realm of politics: the technician and the expert replace the revolutionary. Socialism no longer means the transformation of human relations but economic development, the raising of the standard of living, and the utilization of the labor force as a lever in the struggle for power and world supremacy. Socialism has become an ideology, and in those countries where it has won the day, it is a new form of alienation. The superman has not yet been born, even though men today have a power that a Caesar or an Alexander never dreamed of. Technological man is a combination of Prometheus and Sancho Panza. The American: a titan enamored of progress, a fanatical giant who worships "getting things done" but never asks himself what he is doing nor why he is doing it. His activity is not creative play but mindless sport: he drops bombs in Vietnam and sends messages home on Mother's Day; he believes in sentimental love and his sadism goes by the name of mental hygiene; he razes cities and visits his psychiatrist. He is still tied by his umbilical cord even though he is the explorer

---

* Marxism has lost this power as a philosophy, but not as a revolutionary "ideology" of the "underdeveloped" countries.

of outer space. Progress, solidarity, good intentions, and despicable acts. He does not suffer from hubris; he is simply lawless,
perpetually repentant and perpetually self-satisfied. . . . These
reflections are not a complaint. Our world is no worse than yesterday's, nor will the world of tomorrow be any better. Moreover, there is no possible way of returning to the past. Marx's
and Nietzsche's criticism of our values was so radical that nothing remains of these constructs. Their criticism is our starting
point, our only way of clearing a path that will lead us—where?
Perhaps this *where* is not located in any future time or in any
place further ahead, but there in *this* space and *this* time that
is our very own present. Is there anything left? Art is what remains of religion: the dance above the yawning abyss. Criticism is what remains of dialectics: starting all over again.

Person and Principle

A remarkable recent study of the Hindu caste system by Louis
Dumont (*Homo hierarchicus*, Paris, 1966) is surprising confirmation, for me at least, of the remarks I have ventured with regard to the difficulties of being atheistic in the West and monothe-
istic in India. This French Orientalist points out that castes are
not units or elements in the same sense as the proletariat, the
bureaucracy, the Army, or the Church: that is, corporations,
social bodies, each different from all others. Castes cannot be
described as substances; they are not *classes*, but a system of
relations. Each caste, naturally, has it own distinguishing characteristics: its own territory, occupation, function, diet, marriage
customs, ceremonies, rituals, and so on. But these features are
not what go to make up a caste: they define its relation to other
castes. They are indicative of its position within the whole,
characteristics distinguishing it rather than constituting it. What
constitutes a caste is the over-all system; what defines it is its
position within the system. This conception is the exact opposite

of ours: to our way of thinking, the individual is the basis of society, and both the individual and society are self-sufficient units. In the West, society is either a collection of individuals or a totality, something resembling a collective individual. When politicians call upon the people to "march forward as one," they are not merely mouthing a cliché: they are saying that the group is an individual, what the English tradition calls "the body politic." To us, the nation is a projection of the individual; in India, the individual is a projection of society. Our public law is embodied in a *constitution*, a word that derives from the Latin word *stare*: to stand firmly and immovably in one spot. It denotes the collective will to stand together as a single entity, as an individual. There is nothing similar in India. Every political and moral concept in that country—from the idea of monarchical rule to the hierarchical system that extends from the varnas to dharma—have nothing whatsoever to do with the idea of society as the common will. In the languages of India there is no word to designate the reality that we call a *nation*.

The basic unit of Western thought is an indivisible entity, whether metaphysical (being), psychological (the self), or social (nation, class, political bodies). This model, however, does not correspond to reality, and reality continually destroys it: dialectics, poetry, eroticism, mysticism, and in the realm of history, war and internal conflicts are the violent, spontaneous forms whereby Otherness reminds the One of its existence. The great discovery of modern thought in many different disciplines —from physics and chemistry to linguistics, anthropology and psychology—has in fact been the discovery of relationship; a totality of unstable, evanescent particles has taken the place of an ultimate irreducible element. The basic unit is now multiple, contradictory, insubstantial, ever-changing; hence contemporary thought has failed to corroborate the suppositions underlying the central traditions of the West. The archetype, the basic intellectual framework of India, by contrast, is plurality, flux, relation; just as elements are combinations, the individual is a society. The notions of interdependence and hierarchy are a natural consequence of the basic idea of relation. We look upon the system as an individual; the Hindus look upon the individual as a system. Our notion of the community of nations is that of an assembly of equals, at least potentially if not in actual fact; underlying the caste system is the concept of a hierarchical interdependence. In the West, individualism, equality, rivalry; in India, relation, interdependence, hierarchy. The idea of substance underlies our concepts; the caste system lacks substance: it is a chain of relations. To say that the world of castes is a world of relations is tantamount to saying that

*la caste particulière, l'homme particulier, n'ont pas de substance; ils existent empiriquement, ils n'ont pas d'être. . . . L'individu n'est pas. C'est pourquoi, pour les hindous eux-mêmes, dès qu'ils prennent un point de vue substantialiste, tout, y compris les dieux, est irréel: l'illusionisme est ici en germe, sa popularité et celle du monisme ne sauraient étonner.**

But before taking a look at how philosophical thought dissolves the gods, let us see how the popular imagination conceives of them.

Time and again, my Hindu friends have tried to explain polytheism to me by means of a simple, and essentially European, formula: the gods are manifestations of the divine. But this explanation does not tell us why the gods of India change name from region to region and from caste to caste. To call this phenomenon an instance of syncretism is to offer a handy label for it rather than an interpretation of it; this syncretism would require explanation in turn. What is more, the position of the gods in the hierarchy and their meaning also change: in one place they are creators and in another destroyers. These changes are

---

* ". . . any one caste, any one man has no real existence; they exist empirically, but they have no true essence. . . . There is no such thing as an individual. That is why everything, including the gods, is unreal to the Hindus themselves the moment they adopt a substantialist point of view: this is an embryonic form of illusionism, and the popularity of this concept and that of monism should not surprise us."

related to the calendar: there is a rotation of divinities, a divine revolution similar to that of the planets. The explanation offered by modern Hindus—that the names change but the god remains —is only a partial one, and, moreover, it too is European: it endows the divinities with substance, turns them into individuals. The truth would seem to be precisely the opposite: the gods are interchangeable because they are nonsubstantial. They are at once the same and different because they have no autonomous existence; their being is not really being; it is the embodiment of a momentary conjuncture of relations. The god is merely a cluster of attributes—propitious, harmful, and indifferent—being actualized within a given context. The meaning of the god—the actualization of this set of attributes or that— depends on his position within the over-all system. Since the system perpetually rotates, the position of the gods continually shifts.

There is one other peculiar feature: the god is almost always accompanied by consorts. Duality, a basic feature of Tantrism, permeates all of Hindu religious life: male and female, pure and impure, left and right. Lastly, the god is the possessor of a "vehicle"—Siva's bull, Ganesha's rat, Durga's lion—and is surrounded by a multitude of familiars and parasites. Each couple rules over a great throng of minor divinities. Gods who continually change; a couple; a multitude: not individuals but relations. The Hindu pantheon is a hierarchy of crowds, a system of systems. It thus more or less mirrors the caste system. Nonetheless, it would be an error to consider it a mere reflection of the social structure, as proponents of an elementary sort of Marxism might maintain, for the caste system depends in turn on the distinction between the pure and the impure. Hindu society is religious and Hindu religion social. Everything fits together. The divine is not the godhead; nor is it an impersonal substance, a fluid. The divine is a society: a tissue of relations, a magnetic field, a phrase. The gods are something like the atoms, the cells, or the phonemes of the divine.

I would like to offer a criticism of Dumont's theory here. It seems to me that something essential is missing in his book on Hinduism: the description of what distinguishes human society from divine society. Some distinctive feature, note, or sign must separate the sacred from the profane, the pure from the impure, the castes from the divine multitudes. Dumont tells us how the system functions and describes its structure, but he fails to tell us *what it is*. His definition is not inaccurate: rather, it is formal, and therefore disregards the content of the phenomenon being studied. I will not discuss this point further, because my purpose here is not to examine the phenomenology of Hinduism but to outline the solution to this very same problem that has been arrived at by the Brahmins and Indian philosophy.

The question may be stated, rather roughly, as follows: what is the divine? The answer, one as old as the Upanishads, is simple and clear-cut: there is an impersonal being, forever identical with itself, a being impermeable to change that simply *is*, in which all the gods, all realities, times, and beings are dissolved and reabsorbed: Brahma. This notion reduces the heavenly and the earthly world, time and space, to a phantasmagorical unreality. Later on, a complementary notion appears: the being of man, Atman, is identical with the being of the world. Hence the subject is entirely eliminated. This absolute monism requires a no less absolute denial of reality and time. What is more, this unalterable and indestructible being can be defined only in negative terms. It is not this or that or the other: *neti, neti*. It is neither the whole nor its parts; it is neither transcendence nor immanence; it is nowhere and yet it is always everywhere. Negation opened the door to Samkhya pluralism and Buddhism: the one step required was to apply the criticism of change and reality to the idea of Brahma and its correlative, Atman. Buddhism followed the road to its very end: there is neither being nor individual selves; everything is causal relation. Samkhya pluralism postulated a godless nature (prakriti) and individual souls (purusha). The fan of Hindu thought unfolds between these two extremes: an absolute monism and an equally absolute pluralism. However profound the differences between these many positions may appear to be, they are all dissolved or reconciled in the final phase of philosophical meditation: moksha, nirvana. The annihilation, the reabsorption, or the liberation of the individual ego is tantamount to the disappearance of one of the terms. Change, duality, time, the illusory reality of the self are done away with. Bhakti itself—amorous union of the worshiper with his deity—is no exception: however individual and substantialized Krishna may appear to us to be, he is merely an avatar of Vishnu, a manifestation of impersonal being, as the well-known and impressive passage in the Bhagavad-Gita tells us.

The enormous effort of speculative thought to endow the divine system with substance, to convert a relationship into distinct and self-sufficient being, culminates either in an explicit monism (the Vedanta) or an implicit monism (Madhyamika Buddhism). In all cases, the One wins out. This description would appear to be an oversimplification, but in fact it is not too far from the truth: for all these pluralisms, first, lead to the idea of moksha or nirvana, which cancel out the differences between them; and secondly, the opposition between Hinduism and Buddhism—in their most extreme forms: the monism of Shankara and the relativism of Nagarjuna—is a complementary one. The white and the black version of a single line of thought: two parallel arguments, pursued with equal rigor, the one proving the unreality of everything that is not Being, the other the unreality of everything that is not Change. The affirmation of Being is arrived at through a series of absolute negations: neither this nor that. The affirmation of Change is also negative and absolute: "In primitive Buddhism all elements are interdependent and real; in the new Buddhism, they are unreal because they are interdependent."* Being and sunyata (absolute emptiness) are identical: there is no way to speak of them except uttering the syllable *no*. In Sanskrit *zero* may be spoken of as either *sunya* (empty) or *purna* (full).

* T. Scherbatsky, *Buddhist Logic* (1962).

We now have a clearer idea of what the shift from relation to unity entails. Relation disappears in one of two ways: it is either absorbed in Being or dissolved in Non-Being. It disappears but it is not transformed into a substance. Neither of these two concepts with which it fuses—Being or Emptiness—bears any resemblance to what might appear to be parallel concepts in Western thought: the principle of sufficient reason, the prime cause, the ground. Neither the Being of the Vedanta nor the Emptiness of Buddhism is the ground or source of phenomenal reality: rather, they dissolve it. Man does not begin with them; he ends with them. They are the final truth. They are not at the *beginning*, like being, energy, spirit, or the Christian God; they are *beyond*, in a region that only negation can describe. They are liberation, the unconditioned; neither death nor life, but freedom from the chain of birth and death. In fact, they are not ontological concepts at all, at least not in the Western sense. Translating Brahma as *Being* and sunyata as *Emptiness* is something worse than a misuse of language: it is a spiritual infidelity.

One of the results of this way of thinking is that the problems of time and creation are relegated to the background. The notion of a time that is irreversible and the correlative notion of a god who is the creator of this time are ideas that, strictly speaking, play no part in the logic of the system. They are superfluous ideas, concepts that are the products of illusion or sectarian curiosities. The idea of a personal god admittedly plays a very important role in Hindu religious life, but, as I have already noted, this god always appears as a manifestation or an avatar of another divinity who in turn is only a relation in the whole tissue of relations going to make up the divine system. Within Hindu speculation as a whole, deism is a secondary phenomenon. It is so in two respects: in the first place, as Hajime Nakamura points out, "the ultimate Absolute presumed by the Indian is not a personal god but an impersonal Principle";* and,

* Hajime Nakamura, *Ways of Thinking of Eastern Peoples* (1964).

second, such a deity is a creator by error or inadvertence, a god misled by the power of illusion (maya). Or, as Nakamura puts it: "There is no maya in God himself but when he created the world . . . maya attaches itself to him. God is an illusory state." God has no Being.

The Hindu Brahma does not correspond to our idea of Being: it is an empty, impersonal, substanceless concept—the other pole and the complement of the notion of relation. What I mean is this: the contrary of Being is Non-Being, and Greek and European metaphysics are built on this pair; the contrary of relation is the absence of relation, nullity, zero (sunya). The Hindu Absolute, Brahma, has no relations; the Buddhist Absolute, sunyata, knows nothing but unreal relations. Both are defined by absence, and both eliminate or absorb the contrary term: they cancel out relation. In the West, what is basic is affirmation: we view Non-Being from the point of view of Being. In India what is basic is negation: they see relation—the human world and the divine world—from the point of view of an Absolute that is defined negatively or *is* negation itself. The Non-Being of the West is subordinate to Being; it is *lack* of reality. Hindu relation, the vital flux, is subordinate to zero; it is an unreal *excess*. In the first case, the unity of Being is positive; in the second it is negative. Hence, in essence, Brahma is identical with sunyata: both are the *No* that is the answer of the Absolute both to relation—the world, time, gods—and to discursive thought. We have a tendency to exaggerate the opposition between Brahma and sunyata, between the theory of Atman (Being) and that of Anatta (Non-Being), because we conceive of this opposition in terms of Western metaphysics. Thus Raymundo Panikar regrets that "Between the Parmenides of India and its Heraclitus, no Aristotle has as yet appeared . . . to prove how the being that moves, changes, and is not *Brahma*, at the same time is not an unreal nothingness."* But I repeat: mediation is impossible because the opposition is not between Being and Non-Being, nor

* Raymundo Panikar, *Maya e Apocalisse* (1966).

between Being and Change, but between two concepts that
have their roots in something entirely foreign to the Greek and
European tradition. The thought of the West is based on the
idea of substance, thing, element, being; that of India on relation, interpenetration, interaction, flux. It therefore defines the
Absolute as the cessation of Change, that is to say, as negation
of relation and action. India does not deny Being: it ignores it.
It denies Change: it is maya, illusion. European thought does
not deny relation: it ignores it. It affirms Change: Change is
Being unfolding or manifesting itself.

Negation and the idea of static balance or immobility are two
constant features of Indian thought, both in Hinduism and in
Buddhism. Nakamura points out how fond Indians are of negative expressions; they abound both in Sanskrit and Pali and in
the modern languages of India. While the European speaks of
"victory or defeat," an Indian speaks of "victory or nonvictory."
He does not speak of peace, but of "nonviolence" and what we
would call "diligence" he calls "nonlaziness." Change is "imper-
manence," and the person who has attained illumination or
liberation "goes to a nonencounter with the King of the dead."
The negative abstracts, impersonalizes, sucks the substance from
ideas, names, acts. Nagarjuna summed up his entire doctrine in
Eight Negatives. If the real is negation, change is unreal. For us,
the real is positive and, therefore, change is not a synonym of
unreality. Change may be an imperfect mode of being *in relation to* essence, but it is not an illusion. For the Hindu, change
is an illusion because it *lacks any relation* with the Absolute.

The most notable—and the most basic—feature of Indian
thought is the identification of reality with negation. Its conception of change is also a prominent feature. The Greek says:
everything is in flux; the Hindu says: everything is impermanent.
It is hard for a Westerner to conceive of Nothingness, and
Heidegger has shown that it is literally unthinkable: it is the
fathomless abyss above which metaphysical thought flaps its
wings. In India it is Being that is difficult to conceive. Essence,
the reality of all realities, is formless and nameless. For Plato, the

essence is the *Idea*: a form, an archetype. The Greeks invented geometry; Hindus the zero. To us, Hindu religion is atheistic. A Hindu might well reply that even our science and our atheism are steeped in monotheism. Time and change are real to us because they are modes of being—a being that emerges from chaos or nothingness and unfolds like an apparition. The divinities of the West are presences that radiate energy. Otto's notion of the numinous reflects our instinctive conviction that the godhead is a magnetic presence: the divine is the "fluid" of deity, its emanation, its product. In India, the god is the product of the divine. For us, the divine is concentrated in a Person; for Hindus, it dissolves in the Impersonal.

The Liberated Man and Liberators

Nagarjuna's dialectic is a system of universal negation: the road to emptiness; in Hegel's dialectic, negation is a creative moment within the process and negativity the road to Being. In the Hegelian dialectic, contradiction "does not result in absolute nullity or Nothingness: it is essentially a negation of its own content."* Western philosophy has not been blind to the negativity inherent in the concept, but it has always viewed it as an aspect of the idea, being, or reality rather than an absolute, and certainly never as the Absolute. Hence the West has invented creative negation, revolutionary criticism, the contradiction that affirms the very thing it denies. India has invented liberation by way of negation and made it the nameless mother of all living creatures. These two contrary visions have in turn engendered two types of wisdom, two models of spiritual life: the liberator and the liberated man. For the latter, criticism is a means of letting go: his goal is not self-creation but self-abandonment; for the former, criticism is a means of creation: his goal is re-

* T. Scherbatsky, *Buddhist Logic* (in the chapter on dialectics: "European parallels: Kant and Hegel").

union with himself and with the world. The Hindu practices negation as an inner method: his goal is not to save the world but to destroy the world within himself; the European practices it as a penetration of reality, as a way of appropriating the world: through negation, the concept changes the world and makes him its master. The liberated man approaches criticism as an apprenticeship in silence; the liberator uses it to subject headstrong language to the rule of reason. The Hindu maintains that once language has reached a certain level, it lacks meaning; the Westerner has decided that anything that lacks meaning also lacks reality. In European thought, criticism determines the causes and structures of things and is such a delicate instrument of mediation that it has made indetermination itself a principle of physics. Indian negation, which is no less subtle than that of the West though it is applied to other phenomena, is intended to foster indetermination: its role is to open the door to the unconditioned. . . . But perhaps it would be better to attempt to draw the parallel from the point of view of anthropology. I shall return to Dumont's book, an incomparable guide.

As a way of comparing modern Western society with Hindu society, the French anthropologist, like his mentor Lévi-Strauss, draws up a table of bipolar oppositions. The substantive in India is the religious pair pure-impure, a distinction that serves as the foundation of the social structure: a hierarchical society (interdependence and separation of castes). In the West, the substantive is an a-religious one, the individual, which serves as the basis of an egalitarian society and the idea of nationhood. In India, the social structure is religious; in Europe, it is economic and political. Thus, the adjective in the Hindu world is the economico-political; in the West, the adjective is religious (a private matter). The contradictions, which are also adjectival, are: in India sects, and in the West totalitarianisms, racisms, classes, and social hierarchy (holdovers of an aristocracy, the Army, the Church, etc.). All these oppositions can be summed up in two principal ones: man as a society (hierarchical man), and society as an individual (egalitarian man). Hierarchical society is total but not totalitarian, and thus it has invented a way of escape for the individual man: the free life of the sannyasi, the sadhu, and the Buddhist and Jainist monks. Freedom is attained through renouncing the world: that is to say the duties and advantages of one's caste. Dumont finds no equivalent in the Western tradition. The classical ideal of the sage, in fact, was so closely linked to the idea of the "polis" that there is little need to stress the fact that Greco-Roman wisdom was deeply social in nature. During the heyday of Christianity, the saints and the religious orders were active in this world, even though they were serving a divine cause and a divine truth. In India, on the other hand, the sannyasi lives outside of society: he escapes its rules and his activities are aimed neither at reforming the world nor at saving souls.* Is there anything in the modern Western world comparable to the institution of the sannyasi? Dumont does not think so. I believe there is: the rebel artist and the professional revolutionary.

Both the vagabond seeking liberation and those who aspire to free mankind are outsiders in their respective societies. Thus we must first compare their relations to their worlds. The sannyasi does not fight the world: he denies it; the artist assumes a pose on the sidelines, jeering and scoffing at it; and the revolutionary actively opposes it: his goal is to destroy it and build a better one. The relationship of the sannyasi to his world is a religious

---

* It is quite true that those of us living in New Delhi in 1966 were witness to a popular demonstration headed by several hundred sadhus; a furious pitched battle with the police took place at the entrance to the Indian Parliament. It was a demonstration against the slaughter of cows, and therefore a religious act. I do not deny that in this case, as in others, those involved have been influenced by Western methods, if not Western ideas. Egalitarian ideology has not destroyed the caste system, but it threatens to turn it into something very dangerous: in a number of places the castes are now behaving like individuals and have become closed political corporations. Egalitarianism has undermined the notions of hierarchy and interdependence and has made the castes aggressive entities. Egalitarianism is contradictory: it is an attempt to found social harmony on equality and, at the same time, it opens the door to competition and rivalry. Its real name is envy. The same phenomenon can be observed in the "communalist" struggles, as the struggles among Hindus, Moslems, and Sikhs are called.

one and one of indifference; that of the artist and revolutionary is secular, active, and antagonistic. The reaction of society is also different. The Hindu adopts an attitude of reverence and extreme benevolence toward the sannyasi. He may practice the most extravagant, cruel, or repulsive rites, uphold the most unconventional opinions, wander about either clothed or naked, as he pleases: such behavior in no way lessens his prestige or compromises his respectability. He is an *untouchable*, and, at the same time, his touch does not defile: it illuminates, it purifies. He is the holy exception, the sanctioned violation, the permissible transgression—fiesta incarnated in an individual. He is free of all relations, undefinable in terms of the caste system, a pure soul, wandering where he pleases. The artist is the man misunderstood, the eccentric; he lives in a closed group and even the section of town he lives in with his fellow artists is a dubious sort of place; the bourgeois, the proletarian, and the professor look upon him with suspicion. The revolutionary is the man hounded by the police of every country, the man with no passport and a thousand names, denounced by the press, and sought by the examining magistrate: any step taken to neutralize him is considered legitimate. Another surprising contradiction: once the artist is recognized, he returns to the world, he is a millionaire or a national glory, and if he is Mexican, he is buried in the Pantheon of Illustrious Men when he dies; once the revolutionary has taken over, he immediately sets up a Committee of Public Safety and persecutes dissidents even more cruelly than the former tyrant. The sannyasi, on the other hand, cannot return to the world, for if he does so he risks becoming an untouchable, a real one this time, one of those whose shadow defiles even the sacred waters of the Ganges.

The Hindu ascetic aspires to liberation: ending the cycle of death and birth, destroying the self, dissolving himself in the unlimited and unconditioned, doing away with *this* and *that*, subject and object—entering the dark night of Negation with his eyes wide open. The artist seeks to realize himself or realize a work, rescue beauty or change the language, dynamite men's consciousness or free their passions, do battle with death, communicate with men if only the better to spit on them. The revolutionary seeks to abolish injustice, force us to be free, make us happy or virtuous, increase production and consumption, cast our passions in the perfect mold of geometry. *Changing the world/changing life*: these two formulas of Marx and Rimbaud, which affected Breton so deeply, sum up the modern wisdom of the West. If a sannyasi were to hear them and *understand* them, once he had recovered from his natural astonishment he would greet them with a roar of laughter that would interrupt for the space of an instant the meditation of all the Buddhas and the endless erotic embrace of Siva and Parvati.

3

Revolt, Revolution, Rebellion

The word *revuelta* is not often used in Spanish. Most people prefer to use the words *revolución* and *rebelión*. On first reflection, the contrary would seem more natural: the word *revuelta* is more popular and more expressive. In the year 1611, Covarrubias defines this latter concept as follows: *"Rebolver es ir con chismerías de una parte a otra y causar enemistades y quistiones: y a éste llamamos rebolvedor y reboltoso, rebuelta la cuestión."** The meanings of the Spanish word *revuelta* are numerous, ranging from *return* to *confusion* to a *mixture* of one thing with another; all these meanings have to do with the idea of a recurrence of something accompanied by disorder and irregularity. None of these meanings is a positive one; none of them suggests that *revuelta* is a good thing. In a society such as that of seventeenth-century Spain, *revuelta* was regarded as the root of many evils: the confusion of classes, the return to primordial chaos, agitation, and disorder that threatens the very fabric of society. *Revuelta* was something that reduced distinctions to a formless

---

* Joan Corominas: *Diccionario crítico-etimológico de la lengua castellana.* "*Rebolver* is to go about spreading gossip and causing enmity and quarrels: and we call such a person a *rebolvedor* and a *reboltoso*, and the action, *rebuelta*."

mass. For Bernardo de Balbuena (the sixteenth-century Spanish poet), the foundation of civilization is the establishment of hierarchies, thus creating a necessary inequality between individuals; barbarism is a return to the state of nature, to equality. It is no easy task to determine when the word *revuelta* came to be used with the meaning of a spontaneous uprising of the people. The word *révolte* appears in French around 1500, in the sense of "a change of party," and does not take on the connotation of *rebellion* until a century later. Although the Littré dictionary indicates that *révolte* comes from the Italian *rivoltare* (to turn inside out or upside down), Corominas believes that it may come from the Catalan *revolt, temps de revolt*. Whatever its origin, most Spanish-speaking people now use the word *revolución*, both in conversation and in writing, to refer to public disturbances and uprisings. The word *revuelta* is reserved for riots or agitation with no clearly defined purpose. It is a plebeian word.

There are marked differences in Spanish between the *revoltoso*, the *rebelde*, and the *revolucionario*. The first is a dissatisfied individual who is fond of intrigue and sows confusion; the second is someone who refuses to submit to authority, a disobedient or unruly person; the third is a person who seeks to change institutions through the use of violence. (I use the definitions in our dictionaries even though they seem to be inspired by Police Headquarters.) Despite these differences, the three words are intimately related. This relationship is a hierarchical one: *revuelta* lives in the subsoil of the language; *rebelión* is individualist; *revolución* is an intellectual word and refers more to the uprisings of entire peoples and the laws of history than to the deeds of a rebellious hero. *Rebelión* is a military term; it comes from the Latin *bellum* and evokes the image of civil war. Minorities are rebels; majorities, revolutionaries. Although the origin of *revolución* is the same as that of *revuelta* (as is that of the two English words *revolution* and *revolt*, i.e., Latin *volvere*, to revolve, to turn around, to unroll), and although both words connote a *return* or a *recurrence*, the origin of *revolución* is philosophical and astronomical: the return of the stars and the planets to their earlier position, rotation around an axis, the cycle of the seasons and historical eras. The connotations of *return* and *movement* in the word *revolución* suggest an underlying order; these same connotations in the word *revuelta* suggest disorder. Thus *revuelta* does not imply any cosmic or historical vision; it is the chaotic or tumultuous present. In order for revolt to cease to be a mere passing disturbance and take its place in history, it must be transformed into a revolution. The same is true of rebellion: the acts of the rebel, however daring they may be, are fruitless gestures if they are not based on a revolutionary doctrine. Ever since the end of the eighteenth century, the cardinal word of this triad has been revolution. Bathed in the light of the Idea, it is philosophy in action, criticism that has become an act, violence with a clear purpose. As popular as revolt and as generous as rebellion, it encompasses them and guides them. Revolt is the violence of an entire people; rebellion the unruliness of an individual or an uprising by a minority; both are spontaneous and blind. Revolution is both planned and spontaneous, a science and an art.

The discredit into which the word *revuelta* has fallen is due to a precise historical fact. It is a word that aptly expresses the unrest and the discontent of a people still under the sway of the idea that authority is sacred, even though it may rise up in arms against one specific injustice or another. Although it is egalitarian, revolt respects the divine right of the monarch: *de rey abajo, ninguno.* Its violence is the breaking of the ocean wave against the rocky cliff; the wave bathes the cliff in foam and retreats. The modern meaning of *revolución* in Spain and Hispano-America was an importation by intellectuals. *Revuelta,* a popular, spontaneous word but one that pointed in no particular direction, was replaced by one that had philosophical prestige. The fact that the new word became a very fashionable one is indicative not so much of a historical revolt, a popular uprising, as of the appearance of a new power: philosophy. From the eighteenth century on, reason becomes a subversive political principle. The

revolutionary is a philosopher, or at least an intellectual: a
man of ideas. The word *revolution* calls up many names and
many meanings: Kant, the Encyclopedia, the Jacobin Terror,
and, most vividly of all, the destruction of the order of privileges
and exceptions and the founding of an order based not on authority but on the free exercise of reason. The old virtues went
by the names of faith, fealty, honor. All of them strengthened the
social bond and each of them was related to a universally recognized value: faith in the Church as the incarnation of revealed
truth; fealty to the sacred authority of the monarch; honor to the
tradition based on blood ties. These virtues had their counterpart in the charity of the Church, the magnanimity of the king,
and the loyalty of feudal subjects, whether villeins or great lords.
Revolution is a word for the new virtue: justice. All the other
new virtues—liberty, fraternity, equality—are based on it. It is
a virtue that does not depend on revelation, power, or blood. As
universal as reason, it admits of no exceptions and is equally
far removed from arbitrariness and compassion. Revolution: a
word belonging to the vocabulary of the just and the dealers of
justice. A little later another word suddenly appears, one previously looked upon with horror: rebellion. From the very outset
it was a romantic, bellicose, aristocratic word referring to out-
laws. The rebel: the accursed hero, the solitary poet, lovers who
trample social conventions underfoot, the plebe of genius who
defies one and all, the dandy, the pirate. Rebellion also has religious connotations. It refers not to Heaven but to Hell: the tower-
ing pride of the prince of darkness, the blasphemy of the titan
in chains. Rebellion: melancholy and irony. Art and love were
rebels; politics and philosophy revolutionaries.

   In the second half of the nineteenth century, another word
appears: *reformista*. This word came not from France but
from the English-speaking countries. The word was not a new
one; what was new was its meaning and the aura surrounding
it. An optimistic word and an austere one, an unusual combination of Protestantism and Positivism. This alliance of the old

heresy and the new, of Lutheranism and science, aroused the enmity of both the purists and the conservatives. There were good reasons for their hatred; the word concealed revolutionary contraband beneath its respectable outward trappings. It was a "decent" word. The place where it was heard most often was not in the haunts of the *revoltosos* or in the catacombs of the rebels, but in academic lecture halls and among the editorial staff of periodicals. The revolutionary appealed to philosophy; the reformist to the sciences, commerce, and industry: he was a fanatical admirer of Spencer and the railroads. Ortega y Gasset very cleverly, though perhaps not accurately, points out a basic difference between the revolutionary and the reformist: the former tries to change customary uses; the latter, to correct abuses. If this were true, the reformist would be a rebel who had come to his senses, a Satan who is eager to collaborate with the powers that be. I say this because the rebel, unlike the revolutionary, does not attempt to undermine the social order as a whole. The rebel attacks the tyrant; the revolutionary attacks tyranny. I grant that there are rebels who regard all governments as tyrannical; nonetheless, it is abuses that they condemn, not power itself. Revolutionaries, on the other hand, are convinced that the evil does not lie in the excesses of the constituted order but in order itself. The difference, it seems to me, is considerable. As I see it, the similarities between the revolutionary and the reformist are greater than the differences that separate them. Both are intellectuals, both believe in progress, both reject myths: their faith in reason is unswerving. The reformist is a revolutionary who has chosen the path of evolution rather than violence. His methods are different, but not his goals: the reformist also wants to change institutions. The revolutionary is an advocate of a sudden great leap forward; the reformist of one step at a time. Both believe in history as a linear process and as progress. Both are the offspring of the bourgeoisie, both are modern.

Revolution is a word that implies the notion of cyclical time and therefore that of regular and recurrent change. But the modern meaning of the word does not refer to an eternal return, the circular movement of worlds and stars, but rather to a sudden and *definitive* change in direction of public affairs. Cyclical time is brought to an end and a new rectilinear time begins. The new meaning destroys the old: the past will not return, and the archetype of events is not what has been but what will be. In its original meaning, revolution is a word that affirms the primacy of the past: anything new is a return. The second meaning implies the primacy of the future: the gravitational field of the word shifts from the yesterday that is known to the tomorrow that is yet to be discovered. It is a cluster of new meanings: the pre-eminence of the future, the belief in continuous progress and the perfectibility of the species, rationalism, the discredit of tradition and authority, humanism. All these ideas fuse in that of rectilinear time: history conceived as an onward march. This new cluster of meanings marks the sudden appearance of profane time. Christian time was finite: it began with the Fall and ended in Eternity, the day after the Last Judgment. Modern time, whether revolutionary or reformist, rectilinear or spiral, is infinite.

The change in meaning of the word *revolution* also affects the word *revolt*. Guided by philosophy, it becomes a prerevolutionary activity: it enters the realm of history and the future. The martial word *rebellion*, in turn, absorbs the old meanings of the words *revolt* and *revolution*. Like revolt, it is a spontaneous protest against power; like revolution, it represents cyclical time that ceaselessly reverses top and bottom. The rebel, a fallen angel or a titan in disgrace, is the eternal nonconformist. His action is not engraved upon the rectilinear time of history, the realm of the revolutionary and the reformist, but on the circular time of myth: Jupiter will be dethroned, Quetzalcoatl will reappear, Lucifer will return to heaven. During all of the nineteenth century, the rebel lives on the margin of society. Revolutionaries and reformists look upon him with the same mistrust as Plato passing judgment on poets, and for the same reason: the rebel prolongs the fascination of myth.

The Verbal Round

The meanings of the three words revolt, rebellion, and revolution remained intact, but their position changed. It was a threefold change: these three words that were viewed with suspicion and disapproval ascend to the verbal heaven and replace three other venerable words: king, tradition, God. Within the triangle, revolution becomes the central word; and within each word the secondary meanings become the most important: revolt is not so much confusion as a popular uprising; rebellion ceases to be headstrong disobedience and becomes generous protest; revolution is not a return to origins but the creation of the future. As with the position of chromosomes in hereditary cells, these shifts were the cause of others in our system of beliefs and values. The words and the meanings were the same, but, like choreographic figures in a ballet or the rotation of the stars in the sky, the shift in position of these words revealed a different orientation of society. This change also produced a change in our vital rhythms. Rectilinear time, modern time, now comes to occupy the center of the verbal constellation, and circular time, the image of eternal perfection for Plato and Aristotle, abandons the sphere of reason and degenerates into a more or less unconscious belief. The idea of perfection becomes at once boundless and available to everyone: it is continuous progress, not by the individual but by mankind as a whole. The human species recovers its original innocence, since it is perfectible through its works rather than through divine grace; the individual man loses the possibility of perfection, since it is not he himself, but all of humanity that is the subject of this endless progress. The species goes on although the individual is doomed. Original sin disappears and at the same time Heaven is depopulated. This change in orientation of men's thoughts and actions is accompanied by a corresponding change of rhythm:

rectilinear time is accelerated time. The old time was governed by the past: tradition was the archetype of the present and the future. Modern time considers the past mere ballast, and throws it overboard. Technology has not been the creator of speed: it was the beginning of modern time that made the speed of technology possible. This is the meaning underlying the common phrase, "we live at a faster pace today." The feeling that everything has speeded up stems from the fact that we live face to face with the future, in a horizontal time and in a straight line.

For a protagonist of modern history this shift in position of these three words is a revolution in the political sense: a radical and crucial change. For a spectator standing outside the historical whirlwind this change would also be a revolution—in the astronomical sense: a particular phase in the world's rotation. The second point of view is not absurd. A new shift is occurring within the present pattern of meanings: as we draw further and further away from the nineteenth century and its philosophies, the figure of the revolutionary is losing its bright glow and that of the rebel is ascending on the horizon. This is a phenomenon that is affecting half of contemporary society: the industrial or "developed" countries. The change is noticeable in all the arts, from those that are the most abstract, music and poetry, to those that are the most popular, the novel and films. The change is also evident in public life and in the imagination of the masses. Our heroes and heroines, as always, are exceptional creatures, but unlike those of the past, they not only defy social laws but also make a mockery of them. Our vision of time has changed once more: meaning lies neither in the past nor in the future but in the instant. One by one the old barriers have fallen in the name of the instant; the forbidden, an immense territory a century ago, is today a public square which any youngster in the neighborhood has the right to enter.

Fashion, popular songs, dances, erotic customs, publicity, and entertainment all are bathed in the ambiguous light of subversion. Because our rebellion is ambiguous. A figure halfway between the revolutionary and the tyrant, the modern rebel embodies the dreams and the terrors of a society that for the first time in history is simultaneously experiencing collective abundance and psychological insecurity. A world of mechanical objects obeys our bidding and yet we have never had less confidence in traditional values and utopian values, in religious faith, and in reason. People in industrial societies are not believers: they are credulous. On the one hand, they worship progress and science; on the other, they have ceased to trust in reason. Though they are fascinated by anything new and are antitraditionalists, they have nonetheless completely abandoned the idea of revolution. The disappearance of the values of the past and the future explains why our contemporaries embrace the instant so frantically. They are not aware that they are embracing a phantom; in this respect they are different from both the Epicureans and the Romantics. In the past, worship of the instant was a form of "wisdom" or an act of despair. In Greco-Roman antiquity, it was a philosophy enabling man to confront death; in the Romantic era, it is the passion that transforms the instant into a unique act. The instant represented not only the transitory but the exceptional, what happened to us only once and forevermore: the "fatal instant," that of death or love, the moment of truth. It was not only exceptional and fateful; it was also a *personal* experience. The new rebellion turns the instant into an everyday occurrence and thus robs it of its greatest attraction: surprise. It is no longer something that will happen to us the day we least expect it; it is what happens all the time. It is a promiscuous cult: it encompasses all classes, ages, and sexes. For our forebears the instant was a synonym of separation, a line drawn between *before* and *after*; today it designates the indiscriminate mixture of one thing with another. Not fusion: confusion. The notion of a group, something apart from and opposed to society, is giving way to that of a "wave" that comes to the surface and then immediately disappears again in the liquid mass.

The indifference of the public to present-day leaders is understandable: no head of government in the developed coun-

148 OCTAVIO PAZ

tries has the power to proclaim universal subversion. The love or
the terror inspired by Lenin and Trotsky, Stalin and Hitler seem
to us today to have been collective aberrations. Now that the
breed of great revolutionaries and great despots has died out,
the new heads of government are not leaders or guides but administrators. When a charismatic personality suddenly appears,
the politicians and the masses cannot conceal their anxiety.
Americans mourned Kennedy's death and then breathed freely
again: they could once more live complacent lives. Kennedy's
assassination reflects the state of mind of American society. In
the beginning it was thought that the young President had been
the victim of a conspiracy, either of the right or the left: another
"ideological" crime. But the Warren investigation has apparently
proved that it was the individual act of a confused loner. In
Lope de Vega's play, the judge asks: "Who killed the Comenda-
dor?" and the people answer in chorus: "We all did, as one!"
Everyone killed Kennedy. This "everyone" has no face: he is
the universal nobody. It is not surprising that General de Gaulle
is an exceptional figure in this world of dull functionaries: he
is a holdover from the heroic age. Far from being a revolutionary, he is the very incarnation of tradition, and, at the
same time in his own inimitable way, he represents rebellion: a
head of government with style is something unprecedented in a
world of undistinguished leaders. Khrushchev spoke in proverbs,
like Sancho Panza; Eisenhower could barely repeat the clichés
he borrowed from the *Reader's Digest*; Johnson expresses himself in a hybrid dialect, a mixture of the rhetoric of the New Deal
and the crude speech of a Texas sheriff; others mouth the impersonal and bastard jargon of the U.N. "experts." But the moment
we turn to the Third World, we see something quite different:
Mao Tse-tung or Nasser are something more than heads of government: they are at once leaders and symbols. Their names are
talismans that open the doors of history, symbols of the destiny
of their people. Such figures enjoy both the traditional prestige
of the hero and the more modern prestige of the revolutionary.
They are power and philosophy, Aristotle and Alexander rolled

into one. To find anyone like them in the "developed" countries, we would have to look to the real popular heroes: singers, dancers, actresses, space explorers.

The decline of iron-fisted leaders and revolutionaries with programs as rigid as geometries might appear to be a sign of a renaissance of libertarian and anarchist movements. But this is not what this decline represents: we are the witnesses of the decadence of systems and the twilight of tyrants, not of the appearance of a new brand of critical thought. Nonconformists and rebels abound, but their rebellion is sentimental and emotional, stemming from an instinctive and perhaps legitimate distrust of ideas; it is not a judgment passed on society, but a negation; it is not sustained action, but a series of sporadic outbursts followed by a return to a passive position on the sidelines. Today's rebels come from minority groups; it is not workers or the popular masses, but intellectuals and students who demonstrate against the Vietnam war in the United States. Rebellion is the privilege of groups who enjoy something that industrial society has not yet been able (or willing) to give everyone: leisure and education. The new rebellion is neither proletarian nor popular, and thus yet another indication of the progressive decline in value of two words that accompanied the word revolution in its upward climb and its gradual slide downhill: *people* and *class*. The word *people* summed up a Romantic notion associated with the French Revolution which inflamed people's spirits in the nineteenth century. Marxism replaced this word with a concept that seemed more accurate: classes. But today, these latter are tending to become sectors: the public and private, the industrial and the agricultural. In place of a dynamic image of society as a contradictory totality, sociologists and economists now offer us a classification of human beings according to their occupations.

The City Mouse and
the Country Mouse

Marxism taught us that modern society is defined by the contradiction between capital and labor, the bourgeoisie and the proletariat. Though François Perroux does not deny that society is contradictory, he has established a classification that seems to him to correspond more closely to reality in the industrial era: he divides people into masters and servants of machines. The category of masters does not apply only to the owners of these machines; it also includes administrators, technicians, managers, and experts. This classification offers the advantage of accounting for forms of noncapitalist exploitation that Marx had not foreseen—those of the Soviet regime, for instance. At the same time, it does away with the Marxist vision of history as a conflict bearing a certain resemblance to classical tragedy, with a proletarian Prometheus overthrowing the authority of the gods and inaugurating the reign of freedom over necessity. Instead of classes, Perroux deals with functions; he views history not as nemesis but as *social dialogue*, which, in his words, "obeys a logic all its own, which is different from that of violent struggle." Raymond Aron has evolved another concept that has become widely accepted: the definition of the developed countries, whatever their politico-economic form, as industrial societies. Aron is not blind to the profound differences separating the societies of the West and those of Eastern Europe nor does he minimize their importance, but he rightly maintains that in both the determining factor is not so much the political system as the relation of science and technology to the means of production. Hence Aron proposes that we call this totality of nations and peoples "industrial civilization."

All these conceptions have one feature in common: they replace the old dichotomies—classes, philosophies, civilizations—

with an image of society as a sum of equations. For the ancients, human society was a sort of metaphor of the body, a superior animal (the *body politic* of English political philosophy); Michelet looked on history as epic poetry; to Marx and Nietzsche it was a theatrical performance, or, more exactly, that region where theater ceases to be representation and becomes a living embodiment of the life and death of men and societies. The archetypes today are neither biology nor theater, but communications theory. Inspired by mathematics and symbolic logic, our vision is a formal one: we are not interested in knowing *what* messages say or *who* formulates them, but *how* they are expressed, the form in which they are transmitted and received. Aron writes:

There would be no point in trying to discover what the mental outlook of the manager of an Anglo-American company and the director of a Soviet trust have in common . . . but as economies become industrialized, both must calculate expenses and income, make *long-term plans*—the production schedule—and translate all these data into comparable *quantitative* terms.

The unique nature of the phenomenon, the meaning of the message, is being supplanted by a formal, quantitative conception. Industrial society uses the instruments provided by science, and its methods are no different from those of the laboratory. What counts, therefore, are the means, and not the ends or the goals of each society. History as passion is disappearing.

The concept of class has fared no better within regimes claiming to be Marxist. The idea of the proletariat as a universal class is central to Marxism; without it the entire theory collapses: if there is no universal class, there is no world revolution and no international Socialist society. The idea has been undermined in two ways by Marx's heirs. The first revision took place in Yugoslavia, and has now become quasiofficial Communist doctrine. The proponents of this revised theory maintain that each nation must arrive at Socialism by its own path and its own means.

Marx had emphasized that proletarian internationalism was not a philosophical idea resembling the cosmopolitanism of the Stoics, but rather the consequence of a social reality: the relation between the worker and the means of production. The proletarian, unlike the artisan, not only is not the master of his work and the owner of his work tools; he also sees his existence as a person reduced to the category of an "abstract work force." He therefore is subject to the same process of sheer quantification as the other means of production. Like electricity, coal, or petroleum, the worker knows no nationality and has no local color. Being uprooted is his natural condition and his only tradition is the struggle that links him to others who are uprooted, his fellow proletarians. The new interpretation is a radical inversion of Marx's idea: the nebulous idea of the *nation* becomes predominant and nationalism becomes the way to Socialism. Marx hoped that the proletariat would destroy the boundaries between countries; his heirs have made nationalism respectable again.

The other modification is not an attempt to subordinate the internationalism of the proletariat to nationalism; it aims, rather, at extending this internationalism to other classes. This is the Chinese thesis: exacerbating the conflict between the countryside and the city is the proper strategy for world revolution, the form that the class struggle has taken in the second half of our century. Marx was convinced that it would be the urban proletariat that would resolve the conflict between the countryside and the city once it had seized power; Mao Tse-tung believes that it will be the peasants. Whether correct or not, this idea is anti-Marxist and would have shocked both Lenin and Rosa Luxemburg, both Trotsky and Stalin. The universality of the urban working class is not quantitative (it was not the largest class in Marx's day and never has been); rather, it is the result of its historical position: it is the most advanced class. The daughter of industry and science, it is the most recent human social product, the class that has inherited all the achievements of the bourgeoisie and the other classes that were the masters before it. Therefore it represents the common, general interest:

"The revolutionary class . . . does not present itself as a class but as the representative of the whole of society; it appears as the total mass of society confronting the dominant class."* Just as the bourgeoisie destroyed the narrow particularism of feudalism and built the national State, so the proletariat destroys bourgeois nationalism and establishes an international society. Peasants and workers are natural allies because they are the classes that are most oppressed and largest in number, but this identity of interests does not cancel out their differences: peasants are the oldest class, workers the most recent; the former are a holdover from the preindustrial era and the latter the founders of a new age. Marx never set any store in a Communist revolution by peasants. Late in life, in 1870, he wrote in a letter to Kugelmann: "Only England can serve as a fulcrum for a genuine economic revolution. It is the one country where there are no longer any peasants." He had previously stated: "A Communist movement can never begin in the countryside" (*The German Ideology*). According to Marx, the relation of each class with industry, that is to say with the most advanced and perfect form of the system of production of our age, determines its historical function. The function of the peasant is a passive one: he is a victim of the action of machines as consumers of raw material and natural products, and thus his opposition has no effect. Tied to the land, the farm laborer may rebel, but his rebellion is local, or, at most, national. Though industry is world-wide in scope, the bourgeoisie's relation to it is contradictory: industry is international and the bourgeoisie national; the former is social and the latter private. The proletariat resolves this contradiction because, like industry, it is international and socializes manufactured products.

All this is common knowledge. I have mentioned it not because I believe that every line that Marx wrote is true, but because it is instructive to put his words side by side with those who claim to be his disciples and are doing their utmost to de-

* Karl Marx and Friedrich Engels, *The German Ideology* (1845).

stroy their opponents by labeling them "revisionists." It is obvious that the proletariat has not performed the international revolutionary role assigned it by Marx. Nonetheless, all of Marxist theory is based on this central idea, and therefore none of its proponents ever questioned it. Lenin believed that the struggle for national independence of colonial and semicolonial countries, especially those in Asia, would aggravate the situation of the imperialist countries and dissipate "the entirely false aura of social peace" that reigned in them, thanks to the concessions granted the oppressed masses "at the expense of the conquered countries and the colonial peoples" by the bourgeoisie that had emerged the victor of World War I. This struggle "would culminate in a total crisis of world capitalism." Thus for Lenin the principal axis was still the working class, and revolution was inseparable from a crisis of capitalism. Trotsky was even more explicit, and said in 1939 that World War II would bring on

a proletarian revolution in the advanced countries that will inevitably spread to the Soviet Union, destroy the bureaucracy, and bring about the regeneration of the October Revolution. . . . Nonetheless, if the war does not result in a proletarian revolution—or if the working class takes power, is incapable of retaining it, and hands it over to a bureaucracy—we would be forced to recognize that the trust and hope that Marxism has placed in the proletariat have proved false.

Rosa Luxemburg, who was one of the first to point out the importance of the "underdeveloped" world in the evolution of contemporary history, never doubted that the industrial working class would be the central revolutionary force.

The Channel and the Signs

Marx reduced ideas to reflections of the mode of production and the class struggle; for Nietzsche they were masks that the will to power tears off; Freud described them as sublimations of the unconscious. Now Marshall McLuhan wishes to persuade us that they are products of the communications media. McLuhan is a talented writer, and I am not attempting to use the stupid argument of the authority of these predecessors to demolish him when I cite his name after those of Marx, Nietzsche, and Freud. I mention him because his thoughts on the matter are an example of the fate that these three precursors and critics of modern civilization have suffered. McLuhan is a very popular author, as Spengler was forty years ago. I must add that unlike Spengler, he is not a reactionary; at the same time, he lacks the somber genius of that German author. McLuhan has borrowed Spengler's concept of technology as an extension of the human body; but whereas for Spengler a man's hand is a claw, for McLuhan it is a sign: the former was a prophet of Armageddon and the latter of Madison Avenue. McLuhan's writings abound in paradoxes (usually ingenious ones) and stimulating statements (often quite perceptive ones). We may be disturbed by his emphatic tone, his inordinate fondness for quotations, and the logical inconsistencies of his arguments, but these rhetorical vices are characteristic of his country and our era: McLuhan is a writer typical of his time and his milieu. Hence it is symptomatic, or rather, significant, that the central theme of his writings is *meaning*.

McLuhan's views are an exaggeration and a simplification of what Peirce, Wittgenstein, Heidegger, and Lévi-Strauss, among others, have said. I hasten to add that these authors in no way resemble each other, except for one thing: all four conceive of reality as a tissue of meanings, and all of them are persuaded that there is no such thing as an ultimate meaning to this totality of meanings, or if there is, it is inexpressible. For two of them there is something beyond language which only silence can point to (Wittgenstein), or perhaps poetry (Heidegger); for the other two either are trapped in a net of language that is both transparent and inescapable (Peirce: "The meaning of a symbol is another symbol") or are at best only a link in this unbreakable chain, a sign, a single phrase in the message that nature murmurs to itself (Lévi-Strauss: "Myths communicate with each other through men without their being aware of this fact"). McLuhan reduces these ideas to the level of the advertising industry: the message depends on the medium of communication, and if this medium changes, the meanings also change or disappear.

There is no question that there are crucial differences between participating in a Platonic dialogue and reading the *Symposium* aloud before an audience, between reading the *Critique of Pure Reason* all by oneself and watching a group of professors discussing Kant's critique on television. The differences are not merely formal ones: the change in the medium of communication alters the message. The shift from dialogue to exposition alters the very meaning of the word philosophy. None of this is new, and Max Weber, among others, has given us brilliant descriptions of the interrelation between ideas and social forms. Nor is the idea that technology is the origin of the Logos a radically new one: Engels blithely assigned industry the philosophical role of doing away with Kant's "thing in itself." What is new, however, is making one branch of technology—the communications media—the "motor" of history. Radio and television take the place of Providence and Economics, of the Genius of the world's peoples and the Unconscious. Now, if the changes in the means of communication determine and explain other social changes, who and what is responsible for the changes in the means of communication? McLuhan neither asks this question nor tries to answer it.

Saussure's distinction between the signifier and the signified, a twofold characteristic of all signs, may help to clarify matters. McLuhan begins by identifying the message with the medium of communication, thereby converting the latter into a sign. For McLuhan, the media are signifiers, but what they signify can be reduced to the following tautology: the communications media signify communications media. An example may make my point clearer. In one of the first pages of *Understanding Media*, McLuhan states: ". . . the 'content' of any medium is always another medium. The content of writing is speech, just as the written word is the content of print, and print is the content of the telegraph."* Quite apart from the fact that this is a parody of the sentence of Peirce's that I cited above, it confuses the issue in several ways. McLuhan's application of the concept of form and content to phenomena in the field of communications is misleading. It is obvious that a jar may contain water, wine, or some other liquid. A jar, however, is not *defined* by its content but by its function or by its meaning: a jar is an object used to contain substances, generally liquid ones. The same is true of the media of communication: writing "contains" words, but it may also "contain" numbers, musical notes, and so on. Strictly speaking, writing does not *contain*: it *signifies*. It is a visual sign that points to another sign: the spoken word. To be absolutely precise, we would have to say that the communications media— radio and television for example—in fact have no content at all; they are always empty: they are simply conduits, channels through which signs flow. These signs, in turn, are like capsules containing meanings. The signifier—musical notes, letters, or any other mark—"discharges" its meaning if someone sets the "firing mechanism" in motion: reading, for instance, in the case of the written word.

The notion of content can be applied more accurately to signs than to the channels that transmit them. However, since the old metaphor of form and content introduces dangerous confusions, no one uses it nowadays. The terms *signifier* and *signified* are not identical with *form* and *content*. A jar may contain water, oil, or wine; the linguistic element *Tuesday*, however, refers to the day that comes immediately after Monday and to no other day. The signifier/signified duality also occurs at the level of the sentence, the paragraph, the text, and speech as a whole. Writing does not *contain language*: it *is* language. The same thing is true of the printed text, the Morse code, and the spoken word.

When McLuhan claims that the medium is the message, he is

* *Understanding Media* (1964).

saying that the message is not what we say but what the media say, despite us or without our knowledge. The media become signifiers and produce meaning inevitably and automatically. This idea presupposes a natural or immanent relation between the signifier and what is signified, an idea that goes back as far as Plato. But the truth is precisely the opposite: the relation between the signifier and the signified is conventional. I would say that it is one of the products of the social contract. The sound *pan* in Spanish designates bread, but in Urdu and Hindustani it means betel. To us the sign of the cross is the symbol of Christianity; to a Mayan of the fifth century this sign may well have stood for fertility or some other idea, or may have been simply decorative. The meaning of signs is the product of convention. If the communications media are signs, as McLuhan asserts, their meaning too is necessarily the result of a convention, either an explicit one or a tacit one. The key of meaning therefore does not lie in the communications media but in the structure of the society that has created these media and made them signifiers. Media are not what signify; society is what signifies, and what it signifies is *us*, in and through these media.

McLuhan is quite right when he asserts that the communications media also signify, that they are also messages. It is obvious that any medium can become a sign. But there are many different sorts of media, many different sorts of signs. The spoken word is one medium of communication and radio another. In the case of the spoken word, sign and medium are inseparable: so long as the sound *pan* is not pronounced, the meaning *bread* is not forthcoming. The sound is the signifier by means of which the signified appears. Radio waves, on the other hand, are means by which all sorts of signs appear—including nonverbal signs: music, natural or artificial sounds, and so on. The relation between signifier and signified is an initmate, fundamental one in the case of the spoken word: the former depends on the latter and vice versa. In the case of radio, there is no such relation between signifier and signified. Or, more precisely, this relation is obviously of very little importance. When McLuhan says that the medium is the message, what he is really saying is that the medium—radio, television, and so on—has become a linguistic sign; but if we break down the radio sign into its two components, the signifier and the signified, we find that the one is *radio* and the other is also *radio*. Having arrived at this point, I shall recall what Roman Jakobson has said about linguistic functions. Among these functions, language may take the form of a message whose object is "to establish, prolong, or interrupt communication, to test whether the circuit is functioning." This is a function that is frequently fulfilled in conversation on the telephone: "Hello!" "Can you hear me?" In everyday life it is a ritual: "How are you?" "How nice to see you!" "What's that?" "Er, hmmm, hey there," etc. Among primitive peoples, what Malinowski calls the "phatic function" of language is of prime importance, being both magical and ceremonial. Jakobson points out that it also appears among myna birds, parrots, and other species that "talk." This is the only linguistic function these creatures have in common with us. It is also the first to appear among children when they learn to talk. If we are to believe McLuhan, the era of planetary and interplanetary communications media is that of the return to the tautology of animal language. Like that of talking birds, the object of our communication is to communicate communication.

The spontaneity of history and the universality of reason were conjoined in the word revolution: it was the Logos in action and incarnated among men. Now technology absorbs all these meanings and becomes the active agent of history. Marx had great faith in industry, but he believed that in and of themselves, machines lacked meaning; the function of machines seemed intelligible to him only within the social context: who are their owners and who controls them? It is man who gives his tools meaning. Lévi-Strauss has shown that the invention of writing coincides with the birth of the great empires in Mesopotamia and Egypt: writing was the monopoly of the priestly bureaucracy and an instrument of oppression for centuries thereafter. In the hands of the bourgeoisie, printing broke the clerical monopoly on knowledge and forever ended the status of writing as something *sacred* because it was *secret*. Thus the meaning of writing and printing depended on the social context: it was society that gave them meaning, and not vice versa. In the first half of our century many writers of every political persuasion published books on the technique of revolution; today books and articles on the revolution of technique are published every day. It would be absurd to deny that technology changes us; but it would be equally absurd to disregard the fact that all techniques are the product of a given society and of concrete individuals. There is no point in stressing the undeniable importance of technology in the modern world. What I denounce is our superstitious worship of the *idea* of technology. This notion is as powerful a myth as that of reason or revolution, though it differs from them in one important respect: it is a nihilist myth, neither pointing to nor preaching nor denying a set of values. The systems of the past, from Christianity to Marxism, were at once a criticism of reality and an image of another reality. They were a vision of the world. Technology is not an image of the world but a way of operating on reality. The nihilism of technology lies not only in the fact that it is the most perfect expression of the will to power, as Heidegger believes, but also in the fact that it lacks meaning. *Why?* and *To what purpose?* are questions that technology does not ask itself. What is more, it is not technology, but we ourselves, who should be asking these questions.

Satiety and Nausea

The worship of the idea of technology involves a decline in value of all other ideas. This phenomenon is particularly striking in the realm of art. The new avant-garde makes no attempt to justify itself either rationally or philosophically. Dada claimed to be a metaphysical rebellion. The theoretical literature of Italian Futurism was the most significant feature of that movement. The critical and utopian thought of the Surrealists was as important as the creations of its poets and painters. Today, however, the majority of artists prefer the act to the program, the gesture to the work of art. Mayakovsky extolled technology and Lawrence denounced it; the new artists neither praise nor condemn: they manipulate modern apparatuses and artifacts. Rebellion yesterday was a passionate cry or a deadly silence; today it is a shrug of the shoulders: "why not?" as a reason for being. The aim of poetry, from the Romantics to the Surrealists, was the fusion of contraries, the transformation of an object into its contrary. Creation and destruction were the two poles of one and the same vital energy and the tension between the two sustained modern art. The basis of the new aesthetic is indifference. Not metaphor: juxtaposition, a sort of neutrality between the elements of the painting or poem. Not art or antiart: nonart. The privative *a* reigns supreme over man and his language.

The shift of emphasis in the verbal triangle—from revolt to revolution and from revolution to rebellion—would seem to point to a change in orientation: a shift from utopia to myth, the end of rectilinear time and the beginning of cyclical time. This is not the case. In the West an interregnum has ensued: nothing has yet taken the place of the old principles of faith or reason. The fact that this is the heyday of the rebel, and the fact that his rebellion is ambiguous, indicate that there is something missing. Whatever society he comes from, the rebel is an outsider: if he ceases to be one, he ceases to be a rebel. Hence he cannot be either a source of change or a guide. He is the lonely combatant, the dissident, an isolated fact, and an exception. Industrial society has lost its center, rectilinear time has cut it off from its source and literally uprooted it: it has lost its foundation, that *anterior* principle, that "time immemorial" which is the justification of the present and the future, the reason for being of any and every community. Cut off from the past and continually hurtling toward some vague future at such a dizzy pace that it cannot take root, it merely survives from one day to the next: it is unable to return to its beginnings and thus recover its powers of renewal. Its material abundance and intellectual riches cannot conceal its essential poverty: it is the master of the superfluous but lacks the essential. Being has drained out of it through a bottomless hole, time, which has lost its age-old consistency. This vacuum is experienced as disorientation, and disorientation in turn is experienced as ceaseless movement. And because this movement is completely aimless, it is equivalent to a frantic marking time in one place.

When there are no rules, the exception becomes the rule: the rebel is crowned king in an effort to make the eccentric the center. But the moment the exception becomes the rule, there is a cry for a new exception to take its place. The rule of fashion is extended to ideas, morality, art, and social customs. The restless need to seize upon each new exception that comes along—in order to assimilate it, castrate it, and cast it aside—explains why the powers that be, especially in the United States, are so tolerant of the new rebellion. The ambiguous nihilism of rebel artists is the mirror-image of the complacent, self-satisfied nihilism of those in power. The destiny of the rebel in the past was defeat or submission. Defeat is almost impossible today: the authorities tolerate any sort of rebellion, once they have clipped its nails and claws. I do not regard rebellion as the basic value of art, but it saddens me to see one of man's most generous impulses being simulated or cleverly exploited. It is hard to resign oneself to the corruption of the word *no*, which today has become merely the key or the jimmy to force the doors of fame and fortune. Making the rebel an object of worship is a way of domesticating him. In the past, the rebel was part of an immutable cycle. As the cosmos revolved, glory and punishment were the two faces of his destiny, the recto and the verso: Prometheus and Lucifer, generosity and consciousness. The modern rebel is the offshoot of a society expanding horizontally: a burst of fireworks that glows brightly for a moment and then is suddenly extinguished. Renown and obscurity: his celebrity simply fizzles out. He is a rebel who never experiences one half of his rightful destiny: punishment; hence it is very hard for him to fulfill the other half: awareness.

The history of modern rebellion cannot be reduced to the story of its assimilation by institutions. By a sort of miracle, in a society that for twenty or thirty years now has afforded the majority undreamed-of comforts and well-being, the most favored caste of all, young people, has spontaneously rebelled. Industrial society is proof that abundance is no less cruel than poverty. The abjection of satiety rivals that of privation. The piles of human flesh on Mediterranean or American beaches is no less depressing than the spectacle of the lepers, widows, and beggars of Benares. . . . It takes a certain cynicism to claim that the rebellion of young people is illogical. Of course, it *is* illogical. For the majority of our contemporaries, reason is no longer the Logos, the beginning of all beginnings, but a synonym for efficiency: it is not logical consistency or harmony but power; for a minority, scientists and philosophers, reason has become simply a way of relating and combining messages, a process indistinguishable from those of cells and their acids. In the United States and in the West, ideas have evaporated and in the Socialist countries utopian ideals have been defiled by revolutionary Caesars. If today's spirit of rebellion has little to do with ideas, it is also proof of a splendid indifference toward selfish interests: youngsters want nothing more for themselves, and their gestures of rebellion are not a fight for privilege but a renunciation of privilege.

In the second half of the twentieth century, the only active International is that of young people. It is an International without a program and without leaders. It is fluid, amorphous, and universal. The rebellion of young people and the emancipation of women are perhaps the two great transformations of our day. The second is doubtless more important and more permanent.* It is a change comparable to the one that took place in the

* This was written and published before the advent in the United States of the Women's Liberation Movement.

Neolithic period: the change from hunting to agriculture radically altered man's relation to nature, and the emancipation of women will wreak equally profound changes in human sexual relations, the family, and individual feelings. Rimbaud said that we would have to "reinvent love": perhaps this is the mission of women in our time. The movement of young people is an epiphenomenon, because it is a rebellion that depends on the system against which it is rebelling. It is a protest against the powers that be rather than an attempt to create a new order. The youth movement and the struggles of the ethnic minorities are not really revolutionary. They are rebellions. In our time, we must make a distinction between *rebellion* from within and *revolt* from without. Rebellion from within is a sign of health; a society that examines itself, denies itself, and absorbs its negations is a functioning society. Revolt from without represents a contradiction that thus far has proved insuperable. It is Contradiction itself, the other face of reality. Though it has lessened the tensions between classes, industrial society has failed to do away with the contradiction that has typified it from the beginning. It has merely exteriorized it. The contradiction today is not *within* industrial society but in its relations to the world *outside* it: not the proletariat but the "underdeveloped" countries. And it is not a revolution—it is a revolt.

The Two Forms of Reason

Some forty years ago, Ortega y Gasset wrote a critique of geometrical reason and the revolutionary spirit; Sartre has written an equally penetrating critique of rebellion. Their two points of view represent a sort of symmetrical contradiction; this fact seems to me to merit discussion, for I am not certain that anyone has pointed out the similarities between the French and the Spanish philosopher. Ortega y Gasset's name is seldom mentioned these days, whereas Sartre is famous the world over. This may be because Ortega was a conservative, while Sartre is a revolutionary. Although the views of both have their origin in German phenomenology, this common source is not the only reason for the similarities between them. What makes these two philosophers resemble each other is not so much the ideas they share as their style of attacking them, making them their own, and sharing them with the reader. Though the two of them struck out in opposite directions, each of them in his own way turned modern German thought into a moral and historical meditation. Despite the fact that neither of them cultivates a spoken style, we *hear* them thinking: the tone of their writings is at once passionate and peremptory—a magisterial tone, in both the good and the bad senses of the world. They excite us and irritate us, and thus force us to participate in their demonstrations. Ortega once said that he was only a journalist, and Heidegger has said the same of Sartre. This is quite true: they are not the philosophers of our time, but philosophy in our time.

The French writer is more systematic, and his *œuvre* is more broad in scope and more varied than that of the Spaniard. His public acts have also been more generous and more daring. Sartre has set out to do something that is doomed to failure: to reconcile concrete life and historical life, existentialism and Marxism. His originality as a philosopher does not lie, however, in this immense and disjointed effort to elaborate a synthesis, but rather in the flashes of insight that at times enrich his reflection. Though he may have failed to construct an ethical system, he has reminded us that thinking and writing are not ceremonies but acts. Writing is not simply a chance activity; it is a deliberate choice; beauty creates an atmosphere of responsibility that neither the writer nor the reader can escape with impunity. Ortega's virtues are quite different. A Mediterranean with a Catholic background, while Sartre is Nordic and Protestant, his prose is clear and sensuous. It is not clouded by the "sublimeness" of his German masters, nor is it affected by that underlying religious tension that exacerbates Sartre's prose, betraying his perpetual rebellion against the Protestantism of his childhood.

Sartre has banished God from his system, but not Christianity. Ortega's pessimism is more radical and his recognition of vital human values does not imply the recognition of any sort of transcendence, not even one that has assumed the mask of history. Ortega is a pagan, Sartre an apostate from Christianity. Ortega had a more penetrating understanding of history, and many of his predictions have come true. The same cannot be said of Sartre. This is not the first time that a reactionary philosopher has proved to have strange gifts of prophecy. I have always marveled at the brilliant foresight of Chateaubriand, Tocqueville, Donoso Cortés, Henry Adams. They were clairvoyant despite the fact that their values were those of the past—or perhaps because of that very fact: for them, the old notion of time as cyclical was still a vital concept.

According to Ortega, the bankruptcy of geometrical reason was a portent of the decline of the revolutionary spirit, the child of European rationalism. Reason, the source of utopias and revolutionary projects, had come down to earth and become historical reason: it was no longer a timeless construct but something that unfolds in time. I think he was quite right, and his acuity amazes me: it required an extraordinary perspicacity to foresee the present situation in Europe in the heyday of Bolshevik utopianism. But his critique was superficial, and the new principle that he proclaimed, historical reason, strikes me as no more than a slightly updated version of German vitalism and historicism. As Ortega saw it, our era is one marked by an absence of fundamental principles; but its new principle lies precisely in this absence: its underlying vital or historical cause is simply change itself. The Spanish philosopher neither explains the reason behind this change nor describes the forms that it is taking.

Sartre has encountered a similar obstacle: finding a foundation for dialectics. An heir of reason (whether pure, geometrical, or analytical), dialectics is true historical reason: it is the only method that accounts for society, its changes, and its internal relations (classes) or its relations with nature and other nonhistorical, primitive, or marginal societies. But dialectical reason fails to account for man's concrete existence: there is a part of a man's self, Sartre maintains, that is irreducible to the determinations of history and historical classes. What is more: dialectics cannot explain itself, it is not self-constitutive: the moment it constitutes itself, it is self-divisive. Lévi-Strauss's critique of Sartre is very much to the point: if there is a fundamental opposition between dialectical reason and analytical reason, one of the two must be "less rational"; since the latter is the foundation of the exact sciences, what kind of reason can dialectical reason be? The other alternative is equally contradictory: if dialectics is reason, its only possible foundation is analytical reason. In Lévi-Strauss's view, the difference between these two sorts of reason belongs to the category of complementary opposition: dialectical reason is nothing other than analytical reason, and at the same time it is what enables the latter to understand society and its changes, its institutions and its representations. Lévi-Strauss's critique is half correct: it reveals the contradiction at the heart of Sartre's philosophy, but it neither resolves it nor transcends it. What is the foundation of the new element that appears in analytical reason when it becomes dialectical reason? Vital reason and dialectical reason are philosophical approaches continually searching for a principle of *sufficient* reason.

Ortega studies the reformist as the figure who is the precise opposite of the revolutionary; Sartre the rebel. In his essay on Baudelaire, the French writer takes an idea not very different from Ortega's as his point of departure: the revolutionary seeks to destroy the ruling order and institute another, more just one; the rebel fights against the excesses of power. Ortega had said: the revolutionary wishes to change customary uses; the reformist to correct abuses. Though their points of departure are similar, the conclusions they reach are not: Ortega foresees the decline of revolutions; Sartre unmasks the rebel in order to proclaim the primacy of the revolutionary. I have discussed Ortega's ideas elsewhere; what I would like to do here is follow Sartre's line of argument.

The figure of the rebel quite naturally fascinates and irritates Sartre: for one thing, the rebel was the model that caused him to break with his world in his youth; for another thing, it is an exception that belies the revolutionary rule. To reveal that Baudelaire's refusal to conform in no way undermined the order that he pretended to attack, and that his rebellion was a paradoxical homage to power, is tantamount to demonstrating that the revolutionary rule is universal and that the revolt of artists, from Baudelaire to Surrealism, has been a private quarrel among the bourgeoisie. The rebel is a pillar of power: if that power should crumble, he would be crushed to death. What is more, he is also its parasite. The rebel feeds on power: the iniquity of those above him justifies his blasphemies. His *raison d'être* has its roots in the injustice of his social status; once this injustice ceases, his reason for existing also ceases. Satan does not want God to disappear: if the godhead were to disappear, he, too, would disappear. Diabolism can survive only as an exception, and it therefore confirms the rule. To rebel is to resign oneself to being a prisoner of the rules of power; if the rebel really wanted to be free, he would not challenge the power of the rules but the rules of power; he would not attack the tyrant but power itself. The rebel cannot claim that his reason for being is any sort of special or exceptional status—including that of being a poet, a black, or a proletarian—without contradicting himself, and without being in bad faith in the moral sphere.

Real rebellion must be based on a project that includes others and therefore it must be universal. The black does not seek recognition of his blackness but of his humanity: he fights to make blackness a fundamental, recognized component of the human species, and thus his rebellion becomes part of a universal undertaking: the liberation of mankind as a whole. Rebellion is a pattern of behavior that inevitably leads either to revolution or to self-betrayal. Baudelaire's rebellion was a sort of circular simulation; his protest did not become a cause and the misfortune of others played no part in it. An exaltation of his feelings of humiliation as an individual, it was the counterpart of a tyrannical God. The rebellion of the poet was a comedy in which his ego played a game with power without ever having the courage to destroy it. Baudelaire neither wanted nor tried to be free: if he had really dared to be a free man, he would have ceased to regard himself as an object and ceased to be a *thing*, viewed respectively with scorn and tenderness by the cruel Stepfather and the perfidious Mother. His rebellion was a part of his *dandyism*. The poet wished to be seen. Or rather, he wished to watch others watching him: the gaze of others made him aware of himself and at the same time it turned him to stone. His secret and ambivalent desire was fulfilled in two ways: he became both a heart-rending spectacle for others and an imperturbable statue in his own eyes. His *dandyism* consisted of making himself at once invulnerable and the object of the gaze of others. His rebellion was a nostalgia for childhood and a homage to power: consciousness of separation and a yearning to return to the "green paradise." A paradise he did not believe in. His rebellion condemned him to perpetually peering into a mirror: what he saw in it was not other people but his own gaze gazing back at him.

The Exception to the Rule

Sartre wants Baudelaire to have ceased being what he was and become: who and what? He does not say, though he compares him unfavorably to Victor Hugo. Or rather, to the *idea* of Victor Hugo, for I suspect that deep down Sartre really prefers Baudelaire's poems. More than once, Sartre indulges in what he criticizes most severely: abstractions. In the realm of politics, it was the *idea* of revolution, more than the actual situation in the Soviet Union, that led him around 1950 to defend the entire Soviet regime, including Stalin and his concentration camps. Not because he approved of them, but because in his eyes they did not deny the (ideal) reality: the camps were a blot but they nonetheless did not destroy the Socialist structure of the regime.

The arguments put forth in Sartre's review, *Les Temps Modernes*, were similar to those previously employed by Trotsky at the time of the Soviet-German pact and the invasion of Finland: the latter's notion of a "degenerated workers' State" which nonetheless preserved intact the bases of state ownership of property, was not very different from that of a "stalled revolution" put before the readers of *Les Temps Modernes* by Sartre and Merleau-Ponty. There are other, more grievous examples. For instance, during the Hungarian revolution Sartre made a number of very curious statements:

The most serious error has doubtless been Khrushchev's report, his solemn and public denunciation, the detailed exposure of all the crimes of a sacred person [Stalin], who has long been the symbol of the regime; this is madness when such frankness has not been preceded by any appreciable rise in the standard of living of the population. . . . The masses were not prepared for this sort of revelation of the truth. . . .

To make the masses' ability to understand the truth dependent on their standard of living is to give proof of a quite unrevolutionary conception of the proletariat and a quite unphilosophical conception of truth. . . . Nonetheless, how can we forget Sartre's attitude during the Algerian conflict, and his present position against the war of extermination that Americans are waging in Vietnam?

Sartre's essay on Genet gives us an even clearer picture of his ideas concerning rebellion. I mention this book, perhaps one of his best, not as a model of literary criticism or of psychological analysis but rather as an exposition of some of his ideas on the subject. In Genet's case the rebel has managed to transcend his initial attitude: his absolute negation has been transformed through writing into an affirmation. By embracing his fate as a social outcast, as an ejaculation of society, Genet performs an act of self-projection, of self-ejection—he transfigures himself and thus frees himself. In Sartre's book, the poet Genet becomes a conceptual entity. While concepts are manipulable entities, human beings are irreducible realities: after reading this essay we are much better acquainted with Sartre's thought, but Genet, the real man in the flesh, has evaporated, having been reduced to an example illustrating an argument. Genet chooses "evil" and becomes a "saint"; Saint Teresa chooses "good" and becomes a "whore." I do not know what Genet would think of this statement; I am certain that the Spanish nun would have roared with laughter at it. I suspect that Genet does not believe in the ontological reality of evil, even though the entire line of Sartre's argument is intended to prove that evil is the very basis of Genet's "existential project"; on the other hand, the one reality for Saint Teresa was unquestionably God, who for her was not an ideal reality but a palpable spiritual one. Why is Genet's negation "good" and Saint Teresa's affirmation, which is no less total than Genet's denial, "evil"? Perhaps Sartre is attempting to prove that abjection and sanctity have the same roots and that at a certain point the two fuse. There is some truth in this idea, but examining it here would lead me too far astray. What prevents me from accepting Sartre's judgment of Genet is his conception of the latter's "existential project": if Genet has chosen evil, why does he write and why does he write so well?

The tendency to explain one level of reality by another older, unconscious one—the social order or a person's instinctive life—is something we have inherited from Marx, Nietzsche, and Freud. This way of thinking has changed our view of the world and been responsible for numerous discoveries. But, at the same time, how can we fail to see its limitations? I will mention Polanyi's criticism here: a watch is made up of molecules and atoms governed by the physical laws of matter; if these laws were to momentarily cease functioning, the watch would stop. But this would not be the case if the situation were reversed: if the watch is smashed to bits, the fragments will continue to obey the same laws. . . . Two different levels of meaning are involved here. For Sartre the "project" is a mediation between two realities: the self and its world. In his latest philosophical work the same idea reappears: *"L'homme est médié par les choses dans la mesure même où les choses sont médiées par l'homme."** Since man is not a simple being, mediation implies at least three levels: instinctive or unconscious reality, consciousness, and the world (things and other people). I do not believe that Sartre's method can explain creative works: although they are part of a person's "existential project," their meaning transcends that of this project. There is a gap between a man's works and his biography. This relation between the two is the same as that between the molecules and the watch in Polanyi's analogy. Sartre criticizes our belief in the eternity of creative works because he regards them as historical signs, hieroglyphs of temporality. But even though works may not be eternal—what possible meaning can this word have?—they nonetheless have a longer life span than individuals. They endure for two reasons: they are independent of their authors and their readers; and, since they have a life of their own, their meanings change for each generation and even for each reader. Works are mechanisms for creating multiple meanings, which cannot be reduced to the "project" of the person who writes them.

Sartre condemns literature as an illusion: we write because we cannot live as we would like to. Literature is the expression of a feeling of deprivation, a recourse against a sense of something missing. But the contrary is also true: language is what makes us human. It is a recourse against the meaningless noise and silence of nature and history. Living implies speaking, and without speech man cannot have a full life. Poetry, which is the perfection of speech—language speaking to itself—is an invitation to enjoy the whole of life. Sartre's contempt for language betrays his nostalgia, not for the fullness of human life but for the plenitude of Being: the gods do not speak because they are self-sufficient realities. In his atheism there is a sort of religious frenzy that is absent in the sages and in other atheist philosophers. Though the central word in his philosophy is *free-*

---

* "Man is mediated by things to the very same degree that things are mediated by man."

dom, it must also be said that it is a freedom whose source is a *curse*. For the French writer we are doomed to be free, and that is why we speak, write, and each day begin anew to carve our statue of ourselves out of smoke: an absurd rebellion against our death and an image of our destruction. Sartre's vision of man is that of the Fall: we are flawed, guilty, empty. The "project" is an attempt to fill the yawning hole, the lack of Being. But his conception of the "project" tells us nothing about a reality that reveals our plenitude in the very heart of emptiness: works of art. Thanks to those works, we may enter another world of meanings and see our own intimate self in another light: we escape the prison walls of the self. Genet and Saint Teresa are both authors of an *œuvre*. Genet is an original writer; Saint Teresa is something more, something infinitely more precious: a visionary spirit coupled with an extraordinary critical awareness. (Compare Sartre's autobiographical *Les mots* [*The Words*] with what the Spanish nun tells us of her life.) These works take on a life independent of their authors and are intelligible to us even though the life of their creators may not be.

Baudelaire's answer to Sartre's criticism is his poems. Where does the truth lie: in his letters and other private documents or in his published work? Born of bad faith and the masochistic narcissism of a voyeur, for whom the nakedness of a woman is a mirror that reduces him to a mere reflection and thus preserves him from the gaze of others, does this poetry free us or enslave us, does it lie to us or does it tell us something essential about man and his language? Every great work of art forces us to ask ourselves what language is. This question places the meanings, the world of convictions that sustain the historical man, between parentheses, in order that the *other* may appear. Although Sartre has asked himself this question, he does not believe that it is the task of poetry to pose it and answer it: he is persuaded that the poet turns words into things. But once they are touched by the hand of man, things become suffused with meaning; they become a question or an answer. All human works are languages. The poet does not transform the word into an object: he gives the sign back its multiple meaning as a signifier and obliges the reader to complete his work. A poem is a continual re-creation. Sartre's purpose was not to judge poetry but to unmask the poet, to destroy the myth of the poet. He failed. For one thing, the analysis of Baudelaire's "existential project" sheds no lights on the real meaning of his work; for another, Baudelaire's life is unintelligible without his poems. I do not say that his work explains his life; what I mean to say is that it is an integral part of his life: without his poems Baudelaire would not be Baudelaire. The paradoxical nature of the relations between a life and an *œuvre* stem from the fact that they are complementary realities in only one sense: we can read Baudelaire's poems without knowing a single detail of his biography; but we cannot study his life if we ignore the fact that he was the author of *Les fleurs du mal*.

The Rules of the Exception

Sartre's critique of Baudelaire has a more general interest since in this essay he outlines a distinction between rebels and revolutionaries that seems to me to be central to his political thought. His starting point is not so much the contrast between uses and abuses as between an unjust order and the injustices of order: the uses of the bourgeois regime are genuine abuses, while the abuses of the Socialist regimes are transitory historical evils. The reason for this relativism is not difficult to grasp. Bourgeois society can give us freedoms, but its real structures are essentially a denial of freedom; evil is inherent in its very nature: it stems from the private ownership of the means of production. The morality and the laws of bourgeois society hide its reality: the exploitation of man by man.

Though a Communist regime deprives its subjects of certain rights and freedoms for a more or less extended period of time, its ultimate goal is freedom: it is based on the principle of collective ownership and the cornerstone of its ethic is the universal liberation of mankind. The first question we might ask ourselves is whether the actual situation in China or the Soviet Union bears any real relation to this idea. At this point in history it would seem absurd to maintain that there is such a relationship between the idea and the reality: the claim that human exploitation has disappeared in these countries, or that it is well on its way to disappearing, belongs more to the realm of belief than to the realm of experience and reason. But let us grant the fact that the dichotomy is real. If so, what attitude should Chinese, Russian, or Yugoslavian citizens take with regard to the abuses of their governments? Some will say that the import of their rebellion is different: in a bourgeois regime, customary uses are abuses; in a Socialist regime uses and abuses are two quite different things, and, as a consequence, rebellion is legitimate: it is not merely an instance of bad faith. I shall note that this line of argument justifies the rebellion of citizens in these countries but not the conduct of revolutionary governments. I grant that a revolutionary government may stray from the straight and narrow path from time to time. Nonetheless, the universal rule splits down the middle: there are two types of abuses and two types of rebels, the good and the bad, theirs and ours. The citizen of a Socialist country may be a rebel but not a revolutionary; the citizen of a bourgeois nation must be a revolutionary rather than a rebel. This is the subject of several of Sartre's plays, and it gives rise to another question: what is the proper attitude of a revolutionary in the West toward the rebels of the Socialist countries? Should he condemn them in the name of the universal undertaking that socialism represents, or should he help them by any means at his disposal? The first attitude would be a return to Stalinism, and the second . . .

I am well aware that the actual circumstances are much more complicated and that a number of positions are possible between the two extremes that I have pointed out; what I would like to emphasize is the shakiness of a distinction that at first glance may appear to apply universally. In theory Sartre is quite right: his moral relativism is not all that relative since it is based on a valid rule that applies to everyone in this period of history. This rule is not an ironclad law: it is based on a universal goal, the liberation of all mankind, which is both a consequence of modern history and a matter of free choice. This goal or "project" is the mediation between us and the world we live in. Moral distinctions depend on this project and this project in turn depends on the real situation of the society one belongs to: doing away with the abuses of a bourgeois regime is not enough, because its injustice is radical and built into the system. Nonetheless, the issue becomes clouded the moment we compare the rule to the reality: the dichotomy cannot withstand scrutiny and vanishes in thin air.

In our day a new element has entered the picture, the revolt of the Third World: does the distinction between revolutionaries and rebels apply to us too? It obviously does not, and Sartre has supported movements of rebellion in the European colonies and in Latin America. Hardly any of these movements are Socialist, in the strict sense of the word, and all of them are ardently nationalist. Many of them are a paradoxical combination of both tendencies: Nasser's version of Arab Socialism or that of the Algerians is not an attempt to fuse the pan-Arab movement with Socialism but rather to Arabize the latter. Their rebellion is that of a particularism, precisely the contrary of what Sartre claims to be the case: the dissolution of the exception in the universal rule. The same thing is happening in other nations of Asia and Africa. And in countries where the leaders proclaim themselves disciples of Marx and Lenin, as in Cuba, they nonetheless continue to stress the fact that their national revolutions are original and independent movements. Thus there is a third class of rebels, to which Sartre's distinction is not applicable: their rebellion is an affirmation of their uniqueness.

The dissension among the already well-established powers is equally palpable. The quarrel between the Russians and the Chinese is the most serious one dividing the Socialist states but not the only one. Although these differences take the form of ideological quarrels, their real roots lie in the national particu-larisms and the conflicting political and economic interests of the members of the "Socialist" group. There are also splits within the other bloc and it too threatens to fall apart. The tendencies represented by General de Gaulle are not merely a transitory phenomenon, as the Americans would have us believe, but a sign of the political resurrection of Western Europe. In the not too distant future the nations of Europe, by forming a commu-nity or by concluding bilateral pacts, will establish an inde-pendent policy that will soon cause conflicts of interest with both the Americans and the Russians. Japan will shortly follow the same path. The gradual breaking up of the "free world" alliance is the counterpart in reverse of that taking place in the other bloc: in the West, political and economic differences are the first to make themselves felt, then national ones, and finally ideological ones. And it is significant that the divisions within these two former solid blocs are not the reflection of any sort of transformation of social and economic structures or of a change in political philosophy: one bloc continues to call itself Socialist and the other democratic.

The contradiction in our time is not the one Marxism made us aware of—that between capital and labor—but another one that neither the founders of the doctrine nor their disciples foresaw. This conflict is that between the "developed" and the "under-developed" countries. The irreducible and increasingly severe antagonism between the bourgeoisie and the proletariat that Marx predicted has proven to be more strictly applicable to the relations between these two groups: the rich nations are becom-ing richer and the poor nations poorer every day. But the cate-gories of Marxism do not fit the present situation nor do they explain the new contradiction. The revolt of the Third World is a pluralist movement, and the creation of a universal society is not one of its goals. The political and social forms that it adopts, from State Socialism to a private economy, are not ends in themselves but means to speed up its historical evolution and become modern. Hence they are not a universal model. The

Third World lacks a general revolutionary theory and a program; it has no philosophy nor does it aspire to construct the city of the future according to the dictates of reason or the logic of history; nor is it a doctrine of salvation or liberation as Buddhism, Christianity, the French Revolution, and revolutionary Marxism were in their time. In short, it is a world-wide revolt but it is not ecumenical; it is an affirmation of a particularism through a universalism—and not vice versa. I do not mean to say thereby that it is illegitimate. On the contrary, it not only seems right to me, but I also believe that it is the last chance we Latin Americans have of becoming historical subjects after the great failure of our struggle for independence. It is the only way that we will cease to be objects, to use Sartre's vocabulary, and begin to be our own masters. This is what our revolt is. But it is not a universal project, and as a consequence we cannot deduce any universal rule from it. The distinction between rebels and revolutionaries vanishes because no single goal is discernible in contemporary history. To deny that such a goal exists does not mean that we have regressed to a crude empiricism. If a change in the nature of human time is taking place, as I firmly believe, the phenomenon is affecting our beliefs and systems of thought. What is happening is that rectilinear time is ending and another time is beginning.

The End in the Beginning

The use of the word *revolution* in the sense of a violent and crucial change of society belongs to a period that conceived of history as an endless process. Whether rectilinear, evolutionary, or dialectical, history had a more or less predictable direction. It was of little moment that this process appeared to have the form of a curve or a spiral or a zigzag when examined in detail; in the final analysis it was a straight line: history was a continuous forward march. This idea could not have come to the fore during the reign of the cyclical conception of time, and of the Christian idea of eternity. The destruction of both ideas was the work of reason. But this destruction was possible only because a change in the status of reason had already occurred. Metaphysics regarded reason as the foundation of the order of the universe, the sufficient principle of everything that exists; reason was the guarantee of the coherency of the universe, that is to say its *cohesion*, and thus it was the origin and the center of movement itself. There was a pact, so to speak, between Christian time and Greek geometry: the rectilinear and finite time of mankind ruled on earth; the circular and eternal time of the stars and the angels ruled in the heavens. After the critique of the gods, reason criticized itself and ceased to occupy the center of the cosmos. But it did not lose its privileges thereby: it became the revolutionary principle par excellence. An agent capable of modifying the course of events, reason became active and libertarian. Active: it was movement, an ever-changing, ever-ascending principle; libertarian: it was men's instrument to change the world and change themselves. Human society became the field of operation of reason, and history the unfolding of an idea: a discourse that man had been delivering since the beginning. The first words of history were a stammer; they soon became a march of syllogisms. The progress of society was also that of reason: the story of the feats of technology possessed the clarity and the perfect consistency of a logical demonstration.

Marxism has been the most coherent and most convincing expression of this way of thinking. It combines the prestige of science and that of morality; at the same time it is a total system of thought, like the religions and philosophies of the past. If history is the convergent march of society and reason, revolutionary action will consist in suppressing the contradictions between them at higher and higher levels. Reason must march along with its feet on the ground, and simultaneously society and nature must be humanized: that is, their action must promote freedom and take on the logical necessity of a rational operation. In the bourgeois era the basic contradiction is the divergence between the system of ownership and the system of production: the second is "more rational" than the first. Industrial production tends toward universality, it is energy tamed by man which in turn can tame nature forever; private property stifles the social force of production, the proletariat, and stands in the way of the universal availability of products by withdrawing them from circulation, either through accumulation or through waste. The industrial system creates abundance, but capitalism prevents the masses, either the proletariat or the huge numbers of colonial slaves, from sharing it. The meaning of Communist theory is twofold: Communism frees the forces of production and universalizes the distribution of products. Abundance makes equality possible and the two together bring about authentic, concrete freedom. As the revolutionary process is completed, classes and nations disappear; civil and economic society become one; the contradictions between economics and politics fade away: the State, its morality and its police, wither away. Finally, in its most advanced stage Communism dissolves the fundamental contradiction of what Marx called human "prehistory": the economic system becomes totally social, that is to say rational and universal; and reason becomes socialized. At that moment other contradictions, which are not specified in Communist doctrine, arise. . . . As we all know, the contradictions that actually developed were different, and appeared before the revolutionary process that corresponds to this era was completed. There is no point in drawing up a list of them: the universal class, the proletariat, remained under the sway of reformism and nationalism; no revolutions took place in the developed countries; Nazism triumphed in Germany; in Russia, Stalinism liquidated Lenin's comrades; and in the Third World, the central protagonists of revolt today are the peasants, the petty bourgeoisie, and intellectuals. . . . Apart from the fact that they are not part of the logic of the system, these unexpected contradictions were like the intrusion of another reality, a dissonant, archaic one: something like the appearance of a drunken poet at a meeting of university professors. History began to go astray. It ceased to be a discourse and once again became an enigmatic though perhaps not a totally incoherent text.

After all this, the temptation to bury Marxism is understandable. Nothing could be more difficult, however. In the first place, this philosophy is part of our very selves; it is more or less in our blood. And second, to reject its moral heritage would be to reject at the same time the most lucid and most generous part of modern thought. Marxism has become a point of view. Its position is similar to that of Euclidean geometry: it has turned out not to apply to every sort of space. Nonetheless, its limitation lies not only in the fact that it is not applicable to all societies (primitive ones for example),* but also in the fact that it has not been able to tell us what the over-all meaning of the march of history is. There is a special branch within the modern science of evolution, the biology of microevolution, that studies the changes that occur within cells. It is the central discipline within this area, and the discoveries that researchers in this field have made have radically changed our ideas regarding heredity and the mutation of species. But specialists in microevolution are unable to explain the "direction" of mutations. The comparison of microevolution with Marxism is not a gratuitous one. The essence of my method, Marx states in the preface to *Das Kapital*, "is the force of abstraction." The "social cell" is isolated by analysis and then broken down into its component elements. Marxism has met with much the same failure as microevolutionary theory: it has described the social cell and revealed its internal structure but it has been unable to predict the general direction that society will take.

Precisely because it is the most consistent and most thoroughgoing form of thought corresponding to the era of rectilinear time, Marxism reveals that this time is not the only kind of time there is. And we might perhaps add: if dialectics has proven

---

* See Chapter XVI of Claude Lévi-Strauss's *Anthropologie structurale* on consanguineous relations and economic structures among primitive peoples. (English translation, *Structural Anthropology*, 1963.)

incapable of discovering its constitutive principle it is because, like all modern philosophies, it is built over an abyss. This abyss is the great yawning gap left when the old cyclical time split apart. Our time is that of the search for a foundation, or as Hegel said, that of the consciousness of a split. Marxism has been an attempt to unite what was separated. Its central concern was society: it discovered that the basic cell is a complex organism, a tissue of relations determined by the social process of economic production; it also revealed the interdependence of interests and ideas; and, finally, it demonstrated that societies are not formless amalgams but totalities of unconscious and semiconscious forces (economics, superstructures, and ideologies constantly interacting) which obey certain laws that are independent of our will. But today many of its theories, from the concept of culture as a reflection of the social relations of production to the idea of the universal revolutionary mission of the proletariat, strike us as quite dubious. We have a different view at present of the correspondences and interrelations between the systems of production, philosophies, institutions, and artistic styles of each historical period.

Marx was the founder of the science of social relations. He failed, however, to deal with the morphology of societies and civilizations, with what separates them and distinguishes them above and beyond their economic production. There are many things that have no place within the Marxist schema, from works of art to human passions: everything that is *unique*, either within an individual person or within civilizations. Marx was insensitive to something that was to be one of Nietzsche's discoveries: the physiognomy of cultures, the particular form and the unique mission of each of them. He did not see that the so-called superstructures, far from being mere reflections of the systems of production, are also symbolic expressions and that history, which is a language, is above all else a metaphor. This metaphor is many metaphors: human societies, civilizations. And it is also a single metaphor: the dialogue between man and the world. Marx was unable to account for the "miracle" of

Greek art: it did not correspond to the social system of Greece. What would he have said if he had been intimately acquainted with the arts of primitive peoples or those of the Orient and pre-Columbian America? Yet the nature of these arts is no different from that of the arts of modern times or those of the Renaissance: they are metaphors of man as he confronts the world, metaphors of the world within man. Marxism, finally, has been one of the agents of the historical change of our century, but its explanation of these changes has been inadequate and above all its pronouncements as to its meaning and its predictions as to its direction have proven false. From this point of view, the truth of the matter is precisely the contrary of what Sartre believes: Marxism is not a *body of knowledge* or a *method of investigation* but an *ideology*. It is so on two counts: in the Communist countries, it hides social realities beneath a veil of concepts and thus serves as a coverup for basically unjust social relations; and in the non-Communist countries, as Sartre himself admits, it has turned into a "dogmatic metaphysics."

Although Marxism has become an ideology, it was a critical philosophy in the beginning. The secret of its vitality today and the seeds of its future fertility lie in its critical powers. When I speak of the vitality of critical Marxism today, I am not thinking of Sartre's disquisitions on dialectics or Althusser's ingenious and scholarly variations on Marxist themes, but in the resurrection of the critical spirit in Poland, Czechoslovakia, and other nations of Eastern Europe—if the books and essays by Kolakowski and others are any indication. Sartre is attempting to reconcile Marxism and existentialism; Althusser Marxism and structuralism. Both have made contributions to Marxism as an "ideology": by that I mean that even when they criticize the vulgar versions of Marxism or those considered to be such (the dialectic of nature, "economism," etc.), these authors carefully refrain from criticizing it as "ideology," thereby enhancing its status as a sacred body of writing. Sartre regards Marxism as a historical dialectic and thus distorts it and transforms it into a "method of investigation"—a philosophy with no foundation outside of itself that is continually forced to constitute and reconstitute itself. Althusser attempts to restore the dignity of Marxism as a science and a theory: structure over against history. This interpretation also distorts Marxism, not by transforming it into a "total philosophy" but into a science of sciences. The historical element disappears from Marxism, just as Sartre had previously undermined it as a structure. As François Furet puts it:

Structural analysis is an attempt to extend the methods of the natural sciences to the human sciences, but Althusser and his friends are subtly forcing it in the direction of Marxist dogmatism, which they claim to be an *a priori* of reflection—since from the very beginning they have regarded this latter as an equivalent of the mathematical model.

Althusser's source is Marx's *General Introduction to the Critique of Political Economy* (1857), in whose pages the latter outlines a program for the methodology of this science in terms that to a certain degree anticipate structuralism. (This is not surprising; I have said above that Marx's model was the cell: "merchandise is the cellular economic form," he states in the preface of *Das Kapital*.) But in this same *Introduction* Marx relentlessly hammers home the point that social science is historical: "When we speak of production, it is always a question of production in a specific state of social evolution." Althusser grants that Marx produced new knowledge without being entirely aware that he had done so. This idea is a hundred-per-cent Marxist: science and work *produce* knowledge, they make matter human and intelligible. And precisely because it is a product, this knowledge is historical—it is not a mathematical structure. Sartre regards Marxism as a history and an ethic; Althusser regards it as a science. Both claim that their aim is to make it invulnerable to any sort of criticism. In actual fact, they do not criticize it at all: they set it up as an untouchable model, either of the historical process or of the structures of science.

If the essence of Marxism is criticism, it can be revised only by an act of self-criticism. Criticism of Marxism as an *ideology* is indispensable if there is to be a rebirth of revolutionary thought. The program for this critical revision was outlined by Marx himself, and as Kostas Papaioannou points out* we need only substitute the words *ideological Marxism* for *religion* in the following passage to see how perfectly it applies to our time:

Criticism of religion is the necessary condition of all criticism . . . the foundation of unreligious criticism is this: man makes religion, not religion man. . . . But man is the world of man, the State, society. This State and this society produce religion: an absurd awareness of the world, because they themselves constitute an absurd world. Religion is the general theory of this world, its encyclopedic compendium, its logic in popular form . . . its moral sanction, its general principle of justification and consolation . . . the fight against religion is thus automatically a fight against this world . . . the criticism of religion is inherently that of this vale of tears . . . the criticism of heaven becomes the criticism of earth, the criticism of religion that of law, the criticism of theology that of politics. . . .

I would gladly exchange all the speculations of modern Marxists with regard to dialectics, language, structure, or praxis among Lacandonians for a concrete analysis of the social relations of production in the Soviet Union or China. But the criticism of earth is impossible without the criticism of heaven. No, Marxism is neither a complete philosophy nor an ideology, even though those who govern (and speak) in its name have made it into a "general theory of the world" and an "encyclopedic compendium." In the prologue to his *Critique of Political Economy* (1859), Marx relates how he and Engels decided in 1845 to make their "examination of philosophical conscience." The result was *The German Ideology*. Perhaps someone in our generation will have the courage and the genius to undertake an equally

* *L'Idéologie froide* (1967).

rigorous examination. Until that day, our philosophers, sages, and poets, not content with putting before us the apology of the ideological heaven, will continue to put before us that of the earth and its tyrants.

A Form in Search of Itself

The destiny of the revolutionary, as a hero or an archetype of rectilinear time, has been parallel to that of the theories that have simultaneously expressed and shaped our era, from Machiavelli to Trotsky. When man is confronted with a state of affairs that is unjust he rebels. This rebellion begins as a naysaying and gradually becomes a consciousness: it becomes a critique of the existing order and a determination to bring about a new just, rational, universal order. Criticism is followed by action: waging revolution demands the invention of a technique and an ethic. Revolutionary technique views violence as an instrument and power as a lever. It transforms human relations into physical objects, mechanisms, or forces. Reactionary violence is passionate: it takes the form of punishment, humiliation, vengeance, sacrifice; revolutionary violence is rational and abstract: not a passion but a technique. If violence becomes a technique, a new ethic is needed to justify or reconcile the contradiction between force and reason, freedom and power. Traditional ethics distinguished between means and ends—a theoretical distinction that rarely prevented crime and abuses but a distinction nonetheless. The revolutionary, as Trotsky explains with a sort of icy passion in *Their Morals and Ours*, cannot allow himself the luxury of making such a distinction. Ends and means are not good or bad in themselves: they simply further revolution or they do not. The ethics of the categorical imperative, or any other similar ethic, is viable only in a society that has forever destroyed the sources of coercion and violence: private property and the State. Two extremes: Gandhi and Trotsky. The first was persuaded that the only thing that counts are means: if they are good, the ends will also be good. Trotsky refuses to make a distinction between means and ends: both depend on specific historical situations. Means are ends and ends are means: what counts is the historical context, the class struggle.

Trotsky's ideas may alarm us but we cannot label them immoral without proving ourselves hypocrites or falling into Manichaeism. Everything changes, however, once the revolutionary seizes power. The contradiction between reason and violence, power and freedom, which has been veiled during revolutionary struggle, now becomes blindingly apparent: on assuming authority, the revolutionary is no longer the instrument of the violence of the slave but of the injustice of power. I grant that it is not impossible to justify terror: if the revolutionary State must ward off attacks from its enemies, both within and without, violence is legitimate. But who is to judge whether terror is legitimate: its victims or the theologians in power? This point could be debated endlessly. Whatever our views on the matter, there is one thing that seems to be beyond question: terror is an exceptional means. Its continued use betrays the fact that the revolutionary State has degenerated into a Caesarism. Moreover, when the revolutionary seizes power, he is faced with another problem: the new state of affairs never quite coincides with revolutionary ideas and programs. It would be surprising if it did: these programs are applied not to physical objects but to human societies which by their very nature are unpredictable. In the face of the opacity of the new situation, two paths are open to the revolutionary: rebellion or power, the scaffold or administration. The revolutionary ends up exactly where he began: he must either submit or rebel. Whichever solution he chooses, he ceases to be a revolutionary. The cycle comes to an end and another begins. It is the end of rectilinear time: history is not a continuous march forward.

The end of rectilinear time can be interpreted in two ways. It may be thought of as the absolute end of human history: an atomic holocaust, for instance, might destroy all mankind. This apocalyptic vision, full of disturbing Christian overtones, is the very basis of the Soviet Union's policy of peaceful coexistence. Not without reason, the Chinese find this scandalous and have denounced it as a betrayal of Marxist doctrine. The claim that history may well end in a great burst of fire involves a number of minor heresies and one major one: history ceases to be a dialectical process and the march of reality toward rationality ends in an irrational act, one that is meaningless by definition: a physical explosion. The second way of conceiving of the end of rectilinear time is a much more modest one: we may simply note that the orientation of modern history has changed, and that times literally are changing: a real *revuelta*. To say that rectilinear time is drawing to a close is not an intellectual heresy nor does it betray a nostalgia for myth and its bloody and fateful cycles. Time is changing form and with it our vision of the world, our intellectual concepts, our art and our politics. Perhaps it is premature to try to say what form time is assuming; but we may nonetheless single out, here and there, a few signs pointing to such a change.

Since 1905, the universe has changed shape and the straight line has lost its pre-eminence. "Einstein's space is no longer the stage on which the drama of physics was played out; space today is one of the actors because gravitation is entirely controlled by curvature, a geometrical property of space," Whittaker says. We need hardly mention the modern conception of the structure of the atom: the elementary particles are not really elements but zones of interaction, fields of relations. A similar change can be noted in the other sciences: the biology of microevolution, linguistics, information theory, and Lévi-Strauss's structural anthropology are abandoning linear explanations; all of them view reality as a system of synchronic relations. The cell, the word, the sign, the social group: each of these units is a totality of particles, like those that go to make up the atom; rather than an isolated unit, each of these particles is a relation.

Linguistic analysis, according to Roman Jakobson, distinguishes two levels within language: the semantic level, from the morpheme to the word, the phrase, and the text; and the phonological level: phonemes and distinctive particles. The first level is governed by meaning; the second is a structure that might be called "presignificative," though without it there would be no meaning. The phonemes are "systems of symbolic atoms," each one of which is composed of differentiating particles: although the phonemes and their particles have no meaning in and of themselves, they participate in the process of signification because they serve to distinguish one phonological unit from another. They are units of differentiation: *this* is not *that*. At its simplest level language is a system of relationships of opposition or association, and all the immense wealth of linguistic forms and meanings is based on this binary structure. If we go from the phonemic level to the level of words, we again see that language is a sort of transformation mechanism: the different combinations of words—that is to say, their position within the phrase—produce meaning. This phenomenon is repeated again on the level of the text: the meaning varies according to the position of the sentences. These relations are not "historical," or diachronic: language is a permanent structure. I. A. Richards has recently pointed out that the same combinatory process operates in microbiology: "The molecular, chromosomatic and cellular levels are the counterparts of the morpheme, the phrase and the text in the linguistic hierarchy." The analogy can be extended to anthropology, to communications theory, and to other fields, not excluding artistic and poetic creation.

In a recent book by Stephen Toulmin and June Goodfield (*The Architecture of Matter*), I read: "The distinction between living and non-living things can no longer be drawn in *material* terms. What marks them off from one another is not the stuff of which they are made: the contrast is rather one between systems where organization and activities differ in complexity." An organization, a structure: a circuit of relations. All these conceptions reduce rectilinear time to a variable in the system of relations. Chronology, the order in which one thing follows upon another, is a relation but it is not the only one or the most important one. The modern sciences—physics, linguistics, genetics, anthropology—study synchronic rather than diachronic relations. The model of science is not history. Strictly speaking, *before* and *after* are ways of referring to phenomena: symbolic expressions or metaphors, linguistic devices.

In *The Idea of Progress*, the English historian J. B. Bury describes the efforts of sociologists and historians of the past century to discover the law of motion of civilization. Despite Immanuel Kant's hopes, no Kepler or Newton has yet discovered this historical law. For a time the theory of evolution, rather than physics or astronomy, seemed to offer a solid foundation. Darwin ended his *Origin of Species* with these words:

As all the living forms of life are the lineal descendants of these which lived before the Silurian epoch, we may feel certain that the ordinary succession by generation has never once broken, and that no cataclysm has desolated the whole world. . . . And as natural selection works solely by and for the good of each being, all corporeal and mental environments will tend towards perfection.

But contemporary physics and astronomy, first of all, lean toward the view that the universe has been, and still remains, the theater of continuous explosions and cataclysms; and second, even if it were true that natural selection operates as a Providence "by and for the good of each being"—it is a biological law that is not applicable to human history. On the other hand, by discovering the plurality of societies and civilizations, history and ethnology have shown that the idea of progress, not as a law but as an ideological agent of social change, has had very little influence on mankind, save in the Western world and in modern times. Our civilization has not been (and will not be) the only civilization, and the idea of progress has likewise not been (and will not be) the only one to inspire men. The notion of progress, Bury says, implies "the illusion of deliberate purpose." At the same time it destroys it. If everything is change, the idea of progress is condemned to death by this process itself: "another star, unnoticed now or invisible, will climb up the intellectual heaven, and human emotions will react to its influence, human plans respond to its guidance."

The artistic forms of the past, both classical and Baroque, were closed forms. Intended to present reality, they always had an over-all pattern enclosed within definite boundaries. Since Symbolism, artists have isolated the elements, broken the form, and split the presence. The aim of Symbolism was not so much to convoke reality as to evoke it. Poetry became a liturgy of absence, and later a verbal explosion. The other arts followed in poetry's footsteps. The breaking of closed form was followed by the attack on language; the destruction of meaning by the destruction of the sign; the destruction of the image by that of the painted representation. In extreme forms, as in "concrete poetry," the poem is a typographical composition halfway between the sign and the signified; and painting has ceased to be painting in the strict sense of the word: it is the triumph of the object over representation (Pop Art) and of technique over expression (Op Art). But the history of modern art is not merely the history of the breaking up of closed form. At the end of the last century, shortly before his death, Mallarmé published *Un coup de dés*. In 1965, in *Los signos en rótación* [*Signs in Rotation*], I discussed this text. I shall repeat here that Mallarmé's work represented more than the birth of a style or a movement: it was the appearance of an open form, the purpose of which was to escape linear writing. A form that destroys itself and starts all over: it is reborn only to fall to pieces again and reconstruct itself again. The page also ceases to be mere background: it is a space that participates in the meaning, not because it possesses meaning in and of itself but because it enters into alternate relations of opposition and conjunction with the writing that by turn covers it and leaves it bare. The poem changes meaning as the position of its elements changes: words, phrases, and blanks. The page is writing; the writing space. In constant rotation, in perpetual quest of its ultimate meaning without ever reaching it, the poem is a transformation mechanism, like cells and atoms. These latter are transformers of energy and life; the poem, of symbolic representations. Both are apparatuses for producing metaphors. . . . Any work that really counts as our century goes on, whether in literature, music, or painting, is governed by a similar principle. Neither a circle traced around a fixed center nor a straight line: a wandering duality that expands and contracts, one and a thousand, yet always twofold, an eternal pair in conjunction or opposition, a relation that leads neither to unity nor to separation, meaning destroying itself and being reborn in its contrary. A form in search of itself.

Revolt

A civilization is a system of communicating vessels. There is therefore a certain justification for my translating what I have said above regarding the tendencies of modern thought into historical and political terms. My first observation is this: if history does not march in a straight line, neither is it a circular process. Space moves along with us: it has ceased to be the stage and become one of the actors. The space in which the drama of history has been performed in recent centuries goes by the name of Latin America, Asia, and Africa. In Europe, the various peoples of that continent were, to a certain degree, the agents of history; in our countries they have been the objects of history. It is no exaggeration to say that we have been treated as a landscape, as things, or as inert space. Today this space has come alive and is participating in the drama. This brings me to my second point: if space is an actor, it is also an author. With its continual changes of cast and plot, history is no longer a play written by a philosopher, a party, or a powerful State; there is no such thing as "manifest destiny": no nation or class has a monopoly on the future. History is a daily invention, a permanent creation: a hypothesis, a game, a wager against the unpredictable. Not a science, but a form of wisdom; not a technique, but an art.

The end of rectilinear time is also the end of revolution, in the modern meaning of the word: a crucial change in a neutral space. But in the other, older sense, the end of the straight line confirms the fact that we are participating in a revolution: the wheeling of the stars, the rotation of civilizations and peoples. The shift in position of the words in our verbal universe can help us understand the meaning of what is happening. The word *revolt* was supplanted by the word *revolution*; faithful to its etymology, this latter word is today returning to its old meaning, to its origin: we are living the beginning of a new time. The insurrection of the peoples of the Third World is not a rebellion: whereas rebellions are eccentric, marginal, minority movements, this movement encompasses the greater part of humanity, and even though it began on the periphery of the industrial societies, it has become the focal point of our concerns today. The insurrection of the Third World is not a revolution either. We are witnesses of a pluralistic movement that does not fit our ideas of what a revolution is or ought to be. What it really represents is a popular and spontaneous revolt that is still in search of its ultimate meaning. It is being torn between extremes, and at the same time nourished by them: universal ideas are being used to justify its particularism; the originality of its age-old religions, arts, and philosophies is being used to justify its right to universality. A motley collection of peoples in rags and civilizations in tatters, the heterogeneity of the Third World is becoming a unity as it aligns itself against the West: it is the *other* by definition, its caricature and its conscience, the other face of its inventions, its justice, its charity, its worship of the individual person, and its systems of social security. A reflection of a past that antedates Christ and machines, it is also a determination to be modern; as a traditionalist movement, the prisoner of rites and customs that go back thousands of years, it is unaware of the value and the meaning of its tradi-

tion; as a modernist movement it wavers between Buddha and
Marx, Siva and Darwin, Allah and cybernetics. It feels a fascination and a horror, a love and an envy of its former masters: it
wants to be both like the "developed nations" and unlike them.
The Third World has no idea what it is above and beyond a will
to being.

The industrial societies enjoy a prosperity that no other civilization in the past has ever attained. This abundance is not a
synonym of health: never in history has nihilism been so widespread and so total. I shall not indulge in fateful prophecies of
its imminent collapse. I do not feel that such a collapse is close
at hand. Though I do not believe that the end of industrial societies is in store, neither do I refuse to see what is all too obvious: these societies are moving ahead rapidly, but they no longer
have any idea of where they are going or why. In the last
twenty years we have seen the universalist pretensions of the
Soviet Union crumble. I place great hopes in Russian poets,
sages, and artists. I hope, above all, that the Russian people will
awaken: I would like to hear that deep, rumbling voice like a
great clap of thunder that we sometimes hear when we read
that country's poets and novelists. I believe in the spirit of the
Russian people, but fortunately for them and for us, Moscow is
not Rome. As for the United States, even though it is the most
powerful country on earth, it lacks a philosophy worthy of its
great strength. The political thought of Americans has been borrowed from the English. It suited their needs in the era of Yankee
expansion in Latin America; but today as a global ideology, it
is as antiquated as the doctrine of "free enterprise," the steam-
boat, and other relics of the nineteenth century. The United
States is a unique case in history: an imperialism in search of
universality. Might the secret of the vitality of "isolationist"
tendencies in America not lie in that nation's dim awareness that
there is a profound contradiction between its power and the
political philosophy on which that power is based? I must
confess that my belief in the critical and democratic tradition of
the United States is greater still than my belief in the religious

spirit of the Russians. It is a political and intellectual tradition and, at the same time, a poetic and prophetic tradition. Its roots are in the Reformation, and thus it is a religious tradition and a tradition of criticism of institutionalized religion. It has produced one of the great literatures of the modern era, from Thoreau and Melville to our days. The United States is the world center of economic and political power but it is also the world center of rebellion and self-criticism. This is what Latin Americans seldom see. . . . The United States can no longer aspire to global hegemony, not only because of the existence of the Soviet Union—whose role as a rival has been diminished though not eliminated—but also because of the birth of China and the rebirth of Europe and Japan. The key to the future of the industrial societies, and to a great extent that of the revolt of the Third World, lies in Eastern and Western Europe. Great changes will occur there. An independent European policy would alter the relations between the superpowers and have a decisive effect on history in Africa, Asia, and Latin America. The industrial societies thus might begin a new sort of dialogue between themselves and the rest of the world.

I do know what fate is in store for the revolt of the Third World. Economic and social development is an obsession with the leaders of these nations and their "intelligentsia," almost all of whom have been educated in the former metropolises. Some of them look on the more or less bureaucratic versions of "Socialism" as the most rapid way of reaching the industrial level; others place their trust in a "mixed economy," technology, foreign loans, education, and so on. At this point in history it is no longer possible to have the same confidence in bureaucratic "Socialism" as twenty years ago. Its defects have become obvious. The other solution is equally dubious. Foreign loans, which are always too small and always have strings attached, are frequently counterproductive; they increase the rate of inflation rather than speeding up development, and since it is necessary to administer them, they spawn new armies of bureaucrats and "experts." These latter are the modern form of the plague; while in the past smallpox and malaria decimated the population, this new plague from abroad paralyzes people's minds and imaginations. As for technology: it is not only a method of development, but first and foremost a state of mind, an attitude toward nature and society. The majority of the peoples of Asia and Africa look on technology as a miracle, a form of magic rather than an operation in which a quantitative approach to the world plays the central role.

Modern education has thus far been the dubious privilege of a minority. Its most immediate and most obvious result has been to erect a wall between an elite who have had a Western-style education and the masses who have a traditional culture. Minorities without a people and a people without minorities. What is more, the victims of Western-style education suffer the illness called a "split personality," or in moral terms, "inauthenticity." Hence the most urgent task confronting the Third World is to regain its own being and face up to the realities of its situation. This requires pitiless self-criticism, and an equally rigorous examination of the true nature of its relations to modern ideas. These ideas in many cases have been mere superficial borrowings: they have not been instruments of liberation but masks. Like all masks, their function is to shield us from the gaze of others, and, by a circular process that has often been described, to shield us from our own gaze. By hiding us from others, the mask also hides us from ourselves. For all these reasons, the Third World needs not so much political leaders, a common species, as something far more rare and precious: critics. We need many Swifts, Voltaires, Zamyatins, Orwells. And since in these countries, once the homelands of dionysiac orgies and erotic wisdom, a hypocritical and pedantic puritanism reigns today, we also need a Rabelais and a Restif de la Bretonne.

The great problem that the industrial societies will confront in the next few decades is leisure. Leisure has been both the blessing and the curse of a privileged minority. It will now be that of the masses. This is a problem that will not be resolved without the intervention of poetic imagination, in the strict sense of the words poetry and imagination. In the precapitalist era, people were poorer, but they worked fewer hours and there were more holidays. Time never hung heavy on their hands, thanks to the many ceremonies, festivals, pilgrimages, and religious rites they took part in. Leisure is an art we have forgotten, as we have lost that of meditation and solitary contemplation. The West must rediscover the secret of the incarnation of poetry in collective life: the fiesta. The descent of the Word among men and the sharing of it: Pentecost and Passion. The other alternative is the debased leisures of the great empires, the Roman circus and the Byzantine hippodrome. Although the problems of the "underdeveloped" societies are exactly the contrary, they likewise require the exercise of imagination, both political and poetic. We have to invent models of development that are less costly than those constructed by Western "experts." More viable ones, and above all, ones more in keeping with each country's national character and its history. I mentioned above the need for an Indonesian Swift or an Arab Voltaire; the presence of an active imagination, rooted in native mental soil, is also indispensable: dreaming and working in terms of one's own reality. These peoples were the creators of architectonic complexes that were also centers of human community, points of convergence of imagination and practical action, human passions and contemplation, pleasure and politics, peoples who made the garden a mirror of geometry, the temple a great piece of sculpture palpitating with symbols, the sound of water falling on stone a language rivaling that of the birds—how is it possible that they have denied their history and their destiny so radically? The leaders of these countries, despite their nationalism—or perhaps *because* of this very nationalism, which is yet another European mask—prefer the abstract language that they have learned in schools of economics in London, Paris, or Amsterdam.

In a moment of understandable exasperation, the only Hindu Zamyatin that I know of, Nirad C. Chaudhuri, has written that the first thing that must be done is to expel all foreign experts from India; to reject all foreign aid, which is niggardly, humiliating, and corrupting; to liquidate the handful of elite leaders, whether rightist or leftist, who worship Her Britannic Majesty or the Russian Communist Party, the Pentagon or Chairman Mao . . . and begin all over again, as the Aryan tribes did four thousand years ago. But the Third World is *condemned* to modernity and the task confronting us is not so much to escape this fate as to discover a less inhuman form of conversion. A form that does not bring duplicity and split personalities in its wake, as is the case today. A form that does not bring on the ultimate alienation: the death of the soul. Hence the need for self-criticism and imagination. Self-criticism puts its finger on the wound: falsehood; imagination projects models of development that are models of coexistence: the "standard of living" is an abstract category, whereas real life is concrete and particular. . . . The revolt of the Third World has not discovered its proper form and therefore it has degenerated into different varieties of frenzied Caesarism or languishes beneath the stranglehold of bureaucracies that are both cynical and fuzzy-minded. The leaders don't know exactly what they want or how to achieve the vague goals they have set. What has happened in recent years in Asia, Africa, and Latin America is not encouraging.

As for us Latin Americans: we are face to face with what may well be our last chance historically. We are repeatedly reminded that we are part of the Third World. It should also be pointed out that ours is a unique, borderline situation; like other peoples in the Third World, we have a very low level of industrial development and are more or less completely dependent upon foreign powers (the United States in our case). At the same time, our economic and social situation is different, as is our history. The conquest and domination of Latin America by the Spanish and Portuguese bears little resemblance to that of Asia, and even less to that of Africa, conquered by other European peoples. Nor do our independence movements resemble those of these nations. Unlike what happened in India or Southeast Asia, none of the great pre-Columbian civilizations resisted domination; nor has any non-Christian religion survived among our peoples. The steppingstone to modernity in Latin America is Christianity, not Mohammedanism or Buddhism or Hinduism. The leap into modernity is a natural one for us, in a manner of speaking: modernity began as a criticism of Christianity; it is the daughter of Christianity, not of Islam or of Hinduism. For us, Christianity is a path rather than an obstacle; it involves a *change*, not a *conversion*, as it does in Asia and Africa. The same must be said of the influence that European political thought, especially that of France, has had on our wars of independence and our republican institutions. They were a matter of choice, not a heritage of colonial domination. And, finally, the nature of social conflict is different in our case. However incomplete, imperfect, and riddled with injustices social and cultural integration may be in Latin America, in our countries there are not two societies with opposite values at loggerheads with each other, as in most Asiatic and African countries. There are admittedly minorities and customs that are holdovers from the pre-Hispanic period, but they are not as serious or as burdensome as the caste system in India, tribal loyalties in Africa, and nomadism in other regions. The history of Latin America has made it a case apart. What we really are is an eccentric, backward part of the West.

The subject of Latin America requires separate analysis, and I have therefore refrained from dealing with it at length in the course of these scattered remarks and comments. Many years ago, in the final pages of another book, I pointed out that

No one has bothered to take a good look at the blurred and formless face of agrarian and nationalist revolutions in Latin America in order to try to understand them for what they are: a universal phenomenon that calls for a new interpretation. . . . What is even more depressing is the silence of the Latin American *intelligentsia*, which is living in the center of this whirlwind. . . .*

* *El laberinto de la soledad* (1959; English translation, *The Labyrinth of Solitude*, 1961.)

The Cuban Revolution, which took place after these lines were written, makes such reflection even more urgent. For the present, I will merely say that the task before us is not only to do away with an unjust and anachronistic state of affairs which condemns us to dependency on foreign powers in the international sphere, and on the domestic scene to an endless cycle: dictatorship, followed by anarchy, and a return to dictatorship. Even more importantly, we must also endeavor to recover our true past, which was shattered, dispersed, and sold the day after we won our independence. Latin America has been dismembered: nineteen pseudo-nations created by our "liberators," by oligarchies and, later, by imperialism. The change of our social structures and the recovery of our past—that is to say Latin American unity—are not two different tasks: they are one and the same thing. The present political division of our continent makes no sense either historically or economically. Almost none of our countries, with the exception of the very largest of them, is a viable economic unit by itself. The same is true in the area of politics: the one thing that can save us is an association free of all non-Latin American influence.

I do not know whether the peoples of Latin America will adopt the model of the Mexican or the Cuban Revolution. For different reasons, both these revolutions seem to me to have grave shortcomings. They are not really models but almost accidental forms that two popular movements were forced by internal and external circumstances to assume. In the beginning both lacked a precise ideology. In all likelihood the other peoples of our continent will invent different forms. This is the great task confronting Latin America, one that will test the political imagination of our peoples: viable forms of revolt or reform (whichever best fits the case) must be discovered and new institutions and forms of human community must be created. Development does not merely mean quantitative progress: above all else, it is, or should be, a solution to the over-all problem of social life, including both work and leisure, being together and being by ourselves, individual freedom and popular sovereignty, food and music, contemplation and love, physical and emotional needs. . . . Economic development and the reform of social and juridical structures would be useless without political confederation, without a Latin American alliance. If we fail, we will continue to be what we are now: a hunting and fishing preserve—whether for Americans, as today, or their Russian or Chinese successors.

Cyclical time was fatalistic: the bottom will eventually be the top, the way down is the way up. In order to break the cycle, man had no other recourse than to deny reality, the reality of the world and the reality of time. The most radical and consistent criticism was that of Buddhism. But Buddhism, which began as a criticism of time, soon became a prisoner of circular time. In the West the idea of rectilinear time was based on the notion of identity and homogeneity. It denied, in the first instance, that man's nature is plural, that the self is always *other*. In the second instance, it denied the *others*: colored peoples, yellow peoples, madmen, lovers—all those who were different in some way or other. The answer to circular time was either sanctity or cynicism: Buddha or Diogenes; the answer to rectilinear time was revolution or rebellion: Marx or Rimbaud. I do not know what the form of our age is: all I know is that it is a revolt. Satan does not want God to disappear: he wants to dethrone him, to speak with him as an equal, to re-establish the original relation, which was neither subjection nor annihilation of the other, but complementary opposition. Rectilinear time represented an attempt to eliminate dissimilarities, to suppress differences; contemporary revolt aspires to give *otherness* a place in historical life again.

A new form is emerging amid the present confusion, a moving pattern that is ceaselessly forming and re-forming. Like atoms and cells, this form is dynamic because it is the daughter of the fundamental opposition: the binary relation between the *I* and the *thou*, between us and them. I do not have an idyllic view of dialogue: since it is a confrontation of two points of view whose difference is irreducible, it is more often a struggle than an embrace. This dialogue is history itself: it does not exclude violence, but at the same time it is not merely violence. The revolt of Latin America is not simply an economical and political phenomenon; it is a historical movement and it encompasses those areas rather vaguely defined by the word *civilization*: a style, a language, a vision. Rodó and Darío were not mistaken in their belief that there was a fundamental incompatibility between Latin America and the United States. We are both eccentric offshoots of Europe; we have been shaped by different pasts and our present is no less antagonistic. This incompatibility is not only a product of different systems, ideologies, or techniques but also of something that is irreducible to all of these—something that can only be expressed as a symbol or a metaphor: what was once called a *soul*, that of men and that of civilizations. We fight to preserve our souls; we speak so that the other may recognize our soul and so that we may recognize ourselves in his soul, which is different from ours. The powerful conceive of history as a mirror: in the battered faces of others— the insulted and injured, the conquered or the "converted"— they see their own face reflected. This is the dialogue of masks, that double monologue of the victimizer and the victimized. Revolt is the criticism of masks, the beginning of genuine dialogue. It is also the creation of our own faces. Latin America is beginning to have a face.

Index

BASENJIS
KW-118

The text of this book is the result of the joint effort of the authors and editorial staff of T.F.H. Publications, Inc., which is the originator of all sections of the book except the chapters dealing with the breed history, breed standard, and grooming. Additionally, the portrayal of canine pet products in this book is for general instructive value only; the appearance of such products does not necessarily constitute an endorsement by the author, the publisher, or the owners of the dogs portrayed in this book.

Title page: *The Basenji, the "Barkless Dog," comes from ancient Africa to twentieth-century man, who ofttimes forgets that his favorite hound doesn't howl. Owners, Tom and Judy Matunas. Agent, Michael Zollo.*

Photography: Isabelle Francais, Ron Reagan, Anne Roslin-Williams, Vince Serbin, Robert Smith, Sally Anne Thompson, and Louise van der Meid.

Drawings: Scott Boldt, Richard Crammer, Richard Davis, Andrew Prendimano, John R. Quinn, and Alexandra Suchenko.

Distributed in the UNITED STATES by T.F.H. Publications, Inc., One T.F.H. Plaza, Neptune City, NJ 07753; in CANADA to the Pet Trade by H & L Pet Supplies Inc., 27 Kingston Crescent, Kitchener, Ontario N2B 2T6; Rolf C. Hagen Ltd., 3225 Sartelon Street, Montreal 382 Quebec; in CANADA to the Book Trade by Macmillan of Canada (A Division of Canada Publishing Corporation), 164 Commander Boulevard, Agincourt, Ontario M1S 3C7; in ENGLAND by T.F.H. Publications Limited, Cliveden House/Priors Way/Bray, Maidenhead, Berkshire SL6 2HP, England; in AUSTRALIA AND THE SOUTH PACIFIC by T.F.H. (Australia) Pty. Ltd., Box 149, Brookvale 2100 N.S.W., Australia; in NEW ZEALAND by Ross Haines & Son, Ltd., 82 D Elizabeth Knox Place, Panmure, Auckland, New Zealand; in the PHILIPPINES by Bio-Research, 5 Lippay Street, San Lorenzo Village, Makati Rizal; in SOUTH AFRICA by Multipet Pty. Ltd., Box 235 New Germany, South Africa 3620. Published by T.F.H. Publications, Inc. Manufactured in the United States of America by T.F.H. Publications, Inc.

BASENJIS

JACK SHAFER

and

BOB MANKEY

Basically unchanged since the days when he romped in pharaoh's court, the Basenji still remains elegant, proud and gazelle-like. Additionally, the breed is amazingly clean and hardy.

Contents

1996 EDITION

Introducing the Basenji

In these modern times with man looking to the planets and new worlds to conquer . . . with modern science announcing fantastic new feats . . . the electronics age upon us with everything new, it seems strange that one of the breeds of purebred dogs that is advancing in popularity is a "new" breed of dog that dates back to the days of the Pharaohs and ancient Egypt.

So then, we find modern man can cavort contentedly with his "new" breed of dog just as the Egyptians of the IV Dynasty did in their courts, for engravings show that this "new" breed has a family tree that dates back to some early Egyptian engravings of 3600 B.C.

The breed is a medium-sized one that has found a new world of popularity with people who are situated in three rooms and a bath with neighbors on both sides who object to noisy dogs.

It is a breed of dog whose quietness can be guaranteed and whose shedding is of such short hairs that a few missed in the regular vacuuming wouldn't cause anyone to turn down an invitation to your home. It is a breed of dog that can be dried from a damp day's airing in just a short time and whose cleanliness is such that no objectionable odor ever exists!

This twentieth-century miracle, this unique modern "dream world" dog is a breed of hound, imported from Africa, called the Basenji.

The Basenji is what is termed a "natural breed" of great antiquity—he has not been altered to suit the modern whims and fancies of mankind. The Basenji today is basically the same regal picture he was when he was the favorite of the courts of the Pharaohs. In his native habitat the Basenji is used by the pygmies of the Ituri Forest as a running (finding and chasing), hunting dog. He is in great favor with the natives due to remarkable scenting ability, his cleanliness and his lack of body odor (important in a hunter).

The natives treat their Basenjis with such favor that they carry them about the neck, letting them "ride" to where the hunt is to be, and if the weather becomes inclement, it is not unusual to find the natives out of their huts, leaving the cover to the Basenjis.

APPEARANCE AND TEMPERAMENT

The Basenji is a short-coated, small, lightly built, short-backed, regal appearing dog, with long legs and fine bone structure. In profile the Basenji is a "square

Facing page: *A native of Zaire, the breed possesses independence, resourcefulness and acumen in the hunt, equipping it with an uncanny ability to survive. Today the Basenji is a popular hunting companion who is often referred to as the Congo Dog.*

Like the Basenji, the Pharaoh Hound is recognized in the dog world as a fine pet which has roots in ancient Africa. Both breeds were highly favored by the pharaohs and used for hunting purposes in Egypt. The Pharaoh Hound represents the classic sighthound conformation and is somewhat larger than its cousin, the Basenji.

dog'' in that the measurement from the top of his withers to the ground is approximately equal to, or only slightly less than, his overall body length. His short body and his habit of standing with his feet well under him permits rapid turning and dodging and has contributed to his survival in his native forests. The average height is 16 to 17 inches at the withers and the weight averages about 24 pounds.

There are three colors in the Basenji: red and white; black, tan and white, or tri-color; and black and white. The basic body color of the Basenji is either red or black. Regardless of the basic color, all Basenjis should have white tail tips, white feet and white chests. The amount of white on the face, neck, shoulders, underparts and legs is optional.

Each of the color varieties has a wrinkled forehead. When alert, with upright ears pricked forward, there should be a fine, profuse wrinkle. Wrinkles are more pronounced in puppies, and because of the lack of shadowing, are not as noticeable in tri-colors or black and whites. The whole demeanor of the Basenji is one of poise and alertness.

The Basenji *is* and *should be* an intelligent animal, elegant looking and moving proudly with a gazelle-like grace.

He has been referred to as the

Larger than the Basenji and the Pharaoh Hound is the Ibizan Hound, also a breed of the great Egyptian culture. These versatile sighthounds were brought to Spain and soon became popular pets, race dogs, hunters, and companions. Owner, Judith E. Ford.

"Barkless Dog," and this reference is correct, for the breed is naturally barkless! They are not, however, entirely mute—for they can make sounds common to all dogs. They do have a friendly substitute for the bark—it is a sort of chortle or yodeling sound—and to hear them emit this sound when playing is a joy.

As puppies they *can* whine or cry, but after the usual puppy sounds and correct training by the

Basenji pups are surprisingly trainable and alert. This toddler gracefully inspects his first Nylabone® chew bone.

owner, people are amazed at how quiet they can be.

Since he is a "barkless dog," it has been asked many times, "Can he be a watchdog?" I'd like to see any stranger or intruder come upon your home or yard with the Basenji there to guard it. He can make a noise, one which is seldom heard, but when he does you know that something is surely wrong. Picture an intruder face-to-face with a Basenji, with his hair up on his back, his teeth showing and a deep rumbling growl emanating from his throat. This is sure to discourage anyone bent on trouble.

Children love Basenjis and Basenjis love children even more. They can play together for many hours, romping playfully and tirelessly together. When the evening hours come and the adults of the family want the more docile family pet, one to lie at the feet or on the couch next to them, the Basenji loves the relaxation of their company and plays in his own different way for the elders of the household.

Basenjis rarely ever require bathing, and they actually clean themselves just like cats! Another nice feature Basenji owners discover is that they rarely have more than a minimum of flea or bug problems.

It is a pleasure to note the distinctive Basenji gait . . . for when they walk slowly they are like a trotting horse and their

faster gait is like that of a gazelle.

Basenjis, when very sad, have been known to emit what some believe to be real tears. This occurs many times in the female, during the breeding or whelping process.

Gentle and beguiling, Basenjis make personable household companions that also prove to be competent and dedicated protectors. Owners, Karen Jenkins and M. Greenlee.

Gregarious and companionable, the Basenji enjoys the company of his fellow canines. Here, illustrated with a dog of similar derivation, the Whippet, is a charming and playful Basenji.

THE BASENJI IN ENGLAND

In the *Illustrated Kennel News Of England* of 1908, there was a picture of native dogs from the Congo, and this was in reference to dogs exhibited at the Crufts show of 1895. The dogs which appeared as "Basenji-like" were entered and exhibited as *African Bush Dogs* (also known as Congo Terriers). These dogs were purchased at the show by a W.R. Temple, who was then an associate of H.C. Brooke, who was considered to be one of the foremost experts on foreign dogs. These dogs died a short time after the show, having contracted distemper. Early information on the breed also stated that there was a pair of the same breed exhibited at approximately the same time at the *Jardin d' Acclimatation* in Paris, France.

Basenjis fell to the wayside from this time until the year 1923, when Lady Helen Nutting became enamored with the Zande Dogs, from a region of the Nile, that were favored dogs of the natives. She later transported six of these dogs to England, but the distemper shots given them caused them to fall ill after arriving in England and they later died.

Again following the demise of the six, the Basenji became all but a forgotten breed until it was again transported to England from the Belgian Congo and shown at several shows in England that year. The exhibitor had been chided by some fellow exhibitors that she had crossed the Corgi and the Bull Terrier to produce this "new" breed.

Finally, after much difficulty, the experts of the London Zoo and the experts of the Kennel Club agreed to the purebred aspects of the dogs and thus they were registered under the breed name "Basenji." In the Inter-Territorial Swahili Dictionaries, the closest translation is "Wilde Thing" or "Bushe Thing."

One of the people most responsible for the success and the basic lines of the Basenji was an English woman named Veronica Tudor-Williams (Mrs. Tudor-Williams. is still considered one of the great experts on the Basenji). In 1941 she acquired an exceptional red and white female named Amatangazig. Mrs. Tudor-Williams has stated that without the influence of Amatangazig of the Congo on the breed, the Basenji could have faded out or taken many years longer to be developed. This famous bitch passed away at the age of 14 on New Year's Day of 1952.

The actual dogs that are considered the "foundation stock" of the breed coming from Africa were Bongo of Blean, Bokoto of Blean, Bashele of Blean, Bereke of Blean, Bungwa of Blean and Bakuma of Blean. They were brought to England by another of the famous founders of the breed, Mrs. Oliver Burn, between 1936 and 1937. All of these dogs, with the exception of Bakuma, remained in England to become the foundation stock of the Blean Kennels and the "—of the Congo" Kennels of Veronica Tudor-Williams. Bakuma was later acquired by two of the founders of the breed in the United States, Mr. and Mrs. Alexander Phemister of Kingston, Massachusetts.

The taut and athletic conformation of the Basenji has made him a fine contender in dog races. Dressed in his racing silk, this black/tan Basenji prepares for competition.

Introducing the Basenji

THE BASENJI IN AMERICA

In April 1941, a tramp steamer from the western coast of Africa (possibly Leopoldville) arrived in Boston. In the hold of that ship Alexander Phemister found a Basenji bitch that had been there for almost three weeks. Phemister, who acquired the bitch, said that her condition was such that she weighed only nine pounds on arrival. The next dogs out of Africa were Kindu and Kasenyi, who arrived in the summer of 1941 along with a shipload of gorillas and other animals for a Henry Trefflich of New York. In 1952, Veronica Tudor-Williams imported Wau of the Congo from the southern Sudan, and then a few years later she journeyed to Africa and brought back with her Fula of the Congo. Thus, with the elimination of the dog known as "Simolo" from the early pedigrees, these were the basic dogs that are and should be considered the foundation stock of the American Basenji.

In 1937, a Mrs. Roger brought Bakuma of Blean to New York. In the early summer of 1941, the Alexander Phemisters acquired Bakuma and registered him with the AKC as Phemister's Bois. The next Basenjis who arrived in the United States for breeding purposes were all dogs from the "—of the Congo" strain, named Kwillo, Kikuyu, Koodoo and Kitreve. They all went to a Dr. Richmond, and the first litter of Basenjis born in America was by Koodoo and Kikuyu. The first litter sired by an American dog was by Phemister's Bois x Phemister's Naida (a daughter of Phemister's Congo). It was in June 1941 that another of the early founders of the breed in the U.S. acquired his first Basenji. George Gilkey purchased a bitch named Tanya of Windrush from Dr. Richmond. The Basenji Club of America accepted the standard of the breed as drawn up by the Basenji Club of England. The American Kennel Club then, in 1943, accepted this standard as official and thus accepted the Basenji as acceptable for registration in the AKC Stud Book. Basenjis were shown at the Westminster Kennel Club show in 1945 with an entry of five. They were shown in Miscellaneous Class. The first time a Basenji was shown in the United States in the Hound Group was on June 3, 1945, at the Orange Empire show in California.

The foundation stock of the authors' Cambria Kennels in Santa Ana, California, was first acquired from the Phemisters with the purchase of Ch. Katema of Carmel and Ch. Phemister's Kedar. Kedar became one of the all time top-winning Basenjis in the early history of the breed and lived in retirement at Cambria until his death in June 1966. Among others in the foundation stock of Cambria were the Irish import, Ch. Victory

The combination of the breed's charm, sensitivity, strong protective instincts, and dapper appearance has won it fans around the world. Owners, Karen Jenkins and Margaret Gougelman.

of Syngefield; Ch. My Love of the Congo, who was the dam of 15 American champions; and the tri-color Ch. Bettina's Oryx. The breeding combination of Oryx and My Love produced the all-time winning tri-color Ch. Cambria's Ti-Mungai, who produced nearly 30 champions.

Standard for the Breed

The Basenji, like all other purebred dogs, is measured against a breed standard of perfection, a written description of what the ideal specimen should look like. Each dog-registering organization draws up a standard for each of the breeds of dog it recognizes; however, these standards may vary, in the way they are worded, from registry to registry and from country to country.

AKC STANDARD FOR THE BASENJI

Characteristics—The Basenji should not bark, but is not mute.

The wrinkled forehead and the swift, tireless running gait (resembling a racehorse trotting full out) are typical of the breed.

General Appearance—The Basenji is a small, lightly built, short-backed dog, giving the impression of being high on the leg compared to its length. The wrinkled head must be proudly carried, and the whole demeanor should be one of poise and alertness.

Head and Skull—The skull is flat, well chiseled and of medium width, tapering towards the eyes. The foreface should taper from

A level back, well-sprung ribs and a definable waist befit this lightly built, lithe sportsman.

The captivating grace, sincerity, and natural beauty of the Basenji have cornered many an unsuspecting dog lover and remained embedded in his heart and home.

The standard describes three acceptable color combinations, all of which appear with specified white markings. In their native Zaire, however, Basenjis can be found in a wide variety of colors, including solids and merles.

eye to muzzle and should be shorter than the skull. Muzzle, neither coarse nor snipy, but with rounded cushions. Wrinkles should appear upon the forehead, and be fine and profuse. Side wrinkles are desirable, but should never be exaggerated into dewlap. **Nose:** Black greatly desired. A pinkish tinge should not penalize an otherwise first class specimen, but should be discouraged in breeding. **Eyes:** Dark hazel, almond shaped, obliquely set and far seeing. **Ears:** Small, pointed and erect, of fine texture, set well forward on top of head. **Mouth:** Teeth must be level with scissors bite.

Neck—Of good length, well crested and slightly full at base of throat. It should be well set into flat, laid back shoulders.

Forequarters—The chest should be deep and of medium width. The legs straight with clean fine bone, long forearm and well-defined sinews. Pasterns should be of good length, straight and flexible.

Body—The body should be short and the back level. The ribs well sprung, with plenty of heart room, deep brisket, short coupled, and ending in a definite waist.

Hindquarters—Should be strong and muscular, with hocks well let down, turned neither in nor out, with long second thighs.

Feet—Small, narrow and compact, with well-arched toes.

Tail—Should be set on top and curled tightly over to either side.

Coat—Short and silky. Skin very pliant.

Color—Chestnut red (the deeper the better) or pure black, or black and tan, all with white feet, chest and tail tip. White legs, white blaze and white collar optional.

Weight—Bitches 22 pounds approximately. Dogs 24 pounds approximately.

Size—Bitches 16 inches and dogs 17 inches from the ground to the top of the shoulder. Bitches 16 inches and dogs 17 inches from the front of the chest to the farthest point of the hindquarters.

The importance of breeding for type cannot be over-estimated. The classic Basenji hallmarks include the tightly curled tailed, the erect, pointed ears, and the wrinkled brow—the well-bred Basenji will possess all of these characteristics.

KENNEL CLUB STANDARD FOR THE BASENJI

General Appearance: Lightly built, finely boned aristocratic-looking animal, high on leg compared with its length, always poised, alert and intelligent. Wrinkled head, with pricked ears, proudly carried on a well-arched neck. Deep brisket runs up into a definite waist, tail tightly curled presenting a picture of a well-balanced dog of gazelle-like grace.

Characteristics: Barkless but not mute, its own special noise a mixture of a chortle and a yodel. Remarkable for its cleanliness in every way.

Temperament: An intelligent, independent, but affectionate and alert breed. Can be aloof with strangers.

Head and Skull: Flat, well-chiseled and medium width, tapering towards nose, with slight stop. Distance from top of head to stop slightly more than from stop to tip of nose. Side lines of skull taper gradually towards mouth, giving a clean-cheeked appearance. Fine and profuse wrinkles appearing on forehead when ears pricked, side wrinkles desirable but not exaggerated into dewlap. Wrinkles more noticeable in puppies, but because of lack of shadowing, not as noticeable in tri-colours; black nose desirable.

Eyes: Dark, almond-shaped, obliquely set, far-seeing and rather inscrutable in expression.

Ears: Small, pointed, erect and slightly hooded, of fine texture, set well forward on top of head, tip of ear nearer centre of skull than outside base.

Mouth: Jaws strong, with a perfect, regular and complete scissor bite, i.e., the upper teeth closely overlapping the lower teeth and set square to the jaws.

Neck: Strong and of good length, without thickness, well crested and slightly full at base of throat with a graceful curve accentuating crest. Well-set into shoulders giving head a "lofty" carriage.

Forequarters: Shoulders well laid back, muscular, not loaded.

Although not fundamentally competitive dogs, given the right inspiration (a new Nylabone® chew bone), Basenjis will joust sportingly.

Elbows tucked in against brisket. When viewed from front, elbows in line with ribs and legs should continue in a straight line to ground giving a medium front. Forelegs straight with fine bone

and very long forearms. Pasterns good length, straight and flexible.

Body: Balanced with short, level back. Ribs well sprung, deep and oval. Loin short coupled, deep brisket running up into definite waist.

Hindquarters: Strong and muscular, hocks well let down, turned neither in nor out, with long second thighs and moderately bent stifles.

Feet: Small, narrow and compact, with deep pads, well-arched toes and short nails.

Tail: High set, with posterior curve of buttock extending beyond root of tail giving a reachy appearance to hindquarters. Curls tightly over spine and lies closely to thigh with a single or double curl.

Gait/Movement: Legs carried straight forward with a swift long tireless swinging stride.

Coat: Short, sleek and close, very fine. Skin very pliant.

Colour: Pure black and white, red and white, black, tan and white with tan melon pips and mask, tan and white. The white should be on feet, chest and tail tips. White legs, blaze and white collar optional.

Size: Ideal height—Dogs 43 cm (17 ins) at withers; Bitches 40 cm (16 ins) at withers. Ideal weight— Dogs 11 kg (24 lbs); Bitches 9½ kg (21 lbs).

Dog scholars and writers have always had much to say about the Basenji. The reader will find the coverage of the breed in two all-breed books of tremendous interest: *The Atlas of Dog Breeds of the World* (H-1091) by Chris Walkowicz and Bonnie Wilcox and *The Canine Lexicon* (TS-175) by Andrew De Prisco and James Johnson.

The Basenji's body is short, balanced with his level back; his tail is high set and curls over either side. His expression is invariably intelligent and alert.

Grooming Your Basenji

How fortunate you are with a Basenji when it comes to grooming. With the short hair and the way they like to keep themselves clean all the time, it is no problem to maintain and keep them looking always in the peak of condition. Your grooming takes but a short time to do. If you can arrange to allot yourself a few minutes each day to rub him down

The Basenji is perhaps one of the cleanest of canines, nearly proverbial in the cat-like primping and cleaning of his coat. Therefore, he needs very little in the way of grooming and bathing.

with a small amount of dog grooming oil and then to work over his coat from the ears to the rear with a rubber curry brush, your Basenji will be show-ring ready every day and should have no problems with coat or skin disorders.

A day prior to showing your Basenji, oil his coat down heavily and, should his white parts be dull, chalk them. Use a soft brush (like the type used for brushing a cat) to remove all of the chalk. Wipe the oil off with a damp wash towel. When he is dry, a light coat of oil spray makes him gleam for the ring.

Be sure you have trimmed his whiskers off, using the eye and nose pet scissors your pet dealer has for this purpose.

The claws should be shortened several days before the show and then filed regularly. Long claws not only look bad but can create foot problems, especially if the claws are so long that they touch the ground.

A few "wild" hairs may have to be trimmed around the tail, but great caution should be used in doing this if you are not familiar with the system. Many breeders or handlers can show the novice the

Categorized in the kennel club as a hound, the Basenji can be kept looking clean and sleek by using a simple hound glove on his coat. Regular brushing can virtually eliminate the necessity for bathing.

The Basenji's ears need regular attention to keep them clean and free of wax build-up. Never probe in the ear of any dog further than you can see.

correct way to do this.

The Basenji's beautifully erect ears can also be dust and dirt catchers. Therefore, don't forget to clean the ears. Ear drops for pets can be dropped in the ear and a cotton swab used to clean inside,

but a word of caution here too: only use the type of cotton swab that would be used for babies, i.e., the flexible type, not the hard, stick type, and never go deeper than you can see.

BATHING

It is rare that you will have to bathe your Basenji, but should the need arise, *never* use your own favorite human shampoo for the purpose. Use a good quality pet shampoo, preferably one that is

"Prick up your ears!" Even as a pup, the Basenji has erect and pointy ears, complemented in this pup by an irresistible and assertive alertness.

As part of the grooming procedure, gently wipe around the dog's eyes with a cotton ball to remove dirt and potential stains.

non-toxic. This same care should be given to the use of flea sprays on and around the Basenji. Remember, your Basenji cleans himself as a cat does. In other words, the spray that is used must be of the non-toxic type or a cat-type spray. By following this rule, much trouble can be avoided in the health of your Basenji.

As far as grooming a Basenji is concerned, it is no problem. Just use the proper equipment for what has to be done, give the dog the proper vitamins and the best in coat additives and the few minutes a day from you . . . the result is just what you would want to see.

A STEP-BY-STEP GROOMING PROCEDURE

The following tools and equipment will be necessary to execute the given grooming procedure properly:

- *Pin brush*
- *Sisal (natural bristle brush)*
- *Medicated ear powder*
- *Nail clipper*
- *Eye drops (eye stain remover)*
- *Lanolin coat conditioner*
- *Chamois cloth*
- *Cotton balls*
- *Scissors*

1. Brush the entire coat with the pin brush, thus loosening up the hair; then brush with the sisal brush.

2. Clean the ears using the medicated ear powder.

3. Clean the eyes by wiping with a cotton ball moistened with eye drops. This will also help in removing any stains around the eyes.

4. Clip the toenails with the nail clipper, being careful not to cut the quick.

5. Using the scissors, clip the whiskers from the muzzle, the

Many owners find that clipping the Basenji's whiskers gives the muzzle a cleaner, more defined appearance. This may be the case with many show dogs while other owners allow the whiskers to remain, fondly preserving the breed's cat-like aura.

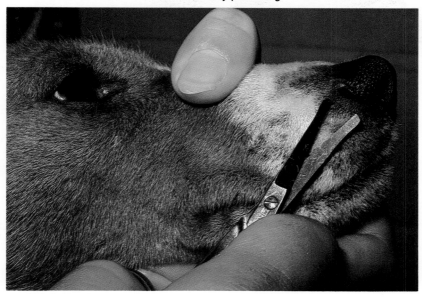

Grooming Your Basenji

chin, the sides of the face, and above the eyes.

6. Putting a cotton ball in each ear prevents water from entering the ear canal. Bathe the dog and cage dry him.

7. Put a few drops of lanolin coat conditioner into the palms of your hands, rub together lightly, and massage gently into the coat.

8. Brush the coat with the sisal brush (to distribute the conditioner) and then lightly rub over the coat with the chamois cloth, thus giving it a nice sheen.

Dogs' nails grow at varying rates, depending on the surfaces on which the dogs run and the frequency of their exercise. Owners must pay close attention to their dogs' feet and clip nails as often as necessary. Be careful not to clip too close to the quick, the nail's blood supply—this can be painful and scarring to your dog.

The Basenji as a show dog has thrived in both the United States and Great Britain. The breed's personable disposition and handsome demeanor have stolen the hearts of many judges and spectators.

The Basenji's grace and beauty are both striking and endearing. Who could not fall in love with such a handsome and beguiling house mate?!

Selecting Your Dog

Now that you have decided which dog breed suits your needs, your lifestyle, and your own temperament, there will be much to consider before you make your final purchase. Buying a puppy on impulse may only cause heartbreak later on; it makes better sense to put some real thought into your canine investment, especially since it is likely that he will share many happy years with you. Which individual will you choose as your adoring companion? Ask yourself some questions as you analyze your needs and preferences for a dog, read all that you can about your particular breed, and visit as many dog shows as possible. At the shows you will be surrounded by people who can give you all the details about the breed you are interested in buying. Decide if you want a household pet, a dog for breeding, or a show dog. Would you prefer a male or female? Puppy or adult?

If you buy from a breeder, ask him to help you with your decision. When you have settled on the dog you want, discuss with him the dog's temperament, the animal's positive and negative aspects, any health problems it might have, its feeding and grooming requirements, and whether the dog has been immunized. Reputable breeders will be willing to answer any questions you might have that pertain to the dog you have selected, and often they will make themselves available if you call for advice or if you encounter problems after you've made your purchase.

Dog and cat lovers alike have found the Basenji a most agreeable companion. This is "Sniff" of White Kennels.

A bit too big?
A little **too** small.
Too fuzzy for me!
Too fat to crawl.

Before you wrap it tight
And crate it home,
Behold its appetite
And room to roam.

A sloppy yap, a barking slur,
Puppy eyes to be let free,
A him? a her? an unmarked cur,
Let's pout to see its pedigree.

The perfect pet quest:
Which pup for me is best?

ANDREW DE PRISCO

35

Most breeders and sellers want to see their dogs placed in loving, responsible homes; they are careful about who buys their animals. So as the dog's new owner, prepare yourself for some interrogation from the breeder.

Buying a puppy should not be an impulsive endeavor; it is never wise to rush out and buy just any puppy that catches your shopping eye. The more time and thought you invest, the greater your satisfaction with your new companion. And if this

The breed is known for its keen eyesight; its eyes are almond shaped and dark hazel in color.

new companion is to be purely a pet, its background and early care will affect its future health and good temperament. It is always essential that you choose a properly raised puppy from healthy, well-bred stock.

You must seek out an active, sturdy puppy with bright eyes and an intelligent expression. If the puppy is friendly, that's a major plus, but you don't want one that is hyperactive nor do you want one that is dull and listless. The coat should be clean and plush, with no signs of fleas or other parasites. The premises should be clean, by sight and smell, and the proprietors should be helpful and knowledgeable. A reputable seller wants his customers satisfied and will therefore represent the puppy fairly. Let good common sense guide your purchase, and choose a reliable, well-recommended source that you know has well-satisfied customers. Don't look for a bargain, since you may end up paying many times over in future veterinarian bills, not to mention disappointments and heartache if your pet turns out not to be well. If you feel that something is lacking in the care or condition of the dogs, it is better to look elsewhere than to buy hastily and regret it afterward. Buy a healthy dog with a good disposition, one that has been

Few breeds of dog delight man like the Basenji. This smiling "Bush Dog" of Yannarella Kennels is a flawless companion and house pet.

properly socialized and likes being around people.

If you cannot find the dog you want locally, write to the secretary of the national breed club or kennel club and ask for names of breeders near you or to whom you can write for information. Puppies are often shipped, sight unseen, from reputable breeders. In these instances, pictures and pedigree information are usually sent beforehand to help you decide.

Breeders can supply you with further details and helpful guidance, if you require it. Many breed clubs provide a puppy referral service, so you may want to look into this before making your final decision.

PET OR SHOW DOG

Conscientious breeders strive to maintain those desirable qualities in their breed. At the same time, they are always working to improve on what they have already achieved, and they do this by referring to the breed standard of perfection. The standard describes the ideal dog, and those animals that come close to the ideal are generally selected as show

Owners of purebred dogs too often forget that all breeds of dog are interrelated. The ancient canine that is the believed ancestor of all dogs is known as Tomarctus. As packs traveled and inhabited various lands, types evolved through the process of adaptation. Later, as dogs and man joined forces, type became further diversified. This chart sketches one commonly accepted theory of the domesticated dog's development. Where does your dog fit in? With a few exceptions, dogs evolve or change as a result of a specific functional need.

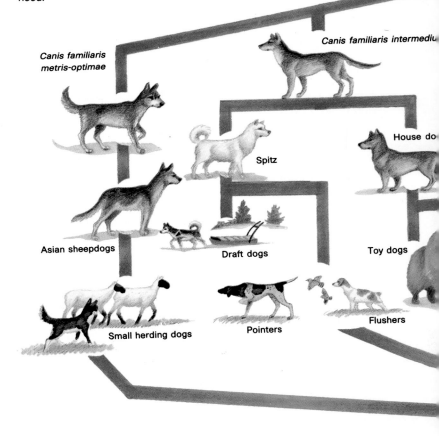

Canis familiaris metris-optimae

Canis familiaris intermediu

Spitz

House do

Asian sheepdogs

Draft dogs

Toy dogs

Small herding dogs

Pointers

Flushers

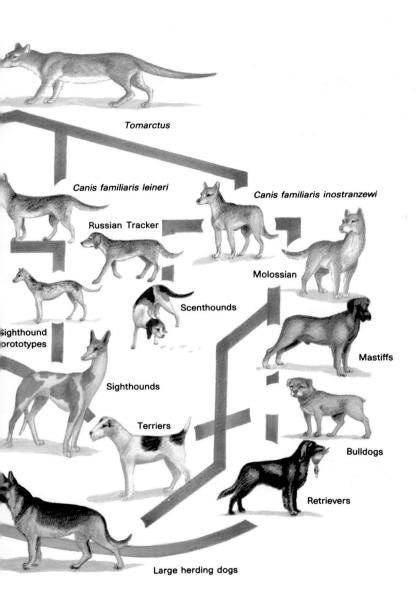

Tomarctus

Canis familiaris leineri

Canis familiaris inostranzewi

Russian Tracker

Molossian

Scenthounds

Sighthound prototypes

Mastiffs

Sighthounds

Terriers

Bulldogs

Retrievers

Large herding dogs

stock; those that do not are culled and sold as pets. Keep in mind that pet-quality purebred dogs are in no way less healthy or attractive than show-quality specimens. It's just that the pet may have undesirable features (such as ears that are too large

Remember that your new Basenji pup has only recently left the warmth and protection of its mother. These pups, but a few weeks of age, still rely on mom heavily for all their needs.

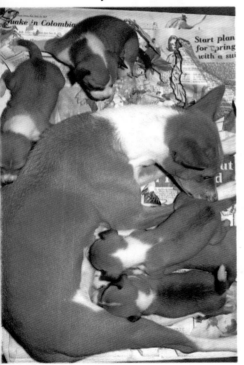

or eyes that are the wrong color for its breed) which would be faults in the show ring. Often these so-called "flaws" are detectable only by experienced breeders or show judges. Naturally the more perfect animal, in terms of its breed standard, will cost more—even though he seems almost identical to his pet-quality littermate.

If you think you may eventually want to show your dog or raise a litter of puppies, by all means buy the best you can afford. You will save expense and disappointment later on. However, if the puppy is strictly to be a pet for the children, or a companion for you, you can afford to look for a bargain. The pup which is not show material, or the older pup for which there is often less demand, or the grown dog which is not being used for breeding are occasionally available and offer opportunities to save money. Remember that your initial investment may be a bargain, but it takes good food and care— and plenty of both—to raise a healthy, vigorous puppy through its adulthood.

Facing page: *Although not required, the white blaze on the Basenji's head is a most prized feature and was perceived by the ancient Egyptians as an indicator of both intelligence and value, symbolizing the living flame of the true Creator.*

The price you pay for your dog is little compared to the love and devotion he will return over the many years he'll be with you. With proper care and affection, your pup should live to a ripe old age; thanks to modern veterinary science and improvements in canine nutrition, dogs today are better maintained and live longer. It is not uncommon to see dogs living well into their teens.

Generally speaking, small dogs live longer than big ones. With love and the proper care any dog will live to its optimum age. Many persons, however, opt for a particular breed because of its proven longevity. This, of course, is purely a personal decision.

MALE OR FEMALE

Let us first disregard the usual generalizations and misconceptions applied to male vs. female dogs and consider the practical concerns. If you intend to show your new dog, a male will likely closer adhere to the

Size variation in the dog family is extreme. The consideration of size must be a high priority when choosing a breed. The amount of housing, exercise, and food required, as well as the animal's lifespan are just some of the factors involved.

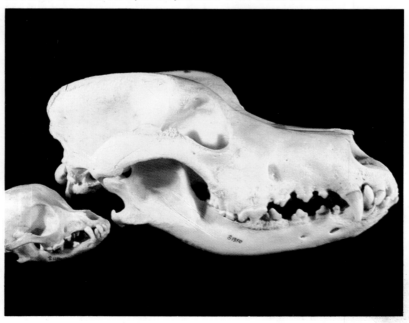

breed standard, though ring competition for males is stiffer. A female chosen to show cannot be spayed and the owner must contend with the bitch's heat period. If it is solely a pet—and pet animals should *not* be bred—castration or spaying is necessary. Neutered pets have longer lifespans and have a decreased risk of cancer. Males are more economical to neuter than are females. You might also consider that females are generally smaller than males, easier to housetrain, may be more family-oriented and protective of home and property. Any dog will roam—male or female—castration will not affect roaming in most cases. Males are larger and stronger, proving better guard-dog candidates. Of course, a dog of either sex, if properly trained, can make a charming, reliable, and loving pet. Male vs. female is chiefly a matter of personal preference—go with your first instinct.

ADULT OR PUP

Whether to buy a grown dog or a young puppy is another question. It is surely an undeniable pleasure to watch your dog grow from a lively pup to a mature, dignified dog. If you don't have the time to spend on the more frequent meals, housebreaking, and other training a puppy needs in order to become a dog you can be

Life Expectancy	
Dog's Age in Years	Comparative Human Age in Years
1	15
2	24
3	28
4	32
5	36
6	40
7	44
8	48
9	52
10	56
11	60
12	64
13	68
14	72
15	76
16	80
17	84
18	88
19	92
20	96
21	100

This chart is designed to provide a comparative view of ages between a dog and its human counterpart. Necessarily it is an oversimplification since larger breeds often have shorter lifespans than do average or medium-sized dogs; likewise working dogs may tend to live shorter lives than the easy-going pet dog. These factors, and many others, must be taken into account when considering this chart.

proud of, then choose an older, partly-trained adolescent or a grown dog. If you want a show dog, remember that no one, not even an expert, can predict with one hundred percent accuracy what a puppy will be like when he grows up. The dog may seem to exhibit show potential *most* of the time, but six months is the earliest age for the would-be exhibitor to select a prospect and know that its future is in the show ring.

If you have a small child, it is best to get a puppy big enough to defend itself, one not less than four or five months old.

Older children will enjoy playing with and helping to take care of a baby pup; but at less than four months, a puppy wants to do little else but eat and sleep, and he must be protected from teasing and overtiring. You cannot expect a very young child to understand that a puppy is a fragile living being; to the youngster he is a toy like his

A silent hunter, the Basenji is called the "Barkless Dog" for good reason. He communicates with a pleasing yodel or a discontented growl—he does not bark!

Standing proudly in the back yard is "Sniff."

stuffed dog. Children, therefore, must learn how to handle and care for their young pets.

We recommend you start with a puppy so that you can raise and train it according to the rules you have established in your own home. While a dog is young, its behavior can be more easily shaped by the owner, whereas an older dog , although trainable, may be a bit set in his ways.

WHAT TO LOOK FOR IN A PUPPY

In choosing a puppy, assuming that it comes from healthy, well-bred parents, look for one that is friendly and outgoing. The biggest pup in the litter is apt to be somewhat coarse as a grown dog, while the appealing "runt of the litter" may turn out to be a timid shadow—or have a Napoleonic complex! If you want a show dog and have no experience in choosing a prospect, study the breed standard and listen carefully to the breeder on the finer points of show conformation. A breeder's prices will be in accord with his puppies' expected worth, and he will be honest with you about each pup's potential because it is to his own advantage. He wants his top-quality show puppies placed in the public eye to reflect glory on him—and to attract future buyers. Why should he sell a potential show champion to someone who just wants a pet?

Now that you have paid your money and made your choice, you are ready to depart with puppy, papers, and instructions. Make sure that you know the youngster's feeding routine, and take along some of his food. For the trip home, place him in a comfortable, sturdy carrier. Do not drive home with a puppy on your lap! If you'll be travelling for a few hours, at the very least bring along a bottle of water from the breeder and a small water dish.

PEDIGREE AND REGISTRATION

Owners of puppies are often misled by sellers with such ruses as leading the owner to believe his dog is something special. The term *pedigree papers* is quite different from the term *registration papers.* A pedigree is nothing more than a statement made by the breeder of the dog;

If you have never been to a dog show, whether you're interested in show dogs or not, by all means—Go! An all-breed dog show will give you hands-on experience with different breeds of dog, the chance to meet their owners and breeders, and the answers to many of your questions.

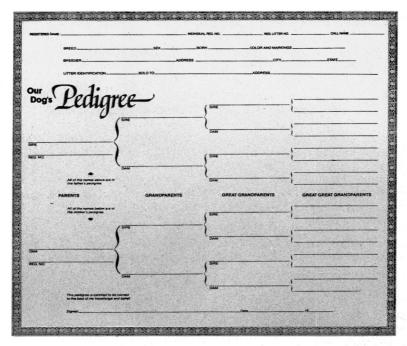

Pedigree papers can trace a dog's lineage back several generations. They do not, however, guarantee that a puppy is purebred, healthy or sound.

and it is written on special pedigree blanks, which are readily available from any pet shop or breed club, with the names of several generations from which the new puppy comes. It records your puppy's ancestry and other important data, such as the pup's date of birth, its breed, its sex, its sire and dam, its breeder's name and address, and so on. If your dog has had purebred champions in his background, then the pedigree papers are valuable as evidence of the good breeding behind your dog; but if the names on the pedigree paper are meaningless, then so is the paper itself. Just because a dog has a pedigree doesn't necessarily mean he is registered with a kennel club.

Registration papers from the American Kennel Club or the United Kennel Club in the United States or The Kennel Club of Great Britain attest to the fact that the mother and father of your puppy were purebred dogs of the breed represented by your puppy and that they were registered with a particular club. Normally every registered dog also has a complete pedigree available. Registration papers, which you receive when you buy a puppy, merely enable you to register your puppy. Usually the breeder has registered only the litter, so it is the new owner's responsibility to register and name an individual pup. The papers should be filled out and sent to the appropriate address printed on the application, along with the fee required for the registration. A certificate of registration will then be sent to you.

Pedigree and registration, by the way, have nothing to do with licensing, which is a local regulation applying to purebred and mongrel alike. Find out what the local ordinance is in your town or city and how it applies to your dog; then buy a license and keep it on your dog's collar for identification.

The breed's intelligence coupled with its natural athletic prowess and above-average trainability have made it excel in show rings and obedience competitions alike.

The New Family Member

The glimmering eyes and wrinkly expression of the Basenji pup will insure his welcome in any home that desires such a loving companion.

At long last, the day you have all been waiting for, your new puppy will make its grand entrance into your home. Before you bring your companion to its new residence, however, you must plan carefully for its arrival. Keep in mind that the puppy will need time to adjust to life with a different owner. He may seem a bit apprehensive about the strange surroundings in which he finds himself, having spent the first few weeks of life with his dam and littermates, but in a couple of days, with love and patience on your part, the transition will be complete.

First impressions are important, especially from the puppy's point of view, and these may very well set the pattern of his future relationship with you. You must be consistent in the

The puppy's bed will provide a place of refuge and privacy. Make sure that the puppy's toilet needs have been met before sending him to bed for the night.

way you handle your pet so that he learns what is expected of him. He must come to trust and respect you as his keeper and master. Provide him with proper care and attention, and you will be rewarded with a loyal companion for many years. Considering the needs of your puppy and planning ahead will surely make the change from his former home to his new one easier.

ADVANCE PREPARATION

In preparing for your puppy's arrival, perhaps more important than anything else is to find out from the seller how the pup was maintained. What brand of food was offered and when and how often was the puppy fed? Has

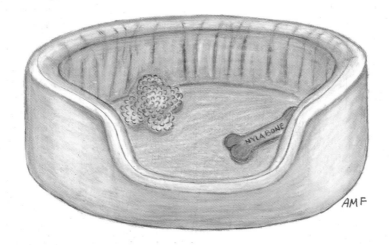

BASIC PUPPY NEEDS

- Canned and dry food/diet schedule
- Feeding and water bowls
- Carrying/sleeping crate
- Bed
- Collar and leash
- Grooming supplies (brushes, shampoo, etc.)
- Outdoor lead and/or pen
- Muzzle/first-aid kit
- Flea collar and preparations
- Safe chew products (Nylabone®, Gumabone®)
- Edible chew products (treats/rewards)

the pup been housebroken; if so, what method was employed? Attempt to continue whatever routine was started by the person from whom you bought your puppy; then, gradually, you can make those changes that suit you and your lifestyle. If, for example, the puppy has been paper trained, plan to stock up on newspaper. Place this newspaper toilet facility in a selected spot so that your puppy learns to use the designated area as his "bathroom." And keep on hand a supply of the dog food to which he is accustomed, as a sudden switch to new food could cause digestive upsets.

Another consideration is sleeping and resting quarters. Be sure to supply a dog bed for your pup, and introduce him to his special cozy corner so that he

This chart lists some of the many items that the dog owner should have on hand before he brings home his new charge.

knows where to retire when he feels like taking a snooze. You'll need to buy a collar (or harness) and leash, a safe chew item (such as Nylabone® or Gumabone®), and a few grooming tools as well. A couple of sturdy feeding dishes, one for food and one for water, will be needed; and it will be necessary, beforehand, to set up a feeding station.

FINDING A VETERINARIAN

An important part of your preparations should include finding a local veterinarian who can provide quality health care in the form of routine check-ups, inoculations, and prompt medical attention in case of illness or an emergency. Find out if the animal you have selected has been vaccinated against canine diseases, and make certain you secure all health certificates at the time of purchase. This information will be valuable to your veterinarian, who will want to know the puppy's complete medical history. Incidentally, don't wait until your puppy becomes sick before you seek the services of a vet; make an appointment for your pup before or soon after he takes up residence with you so that he starts out with a clean bill of health in his new home.

CHILDREN AND PUPPIES

Prepare the young members of the household on pet care. Children should learn not only to love their charges but to respect them and treat them with the consideration one would give all living things. It must be emphasized to youngsters that the puppy has certain needs, just as humans have, and all family members must take an active role in ensuring that these needs are met. Someone must feed the puppy. Someone must walk him a couple of times a day or clean up after him if he is trained to relieve himself on newspaper. Someone must groom nis coat, clean his ears, and clip his nails from time to time. Someone

must see to it that the puppy gets sufficient exercise and attention each day.

A child who has a pet to care for learns responsibility; nonetheless, parental guidance is an essential part of his learning experience. Many a child has been known to "love a pet to death," squeezing and hugging the animal in ways which are irritating or even painful. Others have been found guilty of teasing, perhaps unintentionally, and disturbing their pet while the animal is eating or resting. One must teach a child, therefore, when and how to gently stroke and fondle a puppy. In time, the child can learn how to carefully pick up and handle the pup. A dog should always be supported with both hands, *not* lifted by the scruff of the neck. One hand placed under the chest, between the front legs, and the other hand supporting the dog's rear end will be comfortable and will restrain the animal as you hold and carry him. Always demonstrate to children the proper way to lift a dog.

BE A GOOD NEIGHBOR

For the sake of your dog's safety and well being, don't allow him to wander onto the property of others. Keep him confined at all times to your own yard or indoors where he won't become a nuisance. Consider what

Not only will you receive more companionship and loyalty from two Basenjis but added protection as well. Although the Basenji is not a "man-stopper" as such, his constant wariness and alert way make him a noteworthy watchdog. Owners, Karen Jenkins and Margaret Gougelman. Agent, Gwendolyn Wolforth.

Clockwise from upper right: *pokeweed, jimson weed, foxglove, and yew.* If ingested, any toxic plant can be dangerous to your dog.

ROVER WILL NOT BE HARMED IF YOU FOLLOW MY INSTRUCTIONS

AMF

Dog theft is not an uncommon event. Dognappers will steal either a purebred or mongrel puppy so all owners must always be wary.

dangers lie ahead for an unleashed dog that has total freedom of the great outdoors, particularly when he is unsupervised by his master. There are cars and trucks to dodge on the streets and highways. There are stray animals with which to wrangle. There are poisons all around, such as car antifreeze in driveways or toxic plants and shrubs, which, if swallowed, could prove fatal. There are dognappers and sadistic people who may steal or bring harm to your beloved pet. In short, there are all sorts of nasty things waiting to hurt him. Did you know that if your dog consumes rotting garbage, there is the possibility he could go into shock or even die? And are you aware that a dog left to roam in a wooded area or field could become infected with any number of parasites if he plays with or ingests some small prey, such as a rabbit, that might be carrying these parasitic organisms? A thorn from a rosebush imbedded in the dog's foot pad, tar from a newly paved road stuck to his coat, and a wound inflicted by a wild animal all can be avoided if you take the precaution of keeping your dog in a safe enclosure where he will be protected from such dangers. Don't let your dog run loose; he is likely to stray from home and get into all sorts of trouble.

The New Family Member

GETTING ACQUAINTED

Plan to bring your new pet home in the morning so that by nightfall he will have had some time to become acquainted with you and his new environment. Avoid introducing the pup to the family around holiday time, since all of the extra excitement will only add to the confusion and frighten him. Let the puppy enter your home on a day when the

Resist the temptation to handle him too much during these first few days. And, if there are other dogs or animals around the house, make certain all are properly introduced. If you observe fighting among the animals, or some other problem, you may have to separate all parties until they learn to accept one another. Remember that neglecting your other pets while

routine is normal. For those people who work during the week, a Saturday morning is an ideal time to bring the puppy to his new home; this way he has the entire weekend to make adjustments before being left alone for a few hours, come Monday morning.

Let the puppy explore, under your watchful eye of course, and let him come to know his new home without stress and fear.

Basenjis are both active and quick-thinking. Owners should supervise their activities, especially when outdoors. If bored, the Basenji may occasionally resort to deviltry.

Facing page: *Although the Basenji is particularly celebrated for its keen eyesight, its ears are also impressive. Placed rather prominently on the head, they exude readiness and attentiveness.*

showering the new puppy with extra attention will only cause animosity and jealousy. Make an effort to pay special attention to the other animals as well.

On that eventful first night, try not to give in and let the puppy sleep with you; otherwise, this could become a difficult habit to break. Let him cry and whimper, even if it means a night of restlessness for the entire family. Some people have had success with putting a doll or a hot water bottle wrapped in a towel in the puppy's bed as a surrogate mother, while others have placed a ticking alarm clock in the bed to simulate the heartbeat of the pup's dam and littermates. Remember that this furry little fellow is used to the warmth and security of his mother and siblings, so the adjustment to sleeping alone will take time. Select a location away from drafts and away from the feeding station for placement of his dog bed. Keep in mind, also, that the bed should be roomy enough for him to stretch out in; as he grows older, you may need to supply a larger one.

Prior to the pup's arrival, set up his room and partition it the way you would to keep an infant out of a particular area. You may want to keep his bed, his feeding station, and his toilet area all in the same room—in separate locations—or you may want to set the feeding station up in your kitchen, where meals for all family members are served. Whatever you decide, do it ahead of time so you will have that much less to worry about when your puppy finally moves in with you.

Above all else, be patient with your puppy as he adjusts to life in his new home. If you purchase a pup that is not housebroken, you will have to spend time with the dog—just as you would with a small child—until he develops proper toilet habits. Even a housebroken puppy may feel nervous in strange new surroundings and have an occasional accident. Praise and encouragement will elicit far better results than punishment or scolding. Remember that your puppy wants nothing more than to please you, thus he is anxious to learn the behavior that is required of him.

Feeding Requirements

Perhaps more than any other single aspect of your dog's development, proper feeding requires an educated and responsible dog owner. The importance of nutrition on your dog's bone and muscle growth cannot be overemphasized.

Soon after your puppy comes to live with you, he will need to be fed. Remember to ask the seller what foods were given to the youngster and stay with that diet for a while. It is important for the puppy to keep eating and to avoid skipping a meal, so entice him with the food to which he is accustomed. If you prefer to switch to some other brand of dog food, each day begin to add small quantities of the new brand to the usual food offering. Make the portions of the new food progressively larger until the pup is weaned from his former diet.

What should you feed the puppy and how often? His diet is really quite simple and relatively inexpensive to prepare. Puppies need to be fed small portions at frequent intervals, since they are growing and their activity level is high. You must ensure that your pup gains weight steadily; with an adult dog, however, growth slows down and weight must be regulated to prevent obesity and a host of other problems. At one time, it was thought that home-cooked meals were the answer, with daily rations of meat,

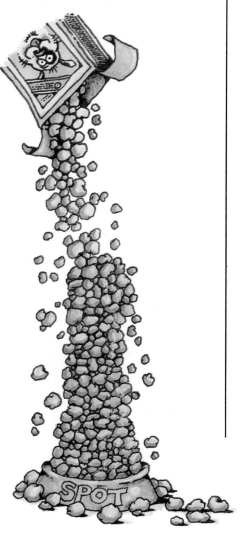

Choosing a quality dog food from your pet shop is easy—deciding how much to feed may not be as straightforward. Feedings must always be carefully monitored.

59

vegetables, egg yolk, cereal, cheese, brewer's yeast, and vitamin supplements. With all of the nutritionally complete commercial dog food products readily available, these time-consuming preparations really are unnecessary now. A great deal of money and research has resulted in foods that we can serve our dogs with confidence and pride; and most of these commercial foods have been developed along strict guidelines according to the size, weight, and age of your dog. These products are reasonably priced, easy to find, and convenient to store.

THE PUPPY'S MEALS

After a puppy has been fully weaned from its mother until approximately three months of age, it needs to be fed four times a day. In the morning and evening offer kibble (dog meal) soaked in hot water or broth, to which you have added some canned meat-based food or fresh raw meat cut into small chunks. At noon and bedtime feed him a bit of kibble or whole-grain cereal moistened with milk (moistening, by the way, makes the food easier to digest, since dogs don't typically chew their food). From three to six months, increase the portion size and

Up until six weeks of age, puppies need to be fed at least three times per day. Proper nourishment is essential to your dog's proper development. Owner, Daniels Kennels.

Basenjis in mid-air amusement. Although small dogs, Basenjis appreciate a lot of open ground to run and play. Owner, White Kennel.

offer just three meals—one milk and two meat. At six months, two meals are sufficient; at one year, a single meal can be given, supplemented with a few dry biscuits in the morning and evening. During the colder months, especially if your dog is active, you might want to mix in some wheat germ oil or corn oil or bacon drippings with the meal to add extra calories. Remember to keep a bowl of cool, fresh water on hand always to help your dog regulate its body temperature and to aid in digestion.

From one year on, you may continue feeding the mature dog a single meal (in the evening, perhaps, when you have your supper), or you may prefer to divide this meal in two, offering half in the morning and the other half at night. Keep in mind that while puppies require foods in small chunks, or nuggets, older dogs can handle larger pieces of food at mealtime. Discuss your dog's feeding schedule with your veterinarian; he can make suggestions about the right diet for your particular canine friend.

COMPARISON SHOPPING

With so many fine dog-food products on the market today, there is something for everyone's pet. You may want to serve dry food "as is" or mix it with warm water or broth. Perhaps you'll choose to combine dry food with fresh or canned preparations. Some canned foods contain all meat, but they are not complete; others are mixtures of meat and grains, which have been fortified with additional nutrients to make them more complete and balanced. There are also various packaged foods that can be served alone or as supplements and that can be left out for a few hours without spoiling. This self-feeding method, which works well for dogs that are not prone to weight problems, allows the animal to serve himself whenever he feels hungry. Many people who work during the day find these dry or semi-moist rations convenient to use, and these foods are great to bring along if you travel with your dog.

Be sure to read the labels carefully before you make your dog-food purchases. Most

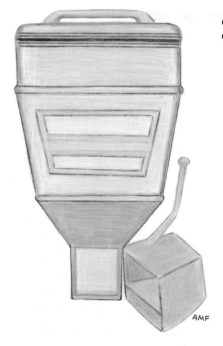

Feeder bins are used by many kennel owners as well as pet owners. These devices help to conveniently store and distribute dry foods in a sanitary, efficient way.

Vitamin/mineral and other food supplements can be formulated for general nutritional value or for particular purposes, such as skin and coat enhancement and/or flea and tick elimination. Photo courtesy of Four Paws.

reputable pet-food manufacturers list the ingredients and the nutritional content right on the can or package. Instructions are usually included so that you will know how much to feed your dog to keep him thriving and in top condition. A varied, well-balanced diet that supplies the proper amounts of protein, carbohydrate, fat, vitamins, minerals, and water is important to keep your puppy healthy and to guarantee his normal development. Adjustments to the diet can be made, under your veterinarian's supervision, according to the individual puppy, his rate of growth, his activity level, and so on. Liquid or powder vitamin and mineral supplements, or those in tablet form, are available and can be given if you need to feel certain that the diet is balanced.

Basically a contented dog, the Basenji thrives on human attention and companionship. He loves to be with his people and takes pride in his ability to communicate his feelings. Owner, Yannarella Kennel.

DEVELOPING GOOD EATING HABITS

Try to serve your puppy his meals at the same time each day and in the same location so that he will get used to his daily routine and develop good eating habits. A bit of raw egg, cottage cheese, or table scraps (leftover food from your own meals) can

Feeding your dog is made easy by the use of sturdy non-tip, easy-clean bowls. Pet shops offer the best selection of colors, styles and sizes.

be offered from time to time; but never accustom your dog to eating human "junk food." Cake, candy, chocolate, soda, and other snack foods are for people, not dogs. Besides, these foods provide only "empty" calories that your pet doesn't need if he is to stay healthy. Avoid offering spicy, fried, fatty, or starchy foods; rather, offer leftover meats, vegetables, and gravies. Get in the habit of feeding your puppy or your grown dog his *own* daily meals of dog food. If ever you are in doubt about what foods and how much to serve, consult your veterinarian.

FEEDING GUIDELINES

Some things to bear in mind with regard to your dog's feeding regimen follow.

● Nutritional balance, provided by many commercial dog foods, is vital; avoid feeding a one-sided all-meat diet. Variety in the kinds of meat (beef, lamb, chicken, liver) or cereal grains (wheat, oats, corn) that

Automatic feeders are handy modern devices, available from most good pet shops. Overfeeding can be a drawback of this method of feeding.

AMF

you offer your dog is of secondary importance compared to the balance or "completeness" of dietary components.

● Always refrigerate opened canned food so that it doesn't spoil. Remember to remove all uneaten portions of canned or moistened food from the feeding dish as soon as the pup has finished his meal. Discard the leftover food immediately and thoroughly wash and dry the feeding dish, as a dirty dish is a breeding ground for harmful germs.

● When offering dry foods, always keep a supply of water on hand for your dog. Water should be made available at all times, even if dry foods are not left out for self-feeding. Each day the water dish should be washed with soap and hot water, rinsed well, and dried; a refill of clean, fresh water should be provided daily.

● Food and water should be served at room temperature, neither too hot nor too cold, so that it is more palatable for your puppy.

● Serve your pup's meals in sturdy hard-plastic, stainless steel, or earthenware containers, ones that won't tip over as the dog gulps his food down. Some bowls and dishes are weighted to prevent spillage, while others fit neatly into holders which offer support. Feeding dishes should be large enough to hold each meal.

- Whenever the nutritional needs of your dog change—that is to say, when it grows older or if it becomes ill, obese, or pregnant; or if it starts to nurse its young—special diets are in order. Always contact your vet for advice on these special dietary requirements.

- Hard foods, such as biscuits and dog meal, should be offered regularly. Chewing on these hard, dry morsels helps the dog keep its teeth clean and its gums conditioned.
- Never overfeed your dog. If given the chance, he will accept and relish every in-between-meal tidbit you offer him. This pampering will only put extra weight on your pet and cause him to be unhealthy.

New treats on the block by Chooz®. These crunchy dog bones are delectable and affordable.

- Feed your puppy at the same regular intervals each day; reserve treats for special occasions or, perhaps, to reward good behavior.

- Do not encourage your dog to beg for food from the table while you are eating your meals.
- Food can be effectively used by the owner to train the dog. Doggie treats are practical and often nutritional—choose your chew treats choosily.

FEEDING CHART

Age and No. of Feedings Per Day	Weight in Lbs.	Weight in Kg.	Caloric Requirement kcal M.E./Day
Puppies—Weaning to 3 months Four per day	1–3 3–6 6–12 12–20 15–30	.5–1.4 1.4–2.7 2.7–5.4 5.4–9.1 6.8–13.6	124–334 334–574 574–943 943–1384 1113–1872
Puppies—3 to 6 months Three per day	3–10 5–15 12–25 20–40 30–70	1.4–4.5 2.3–6.8 5.4–11.3 9.1–18.2 13.6–31.8	334–816 494–1113 943–1645 1384–2352 1872–3542
Puppies—6 to 12 months Two per day	6–12 12–25 20–50 40–70 70–100	2.7–5.4 5.4–11.3 9.1–22.7 18.2–31.8 31.8–45.4	574–943 943–1645 1384–2750 2352–3542 3542–4640
Normally Active Adults One or two per day	6–12 12–25 25–50 50–90 90–175	2.7–5.4 5.4–11.3 11.3–22.7 22.7–40.8 40.8–79.4	286–472 472–823 823–1375 1375–2151 2151–3675

This chart presents general parameters of the dog's caloric requirements, based on weight. The total caloric intake comes from a complete, balanced diet of quality foods. To assist owners, dog food companies generally provide the nutritional information to their product right on the label.

Accommodations

Puppies newly weaned from their mother and siblings should be kept warm at all times. As they get older, they can be acclimated gradually to cooler temperatures. When you purchase your dog, find out from the seller whether he is hardy and can withstand the rigors of outdoor living. Many breeds have been known to adapt well to a surprising number of environments, so long as they are given time to adjust. If your pup is to be an indoor for your pooch; or you may find that a heated garage or finished basement works well as your dog's living quarters. If your breed can tolerate living outside, you may want to buy or build him his own dog house with an attached run. It might be feasible to place his house in your fenced-in backyard. The breed that can live outdoors fares well when given access to some sort of warm, dry shelter during periods of inclement weather. As you begin thinking about where

companion, perhaps a dog bed in the corner of the family room will suffice; or you may want to invest in a crate for him to call his "home" whenever he needs to be confined for short intervals. You might plan to partition off a special room, or part of a room,

A bed for your dog gives him a place to call his own. His bed should be placed in a warm, dry, draft-free area.

Accommodations

your canine friend will spend most of his time, you'll want to consider his breed, his age, his temperament, his need for exercise, and the money, space, and resources you have available to house him.

your puppy something with which to snuggle, such as a laundered towel or blanket or an article of old clothing. Some dogs have been known to chew apart their beds and bedding, but you can easily channel this

THE DOG BED

In preparing for your puppy's arrival, it is recommended that a dog bed be waiting for him so that he has a place to sleep and rest. If you have provided him with his own bed or basket, ensure that it is placed in a warm, dry, draft-free spot that is private but at the same time near the center of family activity. Refrain from placing his bed near the feed and water dishes or his toilet area. You may want to give

Beds can have personality. Pet shops offer many different bedding options to the owner willing to explore.

chewing energy into more constructive behavior simply by supplying him with some safe toys or a Nylabone® pacifier for gnawing. Pet shops stock dog beds, among other supplies that you might need for your pup. Select a bed that is roomy, comfortable, and easy to clean, keeping in mind that you may have to replace the smaller bed with a larger one as the puppy grows to adulthood. Remember to clean and disinfect the bed and sleeping area from time to time, as these can become parasitic playgrounds for fleas, lice, mites, and the like.

THE CRATE

Although many dog lovers may cringe at the mere mention of the word *crate,* thinking of it as a cage or a cruel means of confinement, this handy piece of equipment can be put to good use for puppies and grown dogs alike. Even though you may love your dog to an extraordinary degree, you may not want him to have free reign of the house, particularly when you are not home to supervise him. If used properly, a crate can restrict your dog when it is not convenient to have him underfoot, *i.e.,* when guests are visiting or during your mealtimes.

A surprising number of dog owners, who originally had negative feelings about crating their dogs, have had great success using crates. The crate itself serves as a bed, provided it is furnished with bedding material, or it can be used as an indoor dog house. Not all dogs

The wire crate is a most effective means to accelerate housebreaking and is the safest way to ensure that the puppy is safe when he cannot be supervised.

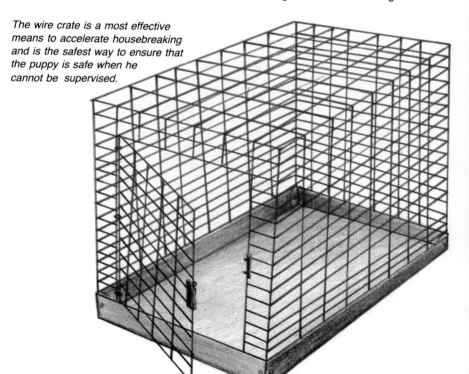

readily accept crates or being confined in them for short intervals, so for these dogs, another means of restriction must be found. But for those dogs that do adjust to spending time in these structures, the crate can be useful in many ways. The animal can be confined for a few hours while you are away from home or at work, or you can bring your

If your living arrangement allows, an outdoor run connected to the house by a swinging pet door can provide an ideal accommodation for your dog.

crated dog along with you in the car when you travel or go on vacation. Crates also prove handy as carriers whenever you have to transport a sick dog to the veterinarian.

Most crates are made of sturdy wire or plastic, and some of the collapsible models can be conveniently stored or folded so that they can be moved easily from room to room or from inside the house to the yard on a warm, sunny day. If you allow your puppy or grown dog to become acquainted with its crate by cleverly propping the door open and leaving some of his favorite toys inside, in no time he

will come to regard the crate as his own doggie haven. As with a dog bed, place the crate away from drafts in a dry, warm spot; refrain from placing food and water dishes in it, as these only crowd the space and offer opportunity for spillage.

If you need to confine your puppy so that he can't get into mischief while you're not home, remember to consider the animal's needs at all times. Select a large crate, one in which the dog can stand up and move around comfortably; in fact, bigger is better in this context. Never leave the animal confined for more than a few hours at a time without letting him out to exercise, play, and, if necessary, relieve himself. Never crate a dog for ten hours, for example, unless you keep the door to the crate open so that he can get out for food and water and to stretch a bit. If long intervals of confinement are necessary, consider placing the unlatched crate in a partitioned section of your house or apartment.

Crates have become the answer for many a dog owner faced with the dilemma of either getting rid of a destructive dog or living with him despite his bad habits. People who have neither the time nor the patience to train their dogs, or to modify undesirable behavior patterns, can at least restrain their pets during the times they can't be

Traveling crates can provide safe and easy transport for your dog. Ventilation for travel is a most important consideration.

there to supervise. So long as the crate is used in a humane fashion, whereby a dog is confined for no more than a few hours at any one time, it can figure importantly in a dog owner's life. Show dogs,

The pet trade offers many commercially made dog houses and other outdoor living structures that make great temporary accommodations for your pet.

incidentally, learn at an early age that much time will be spent in and out of crates while they are on the show circuit. Many canine celebrities are kept in their crates until they are called to ringside, and they spend many hours crated to and from the shows.

THE DOG HOUSE

These structures, often made of wood, should be sturdy and offer enough room for your dog to stretch out in when it rests or sleeps. Dog houses that are elevated or situated on a platform protect the animal from cold and dampness that may seep through the ground. For the breeds that are temperature hardy and will live outdoors, a dog house is an excellent option for daytime occupancy. Owners who cannot provide indoor accommodations for their chosen dog should consider a smaller breed since no dog should lead an exclusively outdoor existence.

If you have no option but to accommodate your dog with only an outdoor house, it will be necessary to provide him with a more elaborate house, one that really protects him from the elements. Make sure the dog's house is constructed of waterproof materials. Furnish him with sufficient bedding to burrow into on a chilly night and provide extra insulation to keep out drafts and wet weather. Add a partition (a kind of room divider which separates the entry area from the main sleeping space) inside his house or attach a swinging door to the entrance to help keep him warm when he is inside his residence. The

Indoor-outdoor dog houses offer pest-free, sanitary conditions for your dog. These attractive living options can be acquired from pet shops, supply outlets or mail-order catalogues.

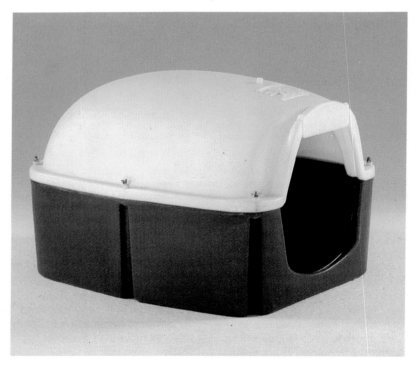

swinging door facilitates entry to and from the dog house, while at the same time it provides protection, particularly from wind and drafts.

Some fortunate owners whose yards are enclosed by high freedom is a dog kennel or run which attaches to or surrounds the dog's house. This restricts some forms of movement, such as running, perhaps, but it does provide ample room for walking, climbing, jumping, and

An anchored lead can provide efficient temporary restraint. This is not a viable substitute for a fenced-in yard and no dog should be left unsupervised on such a lead for any length of time.

fencing allow their dogs complete freedom within the boundaries of their property. In these situations, a dog can leave his dog house and get all the exercise he wants. Of course such a large space requires more effort to keep it clean. An alternative to complete backyard stretching. Another option is to fence off part of the yard and place the dog house in the enclosure. If you need to tether your dog to its house, make certain to use a fairly long lead so as not to hamper the animal's need to move and exercise his limbs.

CLEANLINESS

No matter where your dog lives, either in or out of your home, be sure to keep him in surroundings that are as clean and sanitary as possible. His excrement should be removed and disposed of every day without fail. No dog should be forced to lie in his own feces. If your dog lives in his own house, the floor should be swept occasionally and the bedding should be changed regularly if it becomes soiled. Food and water dishes need to be scrubbed with hot water and detergent and rinsed well to remove all traces of soap. The water dish should be refilled with a supply of fresh water. The dog and his environment must be kept free of parasites (especially fleas and mosquitoes, which can carry disease) with products designed to keep these pests under control. Dog crates need frequent scrubbing, too, as do the floors of kennels and runs. Your pet must be kept clean and comfortable at all times; if you exercise strict sanitary control, you will keep disease and parasite infestation to a minimum.

EXERCISE

A well-balanced diet and regular medical attention from a qualified veterinarian are essential in promoting good health for your dog, but so is

Most cities and towns require dog owners to clean up after their pets. Commercial pooper scoopers can make curbing your dog more convenient and sanitary.

daily exercise to keep him fit and mentally alert. Dogs that have been confined all day while their owners are at work or school need special attention. There should be some time set aside each day for play—a romp with a family member, perhaps. Not everyone is lucky enough to let his dog run through an open meadow or along a sandy beach, but even a ten-minute walk in the fresh air will do Dogs that are house-bound, particularly those that live in apartments, need to

Flying discs are popular with most dog owners, child and adult alike. Many dogs display a natural talent for Frisbee® games.

be walked out-of-doors after each meal so that they can relieve themselves. Owners can make this daily ritual more pleasant both for themselves

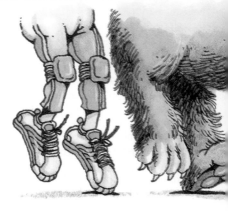

and their canine companions by combining the walk with a little "roughhousing," that is to say, a bit of fun and togetherness.

Whenever possible, take a stroll to an empty lot, a playground, or a nearby park. Attach a long lead to your dog's collar, and let him run and jump and tone his body through aerobic activity. This will help him burn calories and will keep him trim, and it will also help relieve tension and stress that may have had a chance to develop while you were away all day. For people who work Monday through Friday, weekend jaunts can be especially beneficial, since there will be more time to spend with your canine friend. You might want to engage him in a simple game of fetch with a stick or a rubber ball. Even such basic tricks as rolling over, standing on

by all means do it. Don't neglect your pet and leave him confined for long periods without attention from you or time for exercise.

the hindlegs, or jumping up (all of which can be done inside the home as well) can provide additional exercise. But if you plan to challenge your dog with a real workout to raise his heart rate, remember not to push him too hard without first warming up with a brisk walk. Don't forget to "cool him down" afterwards with a rhythmic trot until his heart rate returns to normal. Some dog owners jog with their dogs or take them along on bicycle excursions.

At the very least, however, play with your dog every day to keep him in good shape physically and mentally. If you can walk him outdoors, or better yet run with him in a more vigorous activity,

Fitness and exercise are on the move. Getting in on the trim-and-active side ain't just a doggie obsession—owners should sneak in too!

EXERCISING FOR YOU AND YOUR DOG

Dogs are like people. They come in three weights: overweight, underweight, and the correct weight. It is fair to say that most dogs are in better shape than most humans who own them. The reason for this is that most dogs accept exercise without objection—people do not! Follow your dog's lead towards exercise and the complete enjoyment of the outdoors—your dog is the ideal work-out partner. There are toys

79

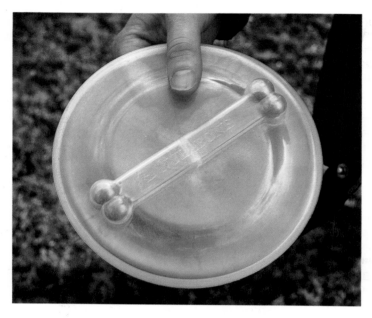

at your local pet shop which are designed just for that purpose: to allow you to play and exercise with your dog. Here are a few recommended exercise toys for you and your dog.

Frisbee® Flying Discs Most dog owners capitalize on the dog's natural instinct to fetch or retrieve, and the Frisbee® flying disc is standard fare for play. The original Frisbee® is composed of polyethylene plastic, ideal for flying and great for games of catch between two humans. Since humans don't usually chew on their flying discs, there is no need for a "chew-worthy" construction material. Dogs, on the other

The most popular in flying discs designed especially for dogs is the Nylabone Frisbee®, a toy that outlasts plastic discs by ten times. The molded dog bone on the top makes for easy retrieves by your dog.

hand, do chew on their Frisbees® and therefore should not be allowed to play with a standard original Frisbee®. These discs will be destroyed quickly by the dog and the rigid plastic can cause intestinal complications.

Nylon Discs More suitable for playing with dogs are the Frisbee® discs that are constructed from nylon. These durable Frisbee® discs are designed especially for dogs and the nearly indestructible manufacturing makes them ideal for aggressive chewing dogs. For play with dogs, the nylon discs called Nylabone Frisbee® are guaranteed to last ten times as long as the regular plastic Frisbee®. Owners should carefully consider the size of the nylon Frisbee® they purchase. A rule of thumb is choose the largest disc that your dog can comfortably carry. Nylabone manufactures two sizes only— toy and large—so the choice should be apparent.

Polyurethane Flexible Floppy Flying Discs The greatest advance in flying discs came with the manufacture of these discs from polyurethane. The polyurethane is so soft that it doesn't hurt you, your dog, or the window it might strike accidentally. The polyurethane Gumadisc® is floppy and soft. It can be folded and fits into your pocket. It is also much tougher than cheap plastics, and most pet shops guarantee that it will last ten times longer than cheap plastic discs.

Making the polyurethane discs even more suited to dog play is the fact that many of the Gumabone® Frisbee® Flexible Fly Discs have the advantage of a dog bone molded on the top. Very often a Frisbee® without the bone molded on the top is difficult for a dog to pick up

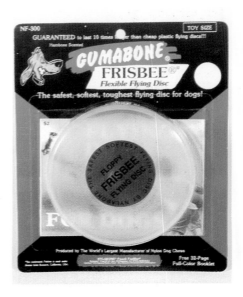

Made of durable and flexible polyurethane, the Gumabone Frisbees® prove chew-worthy and good-smelling to dogs. These and other Nylabone® discs are available in pet shops and other stores.

*Frisbee® is a trademark of the Kransco Company, California, and is used for their brand of flying disc.

when it lands on a flat surface. The molded ones enable the dog to grasp it with his mouth or turn it with his paw. Dogs love pawing at the bone and even chew on it occasionally.

This product has one further capacity—it doubles as a temporary drinking dish while out running, hiking and playing. The Gumabone Frisbee® flyers may also be flavored or scented, besides being annealed, so your dog can find it more easily if it should get lost in woods or tall grass.

with your canine friend. Basically, you play with the dog and the disc so the dog knows the disc belongs to him. Then you throw it continuously,

Toys made for doggie tug-of-wars are popular with lots of pet owners. These tug toys are durable and last a long time.

Flying discs manufactured by the Nylabone® Company may cost more than some of its imitators, but an owner can be assured that the product will last and not be quickly destroyed.

With most flying discs made for dogs comes an instruction booklet on how to use the disc

increasing the distance, so that the dog fetches it and brings it back to you.

The exercise for you comes in when your dog stops fetching it, or when you have a partner. The two of you play catch. You stand as far apart as available space allows—usually 30–35 m (100

Great for the athletic dog and less-active owner are commercially designed retractable leads which give the dog much freedom when exercising in an open field or cleared area.

feet) is more than enough room. You throw the disc to each other, arousing your dog's interest as he tries to catch it. When the disc is dropped or veers off, the dog grabs it and brings it back (hopefully). Obviously you will have to run to catch the disc before your dog does.

There are contests held all over the world where distance, height, and other characteristics are measured competitively. Ask your local pet shop to help you locate a Frisbee® Club near you.

Tug Toys A tug toy is a hard rubber, cheap plastic, or polyurethane toy which allows a

*Frisbee® is a trademark of the Kransco Company, California, and is used for their brand of flying disc.

The more consideration given to the canine's needs, the better the outdoor accommodations will be. Owners planning an outdoor kennel set-up must consider the elements (sun, rain, and wind) as well as sanitation and security.

dog and his owner to have a game of tug-o-war. The owner grips one end while the dog grips the other—then they pull. The polyurethane flexible tug toy is the best on the market at the present time. Your pet shop will have one to show you. The polyurethane toys are clear in color and stay soft forever. Cheap plastic tug toys are indisputably dangerous, and the hard-rubber tug toys get brittle too fast and are too stiff for most dogs; however, there *is* a difference in price—just ask the advice of any pet shop operator.

Balls Nobody has to tell you about playing ball with your dog. The reminder you may need is that you should not throw the ball where traffic might interfere with the dog's catching or fetching of it. The ball should not be cheap plastic (a dog's worst enemy as far as toys are concerned) but made of a substantial material. Balls made of nylon are practically indestructible, but they are very hard and must be rolled, never thrown. The same balls made of polyurethane are great—they bounce and are soft. The Nylaballs® and Gumaballs® are scented and flavored, and dogs can easily find them when lost.

Other manufacturers make balls of almost every substance, including plastic, cotton, and wood. Soft balls, baseballs, tennis balls, and so on, have all been used by dog owners who want their dogs to play with them in a game of catch. A strong caveat is that you use only those balls made especially for dogs.

It pays to invest in entertainment toys and exercise devices which are marketed particularly for dogs. These products outlast everyday play things and are much safer for your pet. The Gumaball® is a great example of a dog toy worth the price of admission.

Housebreaking is required training for all puppies and even some older dogs who come in to new homes. There are many experience-based rules for the housebreaking owner to follow, including the use of a restricted area and close supervision. If approached thoughtfully and intelligently, housebreaking should proceed smoothly to its completion.

Housebreaking and Training

The value of the news may be waning in recent years, but newspaper will always have a worthwhile purpose to the new dog owner.

HOUSEBREAKING

The new addition to your family may already have received some basic house training before his arrival in your home. If he has not, remember that a puppy will want to relieve himself about half a dozen times a day; it is up to you to specify where and when he should "do his business." Housebreaking is your first training concern and should begin the moment you bring the puppy home.

Ideally, puppies should be taken outdoors after meals, as a full stomach will exert pressure on the bladder and colon. What

goes into the dog must eventually come out; the period after his meal is the most natural and appropriate time. When he eliminates, he should be praised, for this will increase the likelihood of the same thing happening after every meal. He should also be encouraged to that your pet will associate the act of elimination with a particular word of your choice rather than with a particular time or place which might not always be convenient or available. So whether you are visiting an unfamiliar place or don't want to go outside with your dog in sub-

Housebreaking pads, used by many cautious owners instead of the ever trusty press, can be purchased in pet shops and pet supply outlets.

use the same area and will probably be attracted to it after frequent use.

Some veterinarians maintain that a puppy can learn to urinate and defecate on command, if properly trained. The advantage of this conditioning technique is zero temperatures, he will still be able to relieve himself when he hears the specific command word. Elimination will occur after this "trigger" phrase or word sets up a conditioned reflex in the dog, who will eliminate anything contained in his bladder or bowel upon hearing it. The shorter the word, the more you can repeat it and imprint it on your dog's memory.

Your chosen command word should be given simultaneously with the sphincter opening events in order to achieve perfect and rapid conditioning. This is why it is important to familiarize yourself with the tell-tale signs preceding your puppy's elimination process. Then you will be prepared to say the word at the crucial moment. There is usually a sense of urgency on the dog's part; he will soon learn to associate the act with the word. One word of advice, however, if you plan to try out this method: never use the puppy's name or any other word which he might frequently hear about the house—you can imagine the result!

Finally, remember that any training takes time. Such a conditioned response can be obtained with intensive practice with any normal, healthy dog over six weeks of age. Even Pavlov's salivating dogs required fifty repetitions before the desired response was achieved.

Crates assist in potty-training the puppy. The dog's natural instinct is never to soil his sleeping area.

may follow a sniffing and circling pattern which you will soon recognize. It is important to use the command in his usual area only when you know the puppy can eliminate, i.e., when his stomach or bladder is full. He Patience and persistence will eventually produce results—do not lose heart!

Indoors, sheets of newspapers can be used to cover the specific area where your dog should relieve himself. These should be placed some distance away from his sleeping and feeding area, as a puppy will not urinate or defecate where he eats. When the newspapers are changed, the bottom papers should be placed on top of the new ones in order to reinforce the purpose of

the run of the house, the sheer size of the place will seem overwhelming and confusing and he might leave his "signature" on your furniture or clothes! There will be time later to familiarize him gradually with his new surroundings.

The choke collar and walking lead are commonly used in training.

the papers by scent as well as by sight. The puppy should be praised during or immediately after he has made use of this particular part of the room. Each positive reinforcement increases the possibility of his using that area again.

When he arrives, it is advisable to limit the puppy to one room, usually the kitchen, as it most likely has a linoleum or easily washable floor surface. Given

PATIENCE, PERSISTENCE, AND PRAISE

As with a human baby, you must be patient, tolerant, and understanding of your pet's mistakes, making him feel loved and wanted, not rejected and isolated. You wouldn't hit a baby for soiling his diapers, as you would realize that he was not yet able to control his bowel movements; be as compassionate with your canine infant. Never rub his nose in his excreta. Never indulge in the common practice of punishing him with a rolled-up newspaper. Never hit a puppy with your hand. He will only become "hand-shy" and learn to fear you. Usually the punishment is meted out sometime after the offense and loses its efficacy, as the bewildered dog cannot connect the two events. Moreover, by association, he will soon learn to be afraid of you and anything to do with newspapers—including, perhaps, that area where he is *supposed* to relieve himself!

A simple dog collar or leash can be deceiving. Never be afraid to ask your pet shop proprietor exactly how a particular device is intended to work.

Most puppies are eager to please. Praise, encouragement, and reward (particularly the food variety) will produce far better results than any scolding or physical punishment. Moreover, it is far better to dissuade your puppy from doing certain things, such as chewing on chair legs or other furniture, by making those objects particularly distasteful to him. Some pet shops stock bitter apple sprays or citronella compounds for application to furniture legs. These products are generally safer than old-fashioned home remedies. An owner may soon discover that application of these products may indeed make it seem as if the object itself was administering the punishment whenever he attempted to chew it. He probably wouldn't need a second reminder and your furniture will remain undamaged.

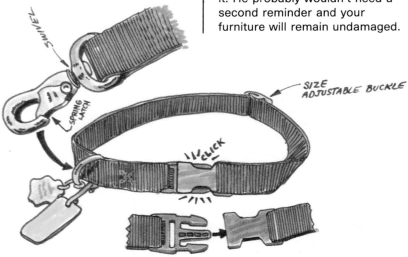

Remember that the reason a dog has housebreaking or behavior problems is because his owner has allowed them to develop. This is why you must begin as you intend to continue, letting your dog know what is acceptable and unacceptable behavior. It is also important that you be consistent in your

A choke collar can be an effective training tool when properly used.

demands; you cannot feed him from the dining room table one day and then punish him when he begs for food from your dinner guests.

TRAINING

You will want the newest member of your family to be welcomed by everyone; this will

not happen if he urinates in every room of the house or barks all night! He needs training in the correct forms of behavior in this new human world. You cannot expect your puppy to become the perfect pet overnight. He needs your help in his socialization process. Training greatly facilitates and enhances the relationship of the dog to his owner and to the rest of society. A successfully trained dog can be taken anywhere and behave well with anyone. Indeed, it is that one crucial word—*training*—which can transform an aggressive animal into a peaceful, well-behaved pet. Now, how does this "transformation" take place?

WHEN AND HOW TO TRAIN

Like housebreaking, training should begin as soon as the puppy enters the house. The formal training sessions should be short but frequent, for example, ten to fifteen minute periods three times a day. These are much more effective than long, tiring sessions of half an hour which might soon become boring. You are building your relationship with your puppy during these times, so make them as enjoyable as possible. It is a good idea to have these sessions *before* the puppy's meal, not after it when he wouldn't feel like exerting himself; the dog will then

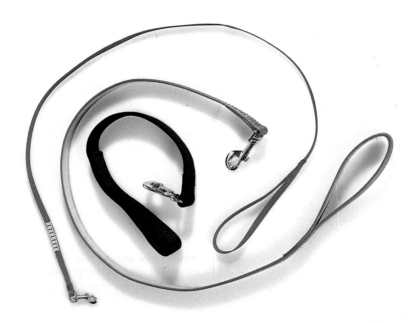

associate something pleasurable with his training sessions and look forward to them.

THE COLLAR AND LEASH

Your puppy should become used to a collar and leash as soon as possible. If he is very young, a thin, choke-chain collar can be used, but you will need a larger and heavier one for training when he is a little older. Remember to have his name and address on an identification tag attached to his collar, as you don't want to lose your pet if he should happen to leave your premises and explore the neighborhood!

Nylon and leather leads are the most popular with pet owners.

Let the puppy wear his collar until he is used to how it feels. After a short time he will soon become accustomed to it and you can attach the leash. He might resist your attempts to lead him or simply sit down and refuse to budge. Fight him for a few minutes, tugging on the leash if necessary, then let him relax for the day. He won't be trained until he learns that he must obey the pull under any circumstance, but this will take a few sessions. Remember that a dog's period of concentration is short, so LITTLE and OFTEN is the wisest course of action—and patience is the password to success.

For safety purposes, as well as the comfort of your pet, be sure to choose the right-sized collar and a sensible leash for your daily walks.

GIVING COMMANDS

When you begin giving your puppy simple commands, make them as short as possible and use the same word with the same meaning at all times, for example, "Heel," "Sit," and "Stay." You must be consistent; otherwise your puppy will become confused. The dog's name should prefix all commands to attract his attention. Do not become impatient with him however many times you have to repeat your command.

A good way to introduce the "Come" command is by calling the puppy when his meal is ready. Once this is learned, you can call your pet to you at will, always remembering to praise him for his prompt obedience. This "reward," or positive reinforcement, is such a crucial part of training that a Director of the New York Academy of Dog Training constructed his whole teaching program upon the methods of "Love, Praise, and Reward." Incidentally, if you use the command "Come," use it every time. Don't switch to "Come here" or "Come boy," as this will only confuse your dog.

It is worth underlining the fact that punishment is an ineffective teaching technique. We have already seen this in housebreaking. For example, if your pup should run away, it would be senseless to beat him when he eventually returns; he would only connect the punishment with his return, not with running away! In addition, it is unwise to call him to you to punish him, as he will soon learn not to respond when you call his name.

Harnesses can be used for daily walks, though some dogs do not find them comfortable. Heavily coated dogs especially may object, and the harness can eventually wear on the dog's coat.

Housebreaking and Training

SOME SPECIFIC COMMANDS

"Sit" This is one of the easiest and most useful commands for your dog to learn, so it is a good idea to begin with it. The only equipment required is a leash, a collar, and a few tasty tidbits. Take your dog out for some exercise before his meal. After about five minutes, call him to you, praise him when he arrives,

Praise must be given when the dog correctly assumes the sit position. If praise is given before sitting or after the dog makes motion to rise, the dog may become confused.

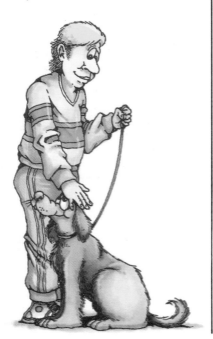

and slip his collar on him. Hold the leash tightly in your right hand; this should force the dog's head up and focus his attention on you. As you say "Sit" in a loud, clear voice, with your left hand press steadily on his rump until he is in a sitting position. As soon as he is in the correct position, praise him and give him the tidbit you have in your hand. Now wait a few minutes to let him rest and repeat the routine. Through repetition, the dog soon associates the word with the act. Never make the lesson too long. Eventually your praise will be reward enough for your puppy. Other methods to teach this command exist, but this one, executed with care and moderation, has proven the most effective.

"Sit-Stay/Stay" To teach your pet to remain in one place or "stay" on your command, first of all order him to the sitting position at your side. Lower your left hand with the flat of your palm in front of his nose and your fingers pointing downwards. Hold the leash high and taut behind his head so that he cannot move. Speak the command "Sit-stay" and, as you are giving it, step in front of him. Repeat the command and tighten the leash so the animal cannot follow you. Walk completely around him, repeating the command and keeping him

Great for the athletic dog and less-active owner are commercially designed retractable leads which give the dog much more freedom when exercising in an open field or cleared area. Photo courtesy of Flexi USA, Inc.

what you do while you are saying it. Give this command in a firm, clear tone, perhaps using a raised forefinger to warn the dog to "stay."

"Heel"
When you walk your dog, you should hold the leash firmly in your right hand. The dog should walk on your left so that the leash crosses your body, giving you greater control over the dog.

Let your dog lead you for the first few moments so that he fully understands that freedom can be his if he goes about it properly. He already knows that when he wants to go outdoors the leash and collar are necessary, so he has respect for the leash. Now, if he starts to pull in one direction while walking, all you do is *stop walking*. He will walk a few steps and then find that he can't walk any further. He will then turn and look into your face. *This is the crucial point!* Just stand there for a moment and stare right back at him . . . now walk another ten feet and stop again. Again your dog will probably walk to the end of the leash, find he can't go any further, and turn around and look again. If he starts to pull and

motionless by holding the leash at arm's length above him to check his movement. When he remains in this position for about fifteen seconds, you can begin the second part of the training. You will have to exchange the leash for a nylon cord or rope about twenty to thirty feet long. Repeat the whole routine from the beginning and be ready to prevent any movement towards you with a sharp "Sit-Stay." Move around him in everwidening circles until you are about fifteen feet away from him. If he still remains seated, you can pat yourself on the back! Remember that the dog makes associations with jerk, just stand there. After he quiets down, bend down and comfort him, as he may be frightened. Keep up this training until he learns not to outwalk you.

Once the puppy obeys the pull of the leash, half of your training is accomplished. "Heeling" is a necessity for a well-behaved dog, so teach him to walk beside you, head even with your knee. Nothing looks sadder than a big dog taking his helpless owner for a walk. It is annoying to passers-by and other dog owners to have a large dog, however friendly, bear down on them and entangle dogs, people, and packages.

To teach your dog, start off walking briskly, saying "Heel" in a firm voice. Pull back with a sharp jerk if he lunges ahead, and if he lags repeat the command and tug on the leash, not allowing him to drag behind. After the dog has learned to heel at various speeds on leash, you can remove it and practice heeling free, but have it ready to snap on again as soon as he wanders.

"Come" Your dog has already learned to come to you when you call his name. Why? Because you only call him when his food is ready or when you wish to play with him or praise him. Outdoors such a response is more difficult to achieve, if he is happily

When in the heel position, the dog should be at your left side. The lead should be held in your right hand, loosely except when checking him back to the desired position.

playing by himself or with other dogs, so he must be trained to come to you when he is called. To teach him to come, let him reach the end of a long lead, then give the command, gently pulling him towards you at the same time. As soon as he associates the word *come* with the action of moving towards you, pull only when he does not respond immediately. As he starts to come, move back to make him learn that he must come from a distance as well as when he is close to you. Soon you may be able to practice without a leash, but if he is slow to come or actively disobedient, go to him and pull him toward you, repeating the command. Always remember to reward his successful completion of a task.

"Down" Teaching the "down" command ideally begins while your dog is still a pup. During

Be gentle and reassuring with your dog, especially during the early stages of the down training—he may not understand what you are doing and may even feel threatened.

If your dog is an aggressive puller, you can get an anti-pulling device at your local pet shop. Photo courtesy of Four Paws.

puppyhood your dog frequently will lie down, as this position is one of the dog's most natural positions. Invest some time, and keep close watch over your pup. Each time he begins to lie, repeat in a low convincing tone the word "down." If for the first day of training, you concur a majority of the dog's sitting with your commands and continue with reinforcement and moderate praise your pup should conquer the "down" command in no time.

Teaching the "down" command to a mature dog likely will require more effort. Although the lying position is still natural to a dog, his being forced into it is not. Some dogs may react with

Once he is in the correct down position, lavish praise will tell him that he is doing well.

fear, anger, or confusion. Others may accept the process and prove quick learners. Have your dog sit and face you. If he is responsive and congenial, gently take his paws, and slowly pull them towards you; give the "down" command as he approaches the proper position. Repeat several times: moderate reinforcement of this procedure should prove successful.

For the dog that responds with anger or aggression, attach a lead (and a muzzle) and have the dog sit facing you at a close distance. There should be a J-loop formed by the lead. With moderate force, relative to the size and strength of your dog, step on the J-loop, forcing the dog down, while repeating the command "down" in a low forceful tone. When the dog is down, moderate praise should be given. If the dog proves responsive, you may attempt extending his legs to the "down" position—leaving the muzzle on, of course. Daily reinforcement of the training method will soon yield the desired results. The keys to remember are: patience, persistence, and praise.

Behavior Modification

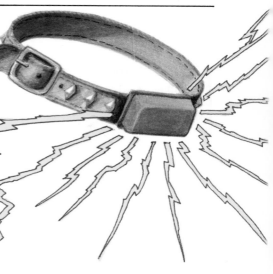

"Problems with the Barking Dog" and "Aggressive Behavior and Dominance" are extracts from the veterinary monograph *Canine Behavior* (a compilation of columns from *Canine Practice,* a journal published by Veterinary Practice Publishing Company).

PROBLEMS WITH THE BARKING DOG

One of the most frequent complaints about canine behavior is barking. Aside from the biting dog, the barking dog is probably the pet peeve of many non-dog owners. I know of at least one city in which owners of dogs that bark excessively, and for which there are complaints on file, are required to take steps to eliminate the barking.

Canine practitioners are drawn into problems with barking when they are asked for their advice in helping an owner come up with a solution or, as a last resort, when they are requested to perform a debarking operation or even euthanasia. In this column I will deal with some of the factors that apparently cause dogs to bark and suggest some corrective approaches.

Barking is, of course, a natural response for many dogs. They have an inherited predisposition to bark as an alarm when other dogs or people approach their territory. Alarm barking makes

Only in the most extreme situations may trainers recommend electric-shock collars for correcting a dog's misbehavior.

many dogs valuable as household watchdogs and is not necessarily undesirable behavior. With a different vocal tone and pattern, dogs bark when they are playing with each other. On occasion dogs have a tendency to bark back at other dogs or join in with other barking dogs.

In addition to inherited barking tendencies, dogs can also learn to bark if the barking is followed, at least sometimes, by a reward. Thus dogs may bark when they wish to come in the house or to get out of a kennel. Some dogs are trained to bark upon hearing the command "speak" for a food reward.

One of the first approaches to take when discussing a barking problem is to determine if the behavior is a manifestation of a natural (inherited) tendency or is learned behavior which has been rewarded in the past.

praise again when it barks after being told to "speak," it will eventually stop this type of barking. This is the process of extinction and it implies that the behavior must be repeated but never again rewarded.

A more practical example of the possible use of extinction

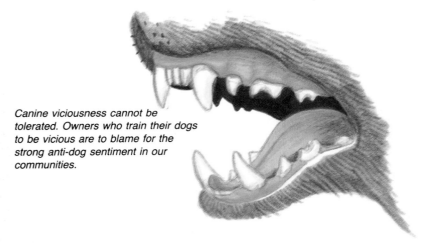

Canine viciousness cannot be tolerated. Owners who train their dogs to be vicious are to blame for the strong anti-dog sentiment in our communities.

Can Barking Be Extinguished?

Extinction, as a way of eliminating a behavioral problem, may be considered when it is clear that the behavior has been learned and when one can identify the specific rewarding or reinforcing factors that maintain the behavior.

For example, the dog that barks upon hearing the command "speak" is periodically rewarded with food and praise. If a dog is never, ever given food or

would be in dealing with the dog that apparently barks because, at least occasionally, it is allowed in the house. By not allowing the dog in the house until the barking has become very frequent and loud, the owners may have shaped the barking behavior to that which is the most objectionable. If the dog is never allowed in the house again when barking, the barking should eventually be extinguished—at least theoretically.

How Should Punishment Be Used? Sometimes it is not feasible to attempt to extinguish barking even if it seems to be the case that the behavior was learned. This brings up the advisability of punishment. Clients who seek advice in dealing with a barking problem may already have employed some type of punishment such as shouting at the dog or throwing something at it. That this type of punishment is ineffective is attested to by the fact that the client is seeking advice. By shouting at a dog or hitting, a person interferes with what effect the punishment may have on the behavior itself through the arousal of autonomic reactions and escape attempts or submissive responses by the dog.

The Water Bucket Approach I am rather impressed by the ingenuity of some dog owners in coming up with ways to punish a dog for barking without being directly involved in administering the punishment. One such harried dog owner I talked to, who was also a veterinarian, was plagued by his dog's barking in the kennel commencing at about 1:30 a.m. every night. A platform to hold a bucket of water was constructed over the area of the kennel in which the dog usually chose to bark. Through a system of hinges, ropes, and pulleys, a mechanism was devised so that

the dog owner could pull a rope from his bedroom window, dumping a bucket of water on the dog when he started to bark. The bucket was suspended such that once it was dumped, it

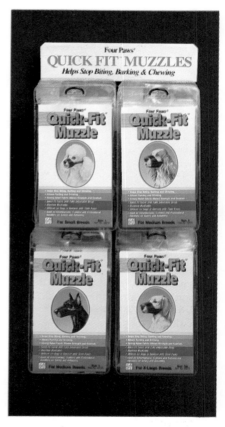

A good nylon muzzle that allows your dog to drink water while wearing is the most humane type. See your local pet supply store for the different types available. Photo courtesy of Four Paws.

Muzzles may prevent biting, but the root cause of biting must be extracted if the dog is to live as a trusted member of the human family.

uprighted itself and the owner could fill it again remotely by turning on a garden hose. After two appropriate dunkings, the dog's barking behavior was apparently eliminated.

In advising a client on the type of punishment discussed above, keep in mind one important consideration. From the time the owner is ready to administer punishment for barking, every attempt should be made to punish all undesirable barking from that point on and not to allow excessively long periods of barking to go unpunished. Thus it may be necessary to keep a dog indoors when away unless the dog will be punished for barking when the owner is gone.

Alternative Responses Barking dogs are, and probably always will be, one of the enduring problems of dog owners. Barking is relatively effortless, and it is such a natural response for many dogs that it is admittedly hard to eliminate with either punishment or a program of conditioning non-barking. In some instances it may be advisable to forget about eliminating barking and to suggest that the problem be dealt with by changing the circumstances which lead to barking. For example, a dog that

Pet shops stock products that aid owners in modifying undesirable behavior on the part of their dogs. The products shown, for example, are among those that keep dogs from biting and chewing by putting a bad taste on the bitten or chewed objects. Photo courtesy of Four Paws.

barks continuously in the backyard while the owners are away may not bark if left in the house while they are gone. But the problem of keeping the dog in the house may be related to inadequate house training or the dog's shedding hair or climbing onto the furniture. It may be easier to correct these latter behavioral problems than it is to change the barking behavior.

AGGRESSIVE BEHAVIOR AND DOMINANCE

Aggressiveness can have many causes. Determining what kind of aggression an animal is manifesting is a prerequisite to successful treatment of the

behavior. A frequent problem that is presented to the practitioner is one of aggression related to dominance.

Dogs, which are social animals, have a hierarchal system of dominance within their pack. This predisposition to take a dominant or submissive position relative to fellow canines also occurs in relationship to people. Only in unusual situations would a submissive dog threaten a dominant animal, and almost never would it physically assault its superior. The dominant dog, however, frequently threatens submissive individuals to maintain its position. In a household setting, a person may be the object of threats, and when the person backs off, the dog's position is reassured. The aggressive behavior is also reinforced, and when behavior is reinforced it is likely to recur.

Case History The following is a typical case history of a dog presented for aggression stemming from dominance.

Max was a two-year-old intact male Cocker Spaniel. He had been acquired by Mr. Smith, one year prior to his owner's marriage, as a puppy. He liked and was well liked by both Mr. and Mrs. Smith. He frequently solicited and received attention from both people. However, several times over the last few months, Max had snapped at Mrs. Smith and repeatedly growled at her. A detailed anamnesis revealed that such incidents usually occurred in situations where the dog wanted his own way or did not want to be bothered. He would growl if asked to move off a chair or if persistently commanded to do a specific task. He growled if Mrs. Smith came between him and a young female Cocker Spaniel acquired a year ago. He also refused to let Mrs. Smith take anything from his possession. Max never showed any of these aggressive behaviors toward Mr. Smith or strangers. Admittedly he did not have much opportunity to demonstrate such

behaviors toward strangers. A description of the dog's body and facial postures and circumstances under which the aggression occurred did not indicate that this was a case of fear-induced aggression, but rather one of assertion of dominance.

Mrs. Smith's reaction to the aggression was always to retreat, and, hence, the dog was rewarded for his assertiveness. She had never physically disciplined the dog and was afraid to do so. To encourage her to physically take control of the dog would likely have resulted in her being bitten. The dominance-submissive relationship had to be reversed in a more subtle manner.

Instructions to Client Mrs. Smith was instructed to avoid all situations which might evoke any aggressive signs from Max. This was to prevent any further reinforcement of his growling and threats.

Both she and her husband were not to indiscriminately pet or show affection towards the dog. For the time being, if Max solicited attention from Mr. Smith, he was to ignore the dog. Mrs. Smith was to take advantage of Max's desire for attention by giving him a command which he had to obey before she praised and petted him. She was also to take advantage of high motivation levels for other activities whenever such situations arose. Max had to obey a command before she gave him anything— before she petted him, before she let him out or in, etc.

Mrs. Smith also was to assume total care of the dog and coveted food rewards as well as praise. These were entirely fun and play sessions—but within a few days the dog had acquired the habit of quickly responding to commands. And this habit transferred over to the non-game situations.

There is a wide variety of collars and harnesses available to the dog owner. Talk with your pet shop proprietor to determine which one best satisfies your needs.

become "the source of all good things in life" for Max. She was to feed him, take him on walks, play with him, etc.

Mrs. Smith also spent 5–10 minutes a day teaching Max simple parlor tricks and obedience responses for

Results Within a few weeks, Max had ceased to growl and threaten Mrs. Smith in situations that he previously had. He would move out of her way or lie quietly when she would pass by him. She could order him off the furniture and handle the female

Cocker Spaniel without eliciting threats from Max.

Mrs. Smith still felt that she would not be able to take the objects from Max's possession. Additional instructions were given to her. She then began placing a series of objects at progressively closer distances to the dog while the dog was in a sit-stay position. After she placed the object on the floor for a short time, she would pick it up. If the dog was still in a sit-stay (which it always was), he received a reward of cheese and verbal praise. Eventually the objects were to be placed and removed from directly in front of the dog. At first she was to use objects that the dog did not care much about and then progressively use more coveted items. This was what she was

Treats can be effective in shaping behavior and establishing a rapport with your pet.

supposed to do, but before she actually had completed the program she called in excitedly to report that she had taken a piece of stolen food and a household ornament from Max's mouth. And he didn't even object! She said she had calmly told Max to sit. He did. He was so used to doing so, in the game and other situations, that the response was now automatic. She walked over, removed the item from his mouth, and praised him.

Mrs. Smith did resume the systematic presentation of objects and put the dog on an intermittent schedule of food and praise reinforcement during the practice sessions. Mr. Smith again began interacting with Max.

A progress check six months later indicated Max was still an obedient dog and had definitely assumed a submissive position relative to both of his owners. The dominance hierarchy between Max and Mrs. Smith had been reversed *without resorting to any physical punishment.* Mrs. Smith was instructed to reinforce her dominance position by frequently giving Max a command and reinforcing him for the appropriate response.

Summary The essential elements in treatment of such cases are as follows. First, of course, there must be a correct

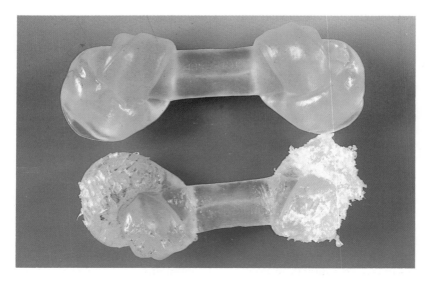

Owners must take an active part in shaping their dog's behavior. Providing a sensible chew device can help alleviate an animal's frustration and thereby eliminate some undesirable behavior.

diagnosis of what kind of aggressive behavior is occurring. During the course of treatment, the submissive person(s) should avoid all situations that might evoke an aggressive attitude by the dog. All other family members should totally ignore the dog during the treatment interim. The person most dominated by the dog should take over complete care of the dog in addition to spending 5–10 minutes a day teaching the dog tricks or simple obedience commands (sit-stay is a useful one to gain control of the dog in subsequent circumstances). These should be fun-and-games

situations. Food rewards are highly recommended in addition to simple praise.

The person submissive to the dog should take the opportunity to give the dog a command, which must be obeyed, before doing anything pleasant for the dog.

It must be emphasized to the owner that no guarantee can be made that the dog will never threaten or be aggressive again. What is being done, as with all other aggression cases, is an attempt to reduce the likelihood, incidence, and intensity of occurrence of the aggressive behavior.

Behavior Modification

DESTRUCTIVE TENDENCIES

It is ironical but true that a dog's destructive behavior in the home may be proof of his love for his owner. He may be trying to get more attention from his owner or, in other cases, may be expressing his frustration at his owner's absence. An abundance of unused energy may also contribute to a dog's destructive behavior, and therefore the owner should ensure that his dog has, at least, twenty minutes of vigorous exercise a day.

As a dog's destructive tendencies may stem from his desire to get more attention from his owner, the latter should devote specific periods each day to his dog when he is actively interacting with him. Such a period should contain practice obedience techniques during which the owner can reward the dog with his favorite food as well as praise and affection.

Planned departure conditioning is one specific technique which has been used to solve the problem of destructive tendencies in a puppy. It eventually ensures the dog's good behavior during the owner's absence. A series of short departures, which are identical to real departures, should condition the dog to behave well in the owner's absence. How is this to be achieved? Initially, the departures are so short (2–5 minutes) that the dog has no opportunity to be destructive. The dog is always rewarded for having been good when the owner returns. Gradually the duration of the departures is increased. The departure time is also varied so that the dog does not know when the owner is going to return. Since a different kind of behavior is now expected, it is best if a new stimulus or "atmosphere" is introduced into the training sessions to permit the dog to distinguish these departures as different from previous departures when he was destructive.

This new stimulus could be the sound of the radio or television. The association which the dog will develop is that whenever the "signal" or "stimulus" is on, the owner will return in an unknown period of time and, if the dog has not been destructive, he will be rewarded. As with the daily owner-dog interaction, the food reward is especially useful.

If the dog misbehaves during his owner's absence, the owner should speak sternly to him and isolate him from social contact for at least thirty minutes. (Puppies hate to be ignored.) Then the owner should conduct another departure of a shorter time and generously reward good behavior when he returns. The owner should progress slowly enough in the program so that once the departure has been initiated, the dog is never given an opportunity to make a mistake.

If planned departures are working satisfactorily, the departure time may gradually be extended to several hours. To reduce the dog's anxiety when left alone, he should be given a "safety valve" such as the indestructible Nylabone® to play with and chew on.

Repellents are excellent training aids that help to avoid destructive behavior by keeping dogs out of forbidden areas. Such products come in a number of different forms and are available for use inside or outside the house. Photo courtesy of Four Paws.

Health Care

From the moment you purchase your puppy, the most important person in both your lives becomes your veterinarian. His

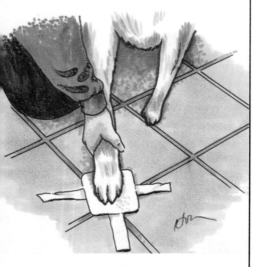

Bandaging a minor cut on the paw pad is one of many basic first-aid techniques that the dog owner should learn.

professional advice and treatment will ensure the good health of your pet. The vet is the first person to call when illness or accidents occur. Do *not* try to be your own veterinarian or apply human remedies to canine diseases. However, just as you would keep a first aid kit handy for minor injuries sustained by members of your family at home, so you should keep a similar kit prepared for your pet.

First aid for your dog would consist of stopping any bleeding, cleaning the wound, and preventing infection. Thus your kit might contain medicated powder, gauze bandages, and adhesive tape to be used in case of cuts. If the cut is deep and bleeding profusely, the bandage should be applied very tightly to help in the formation of a clot. A tight bandage should not be kept in place longer than necessary, so take your pet to the veterinarian immediately.

Walking or running on a cut pad prevents the cut from

Thoroughly clean the injury with peroxide and apply an antibiotic. Then place the injured pad in sterile gauze, secure with first-aid tape, and replace daily.

healing. Proper suturing of the cut and regular changing of the bandages should have your pet's wound healed in a week to ten days. A minor cut should be covered with a light bandage, for you want as much air as possible to reach the wound. Do not apply wads of cotton to a wound, as they will stick to the area and may cause contamination.

You should also keep some hydrogen peroxide available, as it is useful in cleaning wounds and is also one of the best and simplest emetics known. Cotton applicator swabs are useful for applying ointment or removing debris from the eyes. A pair of tweezers should also be kept handy for removing foreign bodies from the dog's neck, head or body.

Nearly everything a dog might contract in the way of sickness has basically the same set of symptoms: loss of appetite, diarrhea, dull eyes, dull coat, warm and/or runny nose, and a high temperature. Therefore, it is most important to take his temperature at the first sign of illness. To do this, you will need a rectal thermometer which should be lubricated with petroleum jelly. Carefully insert it into the rectum, holding it in place for at least two minutes. It must be held firmly; otherwise there is the danger of its being sucked up into the rectum or slipping out, thus giving an

Ugly tear stains can be safely and easily removed with a special shampoo, available at your pet shop. Photo courtesy of Four Paws.

inaccurate reading. The normal temperature for a dog is between 101° and 102.5°F. If your pet is seriously ill or injured in an accident, your veterinarian will advise you what to do before he arrives.

SWALLOWING FOREIGN OBJECTS

Most of us have had experience with a child swallowing a foreign object. Usually it is a small coin; occasionally it may be a fruit pit or something more dangerous. Dogs, *as a general rule,* will not swallow anything which isn't edible. There are, however, many dogs that swallow pebbles or small shiny objects such as pins, coins, and bits of cloth and plastic. This is especially true of dogs that are offered so-called "chew toys."

Chew toys are available in many sizes, shapes, colors and materials. Some even have whistles which sound when the dog's owner plays with it or when the dog chomps on it quickly. Most dogs attack the whistle first, doing everything possible to make it stop squeaking. Obviously, if the whistle is made of metal, a dog can injure its mouth, teeth, or tongue. Therefore, *never* buy a "squeak toy" made with a metal whistle.

Other chew toys are made of vinyl, a cheap plastic which is soft to the touch and pliable. Most of the cute little toys that are figures of animals or people are made of this cheap plastic. They are sometimes hand-painted in countries where the cost of such labor is low. Not only is the paint used dangerous to dogs, because of the lead content, but the vinyl tears easily and is usually destroyed by the dog during the first hour. Small bits of vinyl may be ingested and cause blockage of the intestines. You are, therefore, reminded of these things before you buy anything vinyl for your dog!

Very inexpensive dog toys, usually found in supermarkets and other low-price venues, may

Natural chew bones can splinter and become lodged in a dog's throat. Nylon and polyurethane bones are safer for canine use.

Old discardable shoes should not be included in the dog's toy box. Such items are dangerous to a puppy or an adult dog.

be made of polyethylene. These are to be avoided completely, as this cheap plastic is, for some odd reason, attractive to dogs. Dogs destroy the toy in minutes and sometimes swallow the indigestible bits and pieces that come off. Most pet shops carry only safe toys.

WHAT TOYS ARE SAFE FOR DOGS?

Hard Rubber Toys made of hard rubber are usually safe for dogs, providing the toy is made of 100% hard rubber and not a compound of rubber and other materials. The rubber must be "virgin" and not re-ground from old tires, tubes, and other scrap rubber products. The main problem with rubber, even 100% virgin rubber, is that it oxidizes

quickly, especially when subjected to the ultraviolet rays of the sun and a dog's saliva. The rubber then tends to be brittle, to crack, to dust off, and to be extremely dangerous to dogs that like swallowing things. **Nylon Toys** Toys made of nylon could well be the safest of all toys, *providing the nylon is annealed.* Nylon that is not annealed is very fragile, and if you smash it against a hard surface, it might shatter like glass. The same is true when the weather is cold and the nylon drops below freezing. Thus far there is only one line of dog toys that is made of annealed virgin nylon—Nylabone®. These toys not only are annealed but they are flavored and scented. The flavors and scents, such as hambone, are undetectable by humans, but dogs seem to find them attractive.

Some nylon bones have the flavor sprayed on them or molded into them. These cheaper bones are easy to detect—just smell them. If you

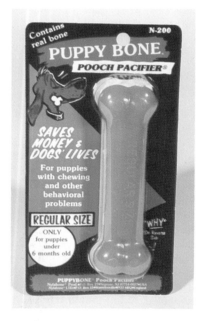

The Puppy Bone® by Nylabone® is multi-purpose, designed for teething, chew-pacification, teeth-cleaning and the elimination of behavioral problems before they become habitual.

discern an odor, you know they are poorly made. The main problem with the nylon toys that have an odor is that they are not annealed and they "smell up"

the house or car. The dog's saliva dilutes the odor of the bone, and when he drops it on your rug, this odor attaches itself to the rug and is quite difficult to remove.

Annealed nylon may be the best there is, but it is not 100% safe. The Nylabone® dog chews are really meant to be Pooch Pacifiers®. This trade name indicates the effect intended for the dog, which is to relieve the tension in your excited puppy or anxious adult dog. Instead of chewing up the furniture or some other object, he chews up his Nylabone® instead. Many dogs ignore the Nylabone® for weeks, suddenly attacking it when they have to relieve their doggie tensions.

The Nylabone® is designed for the most aggressive chewers. Even so, owners should be wary that some dogs may have jaws strong enough to chomp off a piece of Nylabone®, but this is extremely rare. *One word of caution:* the Nylabone® should be replaced when the dog has chewed down the knuckle. Most dogs slowly scrape off small slivers of nylon which pass harmlessly through their digestive tract. The resultant frizzled bone actually becomes a toothbrush.

One of the great characteristics of nylon bones is that they can be boiled and sterilized. If a dog loses interest in his Nylabone®, or it is too hard for him to chew due to his age and the condition of his teeth, you can cook it in some chicken or beef broth, allowing it to boil for 30 minutes. Let it cool down normally. It will then be perfectly sterile and re-flavored for the next dog. *Don't try this with plastic bones, as they will melt and ruin your pot.*

Polyurethane Toys Because polyurethane bones such as the Gumabone® are constructed of the strongest *flexible* materials known, some dogs (and their owners) actually prefer them to the traditional nylon bones. There are several brands on the market: ignore the ones which have scents that you can discern. Some of the scented polyurethane bones have an unbearable odor after the scent has rubbed off the bone and onto your rug or car seat. Again, look for the better-quality polyurethane toy. Gumabone® is a flexible material, the same as used for making artificial hearts and the bumpers on automobiles, thus it is strong and stable. It is not as strong as Nylabone®, but many dogs like it because it is soft.

If your dog is soft-mouthed and a less aggressive, more playful chewer, he will love the great taste and fun feel of the Gumabone® products.

The most popular of the

Gumabone® products made in polyurethane are the tug toys, knots, balls, and Frisbee® flying discs. These items are almost clear in color, have the decided advantage of lasting a long time, and are useful in providing exercise for both a dog and his master or mistress.

Gumabone® is available in different sizes and shapes. These are probably the most popular of all chew toys because dogs love them.

Gumabone® has also introduced new spiral-shaped dental devices under the name Plaque Attacker®. These unique products are fast becoming standards for all aggressive chewers. The Plaque Attacker Dental Device® comes in four fun sizes and each is designed to maximize gum and teeth

Attacker® products are patented and scented with hambone to make them even more enticing for the dog. Clinical findings support the assertion that a significant reduction in calculus accompanies use of the Gumbone® products.

Whatever dog toy you buy, be sure it is high quality. Pet shops

The Plaque Attacker® is a Dental Ball™, not just a plaything, designed to reduce plaque and tartar by use of its revolutionary "dental tips."

massage through its upraised "dental tips," which pimple the surface of the toy. Similarly, the Plaque Attacker Dental Ball® ensures a reduction in plaque and tartar. This one-of-a-kind product provides hours of fun for a dog. It bounces erratically and proves to be the most exciting of all polyurethane toys. All Plaque

and certain supermarkets, as a rule, always carry the better quality toys. Of course there may be exceptions, but you are best advised to ask your local pet shop operator—or even your veterinarian—what toys are suitable for *your* dog.

In conclusion, if your dog is a swallower of foreign objects,

Choose from a variety of ear care products from cleaners to remedies for proper ear hygiene. Photo courtesy of Four Paws.

don't give him anything cheap to chew on. If he swallows a coin, you can hardly blame the Treasury! Unless your dog is carefully supervised, use only the largest size Nylabone® and Gumabone®, and replace them as soon as the dog chews down the knuckles. *Do not let the dog take the Nylabone® outdoors.* First of all he can hide and bury it, digging it up when his tensions rise. Then, too, all nylon becomes more brittle when it freezes, even Nylabone®.

IF YOUR PET SWALLOWS POISON

A poisoned dog must be treated instantly; any delay could cause his death. Different poisons act in different ways and require different treatments. If you know the dog has swallowed an acid, alkali, gasoline, or kerosene, do not induce vomiting. Give milk to dilute the poison and rush him to the vet. If you can find the bottle or container of poison, check the label to see if there is a recommended antidote. If not, try to induce vomiting by giving him a mixture of hydrogen peroxide and water. Mix the regular drugstore strength of hydrogen peroxide (3%) with an equal part of water, but do not attempt to pour it down your dog's throat, as that could cause inhalation pneumonia. Instead, simply pull the dog's lips away from the side of his mouth, making a pocket for depositing the liquid. Use at least a tablespoonful of the mixture for every ten pounds of your dog's weight. He will vomit in about two minutes. When his stomach has settled, give him a teaspoonful of Epsom salts in a little water to empty the intestine quickly. The hydrogen peroxide, on ingestion, becomes oxygen and water and is harmless to your dog; it is the best antidote for phosphorus, which is often used in rat poisons. After you have administered this emergency treatment to your pet and his stomach and bowels have been emptied, rush him to your veterinarian for further care.

Freshen up your pets in between baths with one of the many pleasantly scented colognes available at your pet shop. Photo courtesy of Four Paws.

DANGER IN THE HOME

There are numerous household products that can prove fatal if ingested by your pet. These include rat poison, antifreeze, boric acid, hand soap, detergents, insecticides, mothballs, household cleansers, bleaches, de-icers, polishes and disinfectants, paint and varnish removers, acetone, turpentine, and even health and beauty aids if ingested in large enough quantities. A word to the wise should be sufficient: what you would keep locked away from your two-year-old child should also be kept hidden from your pet.

There is another danger lurking within the home among the household plants, which are almost all poisonous, even if swallowed in small quantities. There are hundreds of poisonous plants around us, among which are: ivy leaves, cyclamen, lily of the valley, rhododendrons, tulip bulbs, azalea, wisteria, poinsettia leaves, mistletoe, daffodils,

There are a number of special tools used by groomers and handlers to maintain a healthy and vibrant coat. See your local pet supply dealer for the tools you need for your dog. Photo courtesy of Four Paws.

Checking for an animal's vital signs in the event of an emergency will help you to provide the veterinarian with the answers to his preliminary questions.

jimson weed—we cannot name them all. Rhubarb leaves, for example, either raw or cooked, can cause death or violent convulsions. Peach, elderberry, and cherry trees can cause cyanide poisoning if their bark is consumed.

There are also many insects that can be poisonous to dogs such as spiders, bees, wasps, and some flies. A few toads and frogs exude a fluid that can make a dog foam at the mouth—and even kill him—if he bites too hard!

There have been cases of dogs suffering nicotine poisoning by consuming the contents of full ashtrays which thoughtless smokers have left on the coffee table. Also, do not leave nails, staples, pins, or other sharp objects lying around. Likewise, don't let your puppy play with plastic bags which could suffocate him. Unplug, remove, or cover any electrical cords or wires near your dog. Chewing live wires could lead to severe mouth burns or death. Remember that an ounce of prevention is worth a pound of cure: keep all potentially dangerous objects out of your pet's reach.

VEHICLE TRAVEL SAFETY

A dog should never be left alone in a car. It takes only a few minutes for the heat to become unbearable in the summer, and to drop to freezing in the winter.

A dog traveling in a car or truck should be well behaved. An undisciplined dog can be deadly in a moving vehicle. The dog should be trained to lie on the back seat of the vehicle. Allowing your dog to stick its head out of the window is unwise. The dog may jump or it may get something in its eye. Some manufacturers sell seat belts and car seats designed for dogs.

Traveling with your dog in the back of your pick-up truck is an unacceptable notion and dangerous to all involved.

PROTECT YOURSELF FIRST

In almost all first aid situations, the dog is in pain. He may indeed be in shock and not appear to be suffering, until you move him. Then he may bite your hand or resist being helped at all. So if you want to help your dog, help yourself first by tying his mouth closed. To do this, use a piece of strong cloth four inches wide and three feet long, depending on the size of the dog.

If you plan on having your dog travel with you, it will be necessary to purchase a device that will secure him in place and prevent him from disturbing driver and passengers. Photo courtesy of Four Paws.

Health Care

Make a loop in the middle of the strip and slip it over his nose with the knot under his chin and over the bony part of his nose. Pull it tight and bring the ends back around his head behind the ears and tie it tightly, ending with a bow knot for quick, easy release. Now you can handle the dog safely. As a dog perspires through his tongue, do not leave the "emergency muzzle" on any longer than necessary.

ADMINISTERING MEDICINE
When you are giving liquid medicine to your dog, it is a good idea to pull the lips away from the side of the mouth, form a lip pocket, and let the liquid trickle past the tongue. Remain at his side, never in front of the dog, as he may cough and spray you with the liquid. Moreover, you must never pour liquid medicine while the victim's tongue is drawn out, as

First aid, in the ideal sense, is the temporary care of an animal or person until professional help can be found. Recognizing the urgency in any given circumstance is the primary concern. Moving an injured animal with utmost care usually requires two persons and a clean blanket.

inhalation pneumonia could be the disastrous result.

Medicine in pill form is best administered by forcing the dog's mouth open, holding his forced to swallow the medicine. As the dog will not be feeling well, stroke his neck to comfort him and to help him swallow his medicine more easily. Do keep

Before attempting to transport an injured dog, be very careful to inspect for apparent wounds, burns or breaks while disturbing the animal as little as possible. Laying the dog in a flat position will make the carrying easier to manage.

head back, and placing the capsule as far back on his tongue as you can reach. To do this: put the palm of your hand over the dog's muzzle (his foreface) with your fingers on one side of his jaw, your thumb on the other. Press his lips hard against his teeth while using your other hand to pull down his lower jaw. With your two fingers, try to put the pill as far back on the dog's tongue as you can reach. Keep his mouth and nostrils closed and he should be an eye on him for a few moments afterward, however, to make certain that he does not spit it out.

IN CASE OF AN ACCIDENT

It is often difficult for you to assess the dog's injuries after a road accident. He may appear normal, but there might be internal hemorrhaging. A vital organ could be damaged or ribs broken. Keep the dog as quiet and warm as possible; cover him with blankets or your coat to let his own body heat build up. Signs of shock are a rapid and weak pulse, glassy-eyed appearance, subnormal temperature, and slow capillary refill time. To determine the last symptom, press firmly against the dog's gums until they turn white. Release and count the number of seconds until the gums return to their normal color. If it is more than 2–3 seconds, the dog may be going into shock. Failure to return to the reddish pink color indicates that the dog may be in serious trouble and needs immediate assistance.

If artificial respiration is required, first open the dog's mouth and check for obstructions; extend his tongue and examine the pharynx. Clear his mouth of mucus and blood and hold the mouth slightly open. Mouth-to-mouth resuscitation involves holding the dog's tongue to the bottom of his mouth with one hand and sealing his nostrils with the other while you blow into his mouth. Watch for his chest to rise with each inflation. Repeat every 5–6 seconds, the equivalent of 10–12 breaths a minute.

If the veterinarian cannot come to you, try to improvise a stretcher to take the dog to him. To carry a puppy, wrap him in a blanket that has been folded into several thicknesses. If he is in shock, it is better to pick him up by holding one hand under his chest, the other under the hindquarters. This will keep him stretched out.

It is always better to roll an injured dog than to try and lift him. If you find him lying beside the road after a car accident, apply a muzzle even if you have to use someone's necktie to make one. Send someone for a blanket and roll him gently onto it. Two people, one on each side, can make a stretcher out of the blanket and move the dog easily.

If no blanket is available and the injured dog must be moved, try to keep him as flat as possible. So many dogs' backs are broken in car accidents that one must first consider that possibility. However, if he can move his hind legs or tail, his spine is probably not broken. Get medical assistance for him immediately.

It should be mentioned that unfortunate car accidents, which can maim or kill your dog, can be avoided if he is confined at all times either indoors or, if out-of-doors, in a fenced-in yard or some other protective enclosure. *Never* allow your dog to roam free; even a well-trained dog may, for some unknown reason, dart into the street—and the result could be tragic.

If you need to walk your dog, leash him first so that he will be protected from moving vehicles.

It is the smooth, efficient execution of first-aid technique that saves lives. Costly mistakes happen when haste and frenzy take over. When moving an injured dog, keep calm and be focused on the situation at hand. Act swiftly and maintain control at all times.

PROTECTING YOUR PET

It is important to watch for any tell-tale signs of illness so that you can spare your pet any unnecessary suffering. Your dog's eyes, for example, should normally be bright and alert, so if the haw is bloodshot or partially covers the eye, it may be a sign of illness or irritation. If your dog has matter in the corners of his eyes, bathe them with a mild eye wash; obtain ointment or eye drops from your veterinarian to treat a chronic condition.

If your dog seems to have something wrong with his ears which causes him to scratch at them or shake his head, cautiously probe the ear with a cotton swab. An accumulation of wax will probably work itself out. Dirt or dried blood, however, is indicative of ear mites or infection and should be treated immediately. Sore ears in the summer, due to insect bites, should be washed with mild soap and water, then covered with a soothing ointment and wrapped in gauze if necessary. Keep your pet away from insects until his ears heal, even if this means confining him indoors.

VACCINATION SCHEDULE

Age	Vaccination
6-8 weeks	Initial canine distemper, canine hepatitis, tracheobronchitis, canine parvovirus, as well as initial leptospirosis vaccination.
10-12 weeks	Second vaccination for all given at 6-8 weeks. Initial rabies and initial Lyme disease to be given at this time.
14-16 weeks	Third vaccination for all given at 6-8 and 10-12 weeks.Re-vaccinate annually, hereafter. Second rabies and second Lyme disease to be given at this time, and then re-vaccinated annually.

INOCULATIONS

Periodic check-ups by your veterinarian throughout your puppy's life are good health insurance. The person from whom your puppy was purchased should tell you what inoculations your puppy has had and when the next visit to the vet is necessary. You must make certain that your puppy has been vaccinated against the following infectious canine diseases: distemper, canine hepatitis, leptospirosis, rabies, parvovirus, and parainfluenza. Annual "boosters" thereafter provide inexpensive protection for your dog against such serious diseases. Puppies should also be checked for worms at an early age.

Vaccination schedules should be confirmed with your vet.

DISTEMPER

Young dogs are most susceptible to distemper, although it may affect dogs of all ages. Some signs of the disease are loss of appetite, depression, chills, and fever, as well as a watery discharge from the eyes and nose. Unless treated promptly, the disease goes into advanced stages with infections of the lungs, intestines, and nervous system. Dogs that recover may be impaired with paralysis, convulsions, a twitch, or some other defect, usually spastic in nature. Early inoculations in puppyhood should be followed by an annual booster to help protect against this disease.

CANINE HEPATITIS

The signs of hepatitis are drowsiness, loss of appetite, high temperature, and great thirst. These signs may be accompanied by swellings of the head, neck, and abdomen. Vomiting may also occur. This disease strikes quickly, and death may occur in only a few hours. An annual booster shot is needed after the initial series of puppy shots.

LEPTOSPIROSIS

Infection caused by either of two serovars, *canicola* or *copehageni,* is usually begun by the dog's licking substances contaminated by the urine or feces of infected animals. Brown rats are the main carriers of *copehageni.* The signs are weakness, vomiting, and a yellowish discoloration of the jaws, teeth, and tongue, caused by an inflammation of the kidneys. A veterinarian can administer the bacterins to protect your dog from this disease. The frequency of the doses is determined by the risk factor involved.

RABIES

This disease of the dog's central nervous system spreads by infectious saliva, which is

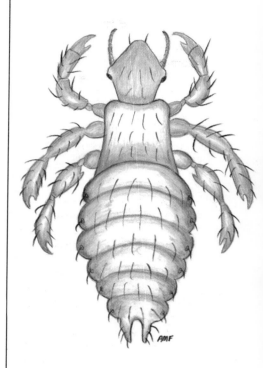

Lice are not a common problem in dogs and usually only infest dogs that are poorly cared for. Proper care of your dog will prevent lice infestation.

transmitted by the bite of an infected animal. Of the two main classes of signs, the first is "furious rabies," in which the dog shows a period of melancholy or depression, then irritation, and finally paralysis. The first period can be from a few hours to several days, and during this time the dog is cross and will change his position often, lose his appetite, begin to lick, and bite or swallow foreign objects. During this phase the dog is spasmodically wild and has impulses to run away. The dog acts fearless and bites everything in sight. If he is caged or confined, he will fight at the bars and possibly break teeth or fracture his jaw. His bark

It is very important to protect your pet from dangerous parasites. See your local pet shop for the myriad of sprays that are designed to defend your dog from fleas, ticks, flies, and mosquitoes. Photo courtesy of Four Paws.

becomes a peculiar howl. In the final stage, the animal's lower jaw becomes paralyzed and hangs down. He then walks with a stagger, and saliva drips from his mouth. About four to eight days after the onset of paralysis, the dog dies.

The second class of symptoms is referred to as "dumb rabies" and is characterized by the dog's walking in a bearlike manner with his head down. The lower jaw is paralyzed and the dog is unable to bite. It appears as if he has a bone caught in his throat.

If a dog is bitten by a rabid animal, he probably can be saved if he is taken to a veterinarian in time for a series of injections. After the signs appear, however, no cure is possible. The local health department must be notified in the case of a rabid dog, for he is a danger to all who come near him. As with the other shots each year, an annual rabies inoculation is very important. In many areas, the administration of rabies vaccines for dogs is required by law.

PARVOVIRUS

This relatively new virus is a contagious disease that has spread in almost epidemic proportions throughout certain sections of the United States. It has also appeared in Australia, Canada, and Europe. Canine parvovirus attacks the intestinal tract, white blood cells, and heart muscle. It is believed to spread through dog-to-dog contact, and the specific course of infection seems to come from fecal matter of infected dogs. Overcoming parvovirus is difficult, for it is capable of existing in the environment for many months under varying conditions and temperatures, and it can be transmitted from place to place on the hair and feet of infected dogs, as well as on the clothes and shoes of people.

Vomiting and severe diarrhea, which will appear within five to seven days after the animal has been exposed to the virus, are the initial signs of this disease. At the onset of illness, feces will be light gray or yellow-gray in color, and the urine might be blood-streaked. Because of the vomiting and severe diarrhea, the dog that has contracted the disease will dehydrate quickly. Depression and loss of appetite, as well as a rise in temperature, can accompany the other symptoms. Death caused by this disease usually occurs within 48 to 72 hours following the appearance of the symptoms. Puppies are hardest hit, and the virus is fatal to 75 percent of puppies that contract it. Death in puppies can be within two days of the onset of the illness.

A series of shots administered by a veterinarian is the best

The stable fly is capable of a painful bite.

preventive measure for canine parvovirus. It is also important to disinfect the area where the dog is housed by using one part sodium hypochlorite solution (household bleach) to thirty parts of water and to keep the dog from coming into contact with the fecal matter of other dogs.

LYME DISEASE

Known as a bacterial infection, Lyme disease is transmitted by ticks infected with a spirochete known as *Borrelia burgdorferi*. The disease is most often

The deer tick is a principal carrier of Lyme disease.

The brown dog tick is the most common tick found on dogs. It is much larger than a deer tick.

acquired by the parasitic bite of an infected deer tick, *Ixodes dammini*. While the range of symptoms is broad, common warning signs include: rash beginning at the bite and soon extending in a bullseye-targetlike fashion; chills, fever, lack of balance, lethargy, and stiffness; swelling and pain, especially in the joints, possibly leading to arthritis or arthritic conditions; heart problems, weak limbs, facial paralysis, and lack of tactile sensation.

Concerned dog owners, especially those living in the United States, should contact a veterinarian to discuss Lyme disease. A vaccination has been developed and is routinely administered to puppies twice before the 16th week, and then annually.

PARAINFLUENZA

Parainfluenza, or infectious canine tracheobronchitis, is commonly known as "kennel cough." It is highly contagious, affects the upper respiratory system, and is spread through direct or indirect contact with already diseased dogs. It will readily infect dogs of all ages that have not been vaccinated or that were previously infected. While this condition is definitely one of the serious diseases in dogs, it is self-limiting, usually lasting only two to four weeks.

The symptoms are high fever and intense, harsh coughing that brings up mucus. As long as your pet sees your veterinarian immediately, the chances for his complete recovery are excellent.

EXTERNAL PARASITES

A parasite is an animal that lives in or on an organism of another species, known as the host, without contributing to the well-being of the host. The majority of dogs' skin problems are parasitic in nature and an estimated 90% of puppies are born with parasites.

Ticks can cause serious problems to dogs where the latter have access to woods, fields, and vegetation in which large numbers of native mammals live. Ticks are usually found clinging to vegetation and attach themselves to animals

passing by. They have eight legs and a heavy shield or shell-like covering on their upper surface. Only by keeping dogs away from tick-infested areas can ticks on dogs be prevented.

The flea is the single most common cause of skin and coat problems in dogs. There are 11,000 kinds of fleas which can transmit specific disorders like tapeworm and heartworm or transport smaller parasites onto your dog. The common tapeworm, for example, requires the flea as an intermediate host for completion of its life cycle.

Fumigating flea bombs are commonly used to de-flea a home. It is essential to follow the manufacturer's instructions to the letter, as this product's fumes can kill more than just insects.

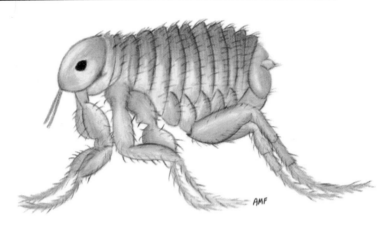

A female flea can lay hundreds of eggs and these will become adults in less than three weeks. Depending on the temperature and the amount of moisture, large numbers of fleas can attack dogs. The ears of dogs, in particular, can play host to hundreds of fleas.

Fleas can lurk in crevices and cracks, carpets, and bedding for months, so frequent cleaning of your dog's environment is absolutely essential. If he is infected by other dogs, then have him bathed and "dipped," which means that he will be put into water containing a chemical that kills fleas. Your veterinarian will advise which dip to use, and your dog must be bathed for at least twenty minutes. These parasites are tenacious and remarkably agile creatures; fleas have existed since prehistoric times and have been found in arctic as well as tropical

Fleas are among the most common external parasites and can be real pests to eliminate from your pet.

climates. Some experts claim that fleas can jump 150 times the length of their bodies; this makes them difficult to catch and kill. Thus, treating your pet for parasites without simultaneously treating the environment is both inefficient and ineffective.

INTERNAL PARASITES

Four common internal parasites that may infect a dog are: roundworms, hookworms, whipworms, and tapeworms. The first three can be diagnosed by laboratory examination of the dog's stool, and tapeworms can be seen in the stool or attached to the hair around the anus. When a veterinarian determines what type of worm or worms are present, he then can advise the best treatment.

Roundworms, the dog's most common intestinal parasite, have a life cycle which permits complete eradication by worming twice, ten days apart. The first worming will remove all adults and the second will destroy all subsequently hatched eggs before they, in turn, can produce more parasites.

A dog in good physical condition is less susceptible to worm infestation than a weak dog. Proper sanitation and a nutritious diet help in preventing worms. One of the best preventive measures is to have clean, dry bedding for the dog, as this diminishes the possibility of reinfection due to flea or tick bites.

Heartworm infestation in dogs is passed by mosquitoes. Dogs with this disease tire easily, have difficulty in breathing, and lose weight despite a hearty appetite. Administration of preventive medicine throughout the spring, summer, and fall months is advised. A veterinarian must first take a blood sample from the dog to test for the presence of the disease, and if the dog is heartworm-free, pills or liquid medicine can be prescribed to protect against any infestation.

CANINE SENIOR CITIZENS
The processes of aging and gradual degenerative changes start far earlier in a dog than often observed, usually at about seven years of age. If we recall that each year of a dog's life roughly corresponds to about seven years in the life of a man,

The fraternity of internal parasites and their eggs: whipworms, hookworms, roundworms and tapeworms.

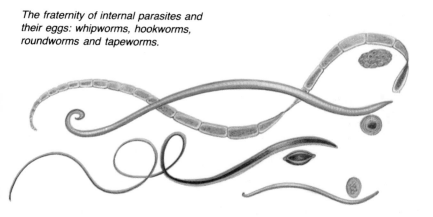

135

by the age of seven he is well into middle age. Your pet will become less active, will have a poorer appetite with increased thirst, there will be frequent periods of constipation and less than normal passage of urine. His skin and coat might become dull and dry and his hair will become thin and fall out. There is a tendency towards obesity in old age, which should be avoided by maintaining a regular exercise program. Remember, also, that your pet will be less able to cope with extreme heat, cold, fatigue, and change in routine.

There is the possibility of loss or impairment of hearing or eyesight. He may become bad-tempered more often than in the past. Other ailments such as rheumatism, arthritis, kidney infections, heart disease, male prostatism, and hip dysplasia may occur. Of course, all these require a veterinarian's examination and recommendation of suitable treatment. Care of the teeth is

Heartworm life cycle: a carrier mosquito bites a dog and deposits microfilariae, which travel through the dog's bloodstream, lodging in the heart to reproduce. The carrier dog is later bitten by an uninfected mosquito, which becomes infected, and bites and infects another dog . . . .

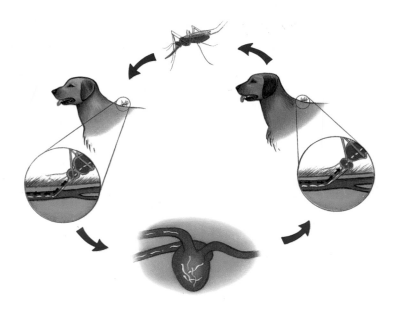

An extensive line of grooming brushes, from slickers to curry brushes to pin brushes, are available from your pet-supply dealer. These are sure to suit the grooming needs of every dog. Photo courtesy of Four Paws.

also important in the aging dog. Indeed, the mouth can be a barometer of nutritional health. Degenerating gums, heavy tartar on the teeth, loose teeth, and sore lips are common. The worst of all diseases in old age, however, is neglect. Good care in early life will have its effect on your dog's later years; the nutrition and general health care of his first few years can determine his lifespan and the quality of his life. It is worth bearing in mind that the older, compared to the younger, animal needs more protein of good biological value, more vitamins A, B-complex, D and E, more calcium and iron, and less fat.

An adult male mosquito. Only female mosquitoes will suck blood from a host animal.

Preventive Dental Care

ALL DOGS NEED TO CHEW

Puppies and young dogs need something with resistance to chew on while their teeth and jaws are developing—to cut the puppy teeth, to induce growth of the permanent teeth under the puppy teeth, to assist in getting

An artist's representation of the calculus index, ranging from index rating **4** *(topmost drawing)* through *index rating* **0** *(lowest drawing).*

4 *Buccal crown covered*

3 *⅔ crown covered*

2 *⅓ crown covered*

1 *Only gingival margin covered*

0 *No calculus evident*

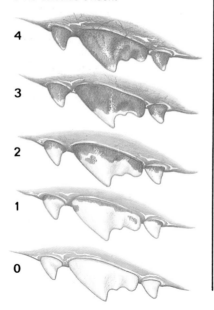

4

3

2

1

0

rid of the puppy teeth on time, to help the permanent teeth through the gums, to assure normal jaw development and to settle the permanent teeth solidly in the jaws.

The adult dog's desire to chew stems from the instinct for tooth cleaning, gum massage, and jaw exercise—plus the need to vent periodic doggie tensions. ... A pacifier if you will!

Dental caries, as they affect the teeth of humans, are virtually unknown in dogs; but tartar (calculus) accumulates on the teeth of dogs, particularly at the gum line, more rapidly than on the teeth of humans. These accumulations, if not removed, bring irritation and then infection, which erode the tooth enamel and ultimately destroy the teeth at the roots. It is important that you take your dog to your local veterinarian for periodic dental examinations.

Tooth and jaw development will normally continue until the dog is more than a year old—but sometimes much longer, depending upon the dog, its chewing exercise, rate of calcium utilization and many other factors, known and unknown, which affect the development of individual dogs. Diseases, like distemper for example, may sometimes arrest development of the teeth and jaws, which may resume months or even years later.

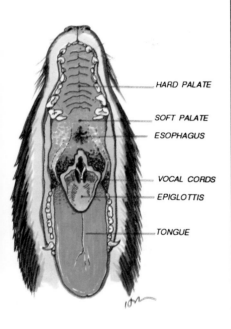

HARD PALATE

SOFT PALATE

ESOPHAGUS

VOCAL CORDS

EPIGLOTTIS

TONGUE

The owner should inspect the dog's mouth regularly to check that all is well.

This is why dogs, especially puppies and young dogs, will often destroy valuable property when their chewing instinct is not diverted from their owners' possessions, particularly during the widely varying critical period for young dogs. Saving your possessions from destruction, assuring proper development of

teeth and jaws, providing for "interim" tooth cleaning and gum massage, and channeling doggie tensions into a non-destructive outlet are, therefore, all dependent upon the dog's having something suitable for chewing readily available when his instinct tells him to chew. If your purposes, and those of your dog, are to be accomplished, what you provide for chewing must be desirable from the doggie viewpoint, have the necessary functional qualities, and, above all, be safe.

It is very important that dogs be prohibited from chewing on anything they can break or indigestible things from which they can bite sizeable chunks. Sharp pieces, such as those from a bone which can be broken by a dog, may pierce the intestinal wall and kill. Indigestible things which can be bitten off in chunks, such as toys made of rubber compound or cheap plastic, may cause an intestinal stoppage; if not regurgitated, they are certain to bring painful death unless surgery is promptly performed.

NATURAL CHEW BONES

Strong natural bones, such as 4- to 8-inch lengths of round shin bone from mature beef—either the kind you can get from your butcher or one of the varieties available commercially in pet stores—may serve your dog's teething needs, if his mouth is large enough to handle them.

You may be tempted to give your puppy a smaller bone and he may not be able to break it when you do, but puppies grow rapidly and the power of their jaws constantly increases until maturity. This means that a growing dog may break one of

excessive chewing on animal bones. Contrary to popular belief, knuckle bones that can be chewed up and swallowed by the dog provide little, if any, useable calcium or other nutrient. They do, however, disturb the digestion of most dogs and might cause them to vomit the nourishing food they really need.

the smaller bones at any time, swallow the pieces and die painfully before you realize what is wrong.

All hard natural bones are highly abrasive. If your dog is an avid chewer, natural bones may wear away his teeth prematurely; hence, they then should be taken away from your dog when the teething purposes have been served. The badly worn, and usually painful, teeth of many mature dogs can be traced to

Roar-Hide™ is the only safe rawhide chew available for dogs. It will outlast other rawhides because the hides are melted and injected into bone molds.

RAWHIDE CHEWS

The most popular material from which dog chews are made is the hide from cows, horses, and other animals. Most of these chews are made in foreign countries where the quality of the hide is not good enough for making leather. These foreign hides may contain lead, antibiotics, arsenic, or insecticides which might be detrimental to the health of your dog . . . or even your children. It is not impossible that a small child will start chewing on a piece of rawhide meant for the dog! Rawhide chews do not serve the primary chewing functions very well. They are also a bit messy when wet from mouthing, and most dogs chew them up rather rapidly. They have been considered safe for dogs until recently.

Rawhide is flavorful to dogs. They like it. Currently, some veterinarians have been attributing cases of acute constipation to large pieces of incompletely digested rawhide in the intestine. Basically it is good for them to chew on, but dogs think rawhide is food. They do not play with it nor do they use it as a pacifier to relieve doggie tension. They eat it as they would any other food. This is dangerous, for the hide is very difficult for dogs to digest and swallow, and many dogs choke on large particles of rawhide that become stuck in their throats. *Before you offer your dog rawhide chews, consult your veterinarian.* Vets have a lot of experience with canine chewing devices; ask them what they recommend.

Annealed nylon and polyurethane chew toys are recommended by veterinarians as proven-safe and effective canine chew devices.

NYLON CHEW DEVICES

The nylon bones, especially those with natural meat and bone flavor added, are probably the most complete, safe, and economical answer to the chewing need. Dogs cannot break them nor bite off sizeable chunks; hence, they are completely safe. And being longer lasting than other things offered for the purpose, they are very economical.

Hard chewing raises little bristle-like projections on the surface of the nylon bones to provide effective interim tooth

The Nylafloss® cannot cure tooth decay, but it is an optimum decay-prevention device. Make your dog's playtime a healthy time and invest in your pet's future.

cleaning and vigorous gum massage, much in the same way your toothbrush does it for you. The little projections are raked off and swallowed in the form of thin shavings, but the chemistry of the nylon is such that they break down in the stomach fluids and pass through without effect.

The toughness of the nylon provides the strong chewing resistance needed for important jaw exercise and effective help for the teething functions; however, there is no tooth wear because nylon is non-abrasive. Being inert, nylon does not support the growth of microorganisms, and it can be washed in soap and water or sterilized by boiling or in an autoclave.

There are a great variety of Nylabone® products available that veterinarians recommend as safe and healthy for your dog or puppy to chew on. These Nylabone® Pooch Pacifiers® usually don't splinter, chip, or break off in large chunks; instead, they are frizzled by the dog's chewing action, and this creates a toothbrush-like surface that cleanses the teeth and massages the gums. At the same time, these hard-nylon therapeutic devices channel doggie tension and chewing frustation into constructive rather than destructive behavior. The original nylon bone (Nylabone®) is not a toy and dogs use it only when in need of pacification. Keeping a bone in each of your dog's recreation rooms is the best method of providing the requisite pacification. Unfortunately, many nylon chew products have been copied. These inferior quality copies are sold in supermarkets and other chain stores. The really good products are sold only through veterinarians, pet shops, grooming salons and places where the sales people really know something about dogs. The good products have the flavor impregnated *into* the bone. This makes the taste last longer. The smell is undetectable to humans. The artificial bones which have a strong odor are poor-quality bones with the odor sprayed on to impress the dog owner (not the dog)! These heavily scented dog toys may impart the odor to your carpets or furniture if an odor-sprayed bone lies there wet from a dog's chewing on it.

revolutionary product that is designed to save dogs teeth and keep them healthy. Even though your dogs won't believe you, Nylafloss® is not a toy but rather a most effective agent in removing destructive plaque

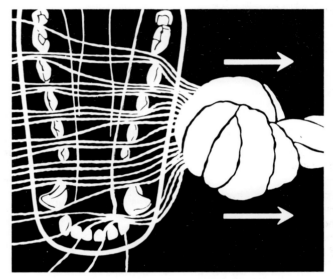

Food particles can be deposited between the teeth, where they can be difficult to remove. Many chew products cannot work to remove these decaying food pieces. For this reason, the Nylafloss® dental device is recommended by professionals as it is the only available mechanism to clean between the dog's teeth.

FLOSS OR LOSS!

Most dentists relay that brushing daily is just not enough. In order to prevent unnecessary tooth loss, flossing is essential. For dogs, human dental floss is not the answer—however, canine dental devices are available. The Nylafloss® is a

between the teeth and *beneath* the gum line where gum disease begins. Gentle tugging is all that is necessary to activate the Nylafloss®. These 100% inert nylon products are guaranteed to outlast rawhide chews by ten times and are available for sale at all pet shops.

Preventive Dental Care

THE IMPORTANCE OF PREVENTION

In order to get to the root of canine dentistry problems, it is important for owners to realize that no less than 75% of all canine dental health problems, serious enough to require a vet's assistance, and nearly 98% of all canine teeth lost are attributable to periodontal disease.

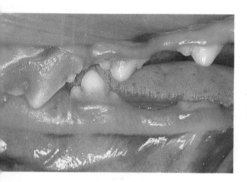

A dog's teeth showing moderate calculus build-up. The moderate calculus build-up on this dog's teeth reflects a certain neglect by the owner. Providing a safe chew item like the Gumabone® can save your dog's teeth.

Periodontal disease not only mars the teeth but also the gums and other buccal tissue in the mouth. Severe cases of periodontal disease involve resultant bacterial toxins which are absorbed into the blood stream and cause permanent damage to the heart and kidneys. In the infected mouth, teeth are loosened; tartar, unsightly and bad smelling, accumulates heavily; and the dog experiences a complete loss of appetite. Long-standing periodontitis can also manifest itself in simple symptoms such as diarrhea and vomiting.

Periodontal disease deserves the attention of every dog owner—a dog's teeth are extremely important to his ongoing health. The accumulation of plaque, food matter mixed with saliva attaching itself to the tooth surface, is a sure sign of potential bacteria build-up. As toxic material gathers, the bone surrounding the teeth erodes. If plaque and calculus continue to reside without attention, bacteria-fighting cells will form residual pus at the root of the teeth, dividing the gum from the tooth. The debris is toxic and actually kills the buccal tissue. This is a most undesirable situation, as hardened dental calculus is one of the most direct causative agents of periodontitis.

In actuality, the disease is a result of a number of contributing factors. Old age, a diet comprised solely of soft or semi-soft foods, dental tartar, constant chewing of hair and even coprophagy (the eating of stool) are among the most common contributors.

Just as regular dental visits and brushing are necessary for humans, regular hygienic care and veterinary check-ups can help control tooth problems in canines. Involved and expensive routines can be performed on the affected, neglected mouth and teeth if decay has begun eroding the enamel and infecting the gums. Cleaning, polishing, and scaling are routine to remove calculus build-up.

Owners must claim responsibility for their dog's health, and tooth care is no small aspect of the care required. Daily brushing with a salt/baking soda solution is the best answer, but many owners find this tedious or just too difficult to perform. The simpler and more proven effective way to avoid, reduce, and fight periodontal disease and calculus build-up is giving the dog regular access to a thermoplastic polymer chew device. The Gumabone® products are the only scientifically proven line that offers the desired protection from calculus and tartar build-up.

CANINE DENTAL BREAKTHROUGH

The independent research of Dr. Andrew Duke, D.V.M., reveals that 70% of the dogs that regularly use Gumabone® experience a reduction of calculus build-up. This find is a breakthrough for the dog world, since the Gumabone® has already resided in the toy boxes

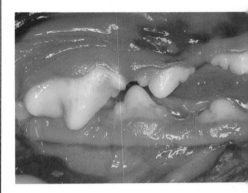

Regular use of the Gumabone® chew products can significantly reduce plaque build-up.

of many dogs as their favorite play item. Little did owners know previously that their dogs were gaining entertainment and unparalleled dental treatment at the same time. Dr. Duke writes: "There is little debate left that dental calculus is an excellent

Teeth of an infected dog showing little to no plaque accumulation after professional cleaning.

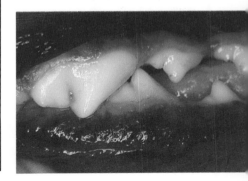

145

indicator of periodontal health in the dog, just as it is in humans. "Calculus does not cause gingivitis and periodontitis, but the plaque and bacteria that cause periodontitis are responsible for the mineral precipitation we know as 'calculus.' All veterinarians who have made a study of dogs' oral health have noticed the middle aged dog who actively chews with excellent gingival health. Many of these dogs that chew hard substances regularly wear the cusps down and even may expose the pulp cavity faster than secondary dentin can be formed. Often these "excellent chewers" are presented with slab fractures of the premolars or apical abcesses.

"The challenge then becomes to find a substance which is effective in removing calculus and plaque but does not wear the enamel excessively. In an attempt to duplicate the chewstuffs enjoyed by dogs in the wild, researchers have used bovine tracheas to demonstrate the inhibition of plaque and gingivitis. Very little else has been done in veterinary medicine

Dental products are available for helping to fight plaque, reduce tartar build-up and control unpleasant breath in dogs. Photo courtesy of Four Paws.

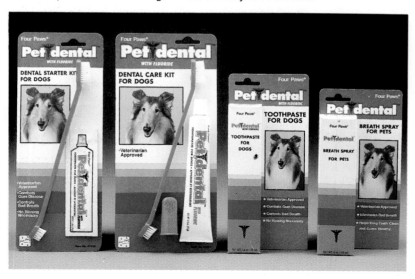

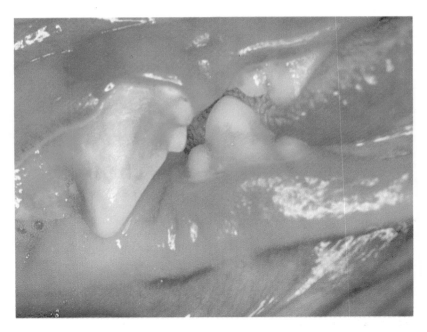

Plaque is formed by the food debris and bacterial deposits left on teeth. Due to the high carbon dioxide and pH levels in the mouth, minerals precipitate quickly on the plaque to form calculus.

to establish a scientific basis for evaluating chewstuffs.

"In the human field it is generally accepted (incorrectly) that fibrous foodstuffs and diet have no effect on oral health. This is a moot point since the practice of brushing is by far a more efficient technique of preventing plaque accumulation, calculus and periodontal disease. Studies in human subjects failed to find any benefits in eating apples, raw carrots, etc. If people are not allowed to brush, it is difficult to conduct clinical trials of more than one week.

"The increased awareness of animals' dental health of recent years has resulted in most veterinary practitioners' recommending some kind of chewstuff to their dog owners. To meet this market demand, there has been a stampede into the market by vendors ready to promote their products. The

The Hercules™ marks a new breakthrough in dog bones. Made of plastic polyurethane, Hercules is designed for powerful chewers. Comes in three sizes to suit any dog breed and fights plaque from every angle!

veterinarian is furnished no scientific data, but is asked to promote rawhide, bounce, and squeaky toys. How would our human colleagues handle this situation? Can Listerine® say that it prevents colds, but not support the claim? Can "Tartar Control Crest®" or "Colgate Tartar Control Formula®" be sold if it is not proven that it does in fact reduce tartar? Of course not.

"To this end, the following study was made.

"*Method:* Twenty dogs of different breeds and age were selected from a veterinary

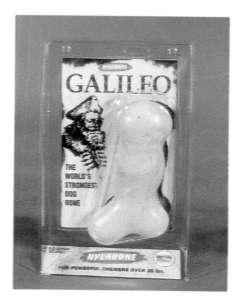

Galileo™ is the strongest nylon bone in the world. Its unique shape and solid nylon construction make it the most durable of all Nylabones.

CUMULATIVE CALCULUS INDEX SCORES

Dog	Without Gumabone®	With Gumabone®	Difference
1.	20	9	11
2.	19	23	- 4
3.	49	26	23
4.	21	15	6
5.	34	11	23
6.	36	21	15
7.	44	31	13
8.	25	25	0
9.	34	28	6
10.	44	23	21
11.	22	15	7
12.	23	33	-10
13.	26	23	3
14.	22	14	8
15.	20	20	0
16.	23	13	10
17.	24	14	10
18.	24	17	7
19.	24	31	-7
20.	15	30	-15

As supported by Dr. Duke's study on reducing calculus build-up, the effectiveness of a chewing device can be measured by assigning numerical values to the accumulation when the Gumabone® device is used and not used. Seventy percent of dogs chewing Gumabone® (14 out of 20 dogs) showed a reduction in calculus build-up.

practice's clientele. Although most were from multiple pet households, none were colony dogs. The owners were asked if they would allow their dogs to be anesthetized for two prophylactic cleanings which included root planing, polishing, and gingival debridement necessary to insure good oral hygiene.

"The dogs were divided into two groups of 10. Their teeth were cleaned and their calculus index converted to 0. One group was allowed only their normal dry commercial dog ration for 30 days. The other was allowed to have free choice access to Gumabone® products of the appropriate size.

"After 30 days, photoslides were made of the upper 3rd premolar, upper 4th premolar, and the lower 4th premolar on both sides of the dog's mouth. The dogs were again subjected to a prophylactic cleaning and the group reversed. After the second 30 days, photoslides were again made. A total of six teeth in each mouth were evaluated on each dog. This was 80 slides representing 240 teeth."

Fourteen out of 20 dogs (or 70%) experienced a reduction in calculus build-up by regularly using the Gumabone® product. These products are available in a variety of sizes (for different size dogs) and designed in interesting shapes: bones, balls,

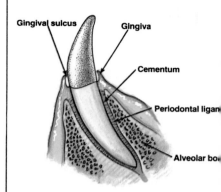

Comparative look at healthy gums (above) and affected gums (below) in a dog's mouth. Instinctively dogs need to massage their gums—and the Gumabone® can satisfy this doggie craving.

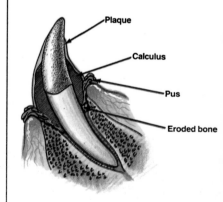

The Gumaring® and Tug Toy® have a high entertainment value plus the plaque-fighting advantage.

knots and rings (and even a tug toy). The entertainment value of the Gumabone® products is but an added advantage to the fighting of tooth decay and periodontitis. The products are ham-flavored and made of a thermoplastic polymer that is designed to outlast by ten times any rawhide, rubber or vinyl chew product, none of which can promise the proven benefit of the Gumabone®.

If your dog is able to chew apart a Gumabone®, it is probable that you provided him with a bone that is too small for him. Replace it with a larger one and the problem should not re-materialize. Economically, the Gumabone® is a smart choice, even without comparing it to the cost of extensive dental care.

Of course, nothing can *substitute* for periodic professional attention to your dog's teeth and gums, no more than your toothbrush can replace your dentist. Have your dog's teeth cleaned by your veterinarian at least once a year—twice a year is better—and he will be healthier, happier, and a far more pleasant companion.

Gumabones® are available through veterinarians and pet shops.

PERPETUAL WHELPING CHART

	1	2	3	4	5	6	7	8	9	10	11	12	13	14	15	16	17	18	19	20	21	22	23	24	25	26	27	28	29	30	31
Bred—Jan.	1	2	3	4	5	6	7	8	9	10	11	12	13	14	15	16	17	18	19	20	21	22	23	24	25	26	27	28	29	30	31
Due—March	5	6	7	8	9	10	11	12	13	14	15	16	17	18	19	20	21	22	23	24	25	26	27	28	29	30	31	1	2	3	4
Bred—Feb.	1	2	3	4	5	6	7	8	9	10	11	12	13	14	15	16	17	18	19	20	21	22	23	24	25	26	27	28			
Due—April	5	6	7	8	9	10	11	12	13	14	15	16	17	18	19	20	21	22	23	24	25	26	27	28	29	30	1	2			
Bred—Mar.	1	2	3	4	5	6	7	8	9	10	11	12	13	14	15	16	17	18	19	20	21	22	23	24	25	26	27	28	29	30	31
Due—May	3	4	5	6	7	8	9	10	11	12	13	14	15	16	17	18	19	20	21	22	23	24	25	26	27	28	29	30	31	1	2
Bred—Apr.	1	2	3	4	5	6	7	8	9	10	11	12	13	14	15	16	17	18	19	20	21	22	23	24	25	26	27	28	29	30	
Due—June	3	4	5	6	7	8	9	10	11	12	13	14	15	16	17	18	19	20	21	22	23	24	25	26	27	28	29	30	1	2	
Bred—May	1	2	3	4	5	6	7	8	9	10	11	12	13	14	15	16	17	18	19	20	21	22	23	24	25	26	27	28	29	30	31
Due—July	3	4	5	6	7	8	9	10	11	12	13	14	15	16	17	18	19	20	21	22	23	24	25	26	27	28	29	30	31	1	2
Bred—June	1	2	3	4	5	6	7	8	9	10	11	12	13	14	15	16	17	18	19	20	21	22	23	24	25	26	27	28	29	30	
Due—August	3	4	5	6	7	8	9	10	11	12	13	14	15	16	17	18	19	20	21	22	23	24	25	26	27	28	29	30	31	1	
Bred—July	1	2	3	4	5	6	7	8	9	10	11	12	13	14	15	16	17	18	19	20	21	22	23	24	25	26	27	28	29	30	31
Due—September	2	3	4	5	6	7	8	9	10	11	12	13	14	15	16	17	18	19	20	21	22	23	24	25	26	27	28	29	30	1	2
Bred—Aug.	1	2	3	4	5	6	7	8	9	10	11	12	13	14	15	16	17	18	19	20	21	22	23	24	25	26	27	28	29	30	31
Due—October	3	4	5	6	7	8	9	10	11	12	13	14	15	16	17	18	19	20	21	22	23	24	25	26	27	28	29	30	31	1	2
Bred—Sept.	1	2	3	4	5	6	7	8	9	10	11	12	13	14	15	16	17	18	19	20	21	22	23	24	25	26	27	28	29	30	
Due—November	3	4	5	6	7	8	9	10	11	12	13	14	15	16	17	18	19	20	21	22	23	24	25	26	27	28	29	30	1	2	
Bred—Oct.	1	2	3	4	5	6	7	8	9	10	11	12	13	14	15	16	17	18	19	20	21	22	23	24	25	26	27	28	29	30	31
Due—December	3	4	5	6	7	8	9	10	11	12	13	14	15	16	17	18	19	20	21	22	23	24	25	26	27	28	29	30	31	1	2
Bred—Nov.	1	2	3	4	5	6	7	8	9	10	11	12	13	14	15	16	17	18	19	20	21	22	23	24	25	26	27	28	29	30	
Due—January	3	4	5	6	7	8	9	10	11	12	13	14	15	16	17	18	19	20	21	22	23	24	25	26	27	28	29	30	31	1	
Bred—Dec.	1	2	3	4	5	6	7	8	9	10	11	12	13	14	15	16	17	18	19	20	21	22	23	24	25	26	27	28	29	30	31
Due—February	2	3	4	5	6	7	8	9	10	11	12	13	14	15	16	17	18	19	20	21	22	23	24	25	26	27	28	1	2	3	4

Breeding

As the owner of a purebred dog, you may have considered breeding your pet at one time or another. If your dog is a beloved family pet, and not a show dog, you should *not* breed your dog. Breeding is not a hobby for pet owners, but rather a demanding, complicated vocation that is not to be dabbled with. Many people have thought of breeding as an easy-money opportunity: buy two dogs and let them do the work. The rule of thumb is: if you're making money by breeding dogs, you're doing something wrong!

Consider the time and money involved just to get your bitch into breeding condition and then to sustain her throughout pregnancy and afterwards while she tends her young. You will be obligated to house, feed, groom, and housebreak the puppies until good homes can be found for them; and, lest we forget, there will be periodic trips to the vet for check-ups, wormings, and inoculations. Common sense should tell you that it is indeed cruel to bring unwanted or unplanned puppies into an already crowded canine world; only negligent pet owners allow this to happen. Recognizing the number of dogs, purebred and mixed breeds, pet-, show- and breeding-quality, that are put to sleep annually, responsible breeders require that all pet animals be neutered. This condition most often is

incorporated into the selling contract. The motives of good breeders are clear: avoid the manufacturing and mass-producing of average and below-average dogs; control the overblown canine population; concentrate on the improvement of purebred bloodlines. Breeding is a noble calling and unless you can improve the breed, you should not consider breeding your animal. Despite all of the obvious virtues of breeding texts, no book could ever prepare a person for breeding. What a heart-breaking and tragic experience to lose an entire litter because a good-intentioned pet owner wasn't aware of potential genetic complications, didn't recognize a breech birth, or couldn't identify the signals of a struggling bitch! Possibly the dam could be lost as well!

Before you take any step towards mating your bitch, think carefully about why you want her to give birth to a litter of puppies. If you feel she will be deprived in some way if she is not bred, if you think your children will learn from the experience, if you have the mistaken notion that you will make money from this great undertaking, think again. A dog can lead a perfectly happy, healthy, normal life without having been mated; in fact, spaying a female and neutering a male helps them become better, longer-lived pets, as they are not

Breeding

so anxious to search for a mate in an effort to relieve their sexual tensions and have a diminished risk of cancer. As for giving the children a lesson in sex education, this is hardly a valid reason for breeding your dog. And on an economic level, it takes not only years of hard work (researching pedigrees and bloodlines, studying genetics, among other things), but it takes plenty of capital (money, equipment, facilities) to make a decent profit from dog breeding.

Why most dedicated breeders are lucky just to break even. If you have only a casual interest in dog breeding, it is best to leave this pastime to those who are more experienced in such matters, those who consider it a serious hobby and a real vocation. If you have bought a breeder– or show-quality canine, one that may be capable of producing champions, and if you are just starting out with this breeding venture, seek advice from the seller of your dog, from

Breeding dogs requires more than book knowledge. In dogs, breech presentation is not uncommon and the breeder must be prepared to handle this situation and guide the puppy so that neither the pup nor the bitch is injured.

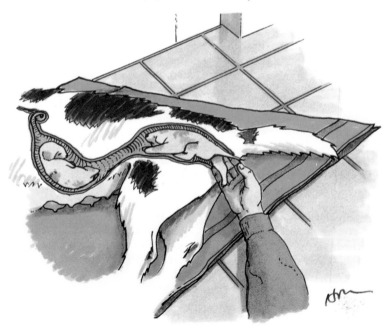

other veteran breeders, and from your veterinarian before you begin.

The following sections on reproduction are intended for academic value only. This is not a "How-to" chapter on breeding, nor a step-by-step approach for the novice for getting started. Hopefully the reader will understand the depth and complexity of breeding as well as the expected ethical and moral obligations of persons who choose to do so—and never attempt it.

THE FEMALE "IN SEASON"

A bitch may come into season (also known as "heat" or estrus) once or several times a year, depending on the particular breed and the individual dog. Her first seasonal period, that is to say, the time when she is capable of being fertilized by a male dog, may occur as early as six months with some breeds. If you own a female and your intention is *not* to breed her, by all means discuss with the vet the possibility of having her spayed: this means before she

Ideally the puppy will be delivered in the normal, head-first position.

155

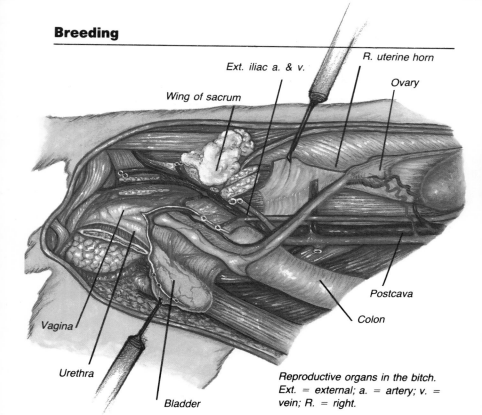

Ext. iliac a. & v.

R. uterine horn

Ovary

Wing of sacrum

R. uterine horn

Postcava

Colon

Vagina

Urethra

Bladder

Reproductive organs in the bitch.
Ext. = external; a. = artery; v. =
vein; R. = right.

The reproductive system of the female dog consists of a highly specialized system of organs situated to the rear of the animal.

reaches sexual maturity.

The first sign of the female's being in season is a thin red discharge, which may increase for about a week; it then changes color to a thin yellowish stain, which lasts about another week. Simultaneously, there is a swelling of the vulva, the exterior portion of the female's reproductive tract; the soft, flabby vulva indicates her readiness to mate. Around this second week or so ovulation

occurs, and this is the crucial period for her to be bred, if this is what you have in mind for her. It is during this middle phase of the heat cycle when conception can take place. Just remember that there is great variation from bitch to bitch with regard to how often they come into heat, how long the heat cycles last, how long the period of ovulation lasts, and how much time elapses between heat cycles. Generally, after the third week of heat, the vulval swelling decreases and the estrus period ceases for several months.

It should be mentioned that the female will probably lose her puppy coat, or at least shed part of it, about three months after she has come into season. This is the time when her puppies would have been weaned, had she been mated, and females generally drop coat at this time.

With female dogs, there are few, if any, behavioral changes during estrus. A bitch may dart out of an open door to greet all available male dogs that show an interest in her, and she may occasionally raise her tail and assume a mating stance, particularly if you pet her lower back; but these signs are not as dramatic as those of the sexually mature male. He himself does

Each egg within the female is surrounded by a wall that normally takes many sperm to penetrate. In this way, it is more likely that only the strongest sperm will fertilize the egg. A fertile female in season usually has a number of eggs, known as gametes.

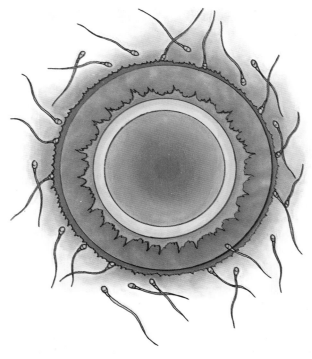

not experience heat cycles; rather, he is attracted to the female during all phases of her seasonal period. He usually becomes more aggressive and tends to fight with other males, especially over females in heat. He tends to mark his territory with urine to attract females and at the same time to warn other competitive males. It is not uncommon to see him mount various objects, and people, in an effort to satisfy his mature sexual urges.

If you are a homeowner and you have an absolutely climb-proof and dig-proof run within your yard, it may be safe to leave your bitch in season there. But then again it may not be a wise idea, as there have been cases of males mating with females right through chain-link fencing! Just to be on the safe side, shut her indoors during her heat periods and don't let her outdoors until you are certain the estrus period is over. Never leave a bitch in heat outdoors, unsupervised, even for a minute so that she can defecate or urinate. If you want to prevent the neighborhood dogs from hanging around your doorstep, as they inevitably will do when they discover your female is in season, take her some distance away from the house before you let her do her business. Otherwise, these canine suitors will be attracted to her by the arousing odor of her urine, and they will know instinctively that she isn't far from her scented "calling card." If you need to walk your bitch, take her in the car to a nearby park or field for a chance to stretch her legs. Remember that after about three weeks, and this varies from dog to dog, you can let her outdoors again with no worry that she can have puppies until the next heat period.

If you are seriously considering breeding your dog, first talk to as many experienced breeders as possible and read up on the subject in specific books and articles. Only when you are fully aware of the demands and responsibilities of breeding should you make your final decision. It must be stated here that there is no shortage of fine dogs in need of good homes, nor is there likely to be in the foreseeable future. So, if your object in breeding is merely to produce more dogs, you are strongly encouraged to reconsider your objective.

WHEN TO BREED

It is usually best to breed a bitch when she comes into her second or third season. Plan in advance the time of year which is best for you, taking into account your own schedule of activities (vacations, business trips, social engagements, and so on). Make sure you will be able to set aside plenty of time to assist with whelping of the newborn pups and caring for the dam and her litter for the next few weeks. At

The male reproductive system includes the penis and testicles. When not excited, the penis is withdrawn into the dog's body.

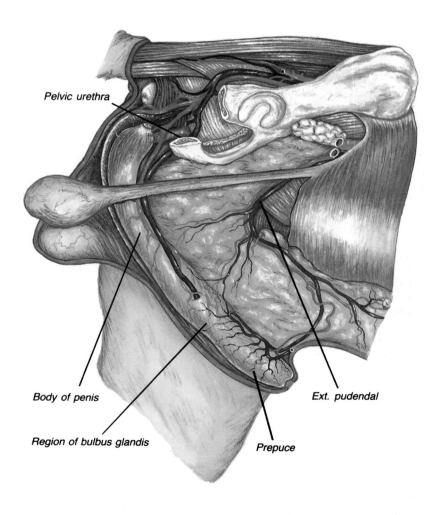

Pelvic urethra

Body of penis

Region of bulbus glandis

Prepuce

Ext. pudendal

the very least, it probably will take an hour or so each day just to feed and clean up after the brood—but undoubtedly you will find it takes much longer if you stop to admire and play with the youngsters periodically! Refrain from selling the litter until it is at least six weeks old, keeping in mind that a litter of pups takes up a fair amount of space by then. It will be your responsibility to provide for them until they have been weaned from their mother, properly socialized, housebroken, and ready to go to new homes (unless you plan to keep them all). Hopefully, as strongly recommended, you will have already lined up buyers for the pups in advance of their arrival into this world.

CHOOSING THE STUD

You can plan to breed your female about six-and-one-half months after the start of her last season, although a variation of a month or two either way is not unusual. Do some research into the various bloodlines within your breed and then choose a stud dog and make arrangements well in advance. If you are breeding for show stock, which will command higher prices than pet-quality animals, a mate should be chosen very carefully. He should complement any deficiencies (bad traits) that your female may have, and he should have a good show record

or be the sire of show winners, if he is old enough to have proven himself. If possible, the bitch and stud should have several ancestors in common within the last two or three generations, as such combinations have been known, generally, to "click" best.

The owner of a stud dog usually charges a stud fee for use of the animal's services. This does not always guarantee a litter, but if she fails to conceive, chances are you may be able to breed your female to that stud again. In some instances the owner of the stud will agree to take a "first pick of the litter" in place of a fee. You should, of course, settle all details beforehand, including the possibility of a single puppy surviving, deciding the age at which the pup is to be taken, and so forth.

If you plan to raise a litter that will be sold exclusively as pets, and if you merely plan to make use of an available male (not a top stud dog), the most important selection point involves temperament. Make sure the dog is friendly, as well as healthy, because a bad disposition can be passed on to his puppies—and this is the worst of all traits in a dog destined to be a pet. If you are breeding pet-quality dogs, a "stud fee puppy," not necessarily the choice of the litter, is the usual payment. Don't

Whelping box prepared with "pig rails," bars on either side of the box to prevent the bitch from rolling on the puppies.

breed indiscriminately; be sure you will be able to find good homes for each of the pups.

PREPARATION FOR BREEDING

Before you breed your female, make sure she is in good health. She should be neither too thin nor too fat. Any skin disease *must* be cured first so that it is not passed on to the puppies. If she has worms, she should be wormed before being bred or within three weeks after the mating. It is generally considered a good idea to revaccinate her against distemper and hepatitis before the puppies are born.

The female will probably be ready to breed twelve days after the first colored discharge appears. You can usually make arrangements to board her with the owner of the stud for a few days, to insure her being there at the proper time; or you can take her to be mated and bring her home the same day if you live near enough to the stud's owner. If the bitch still appears receptive she may be bred again two days later, just to make certain the mating was successful. However, some females never show signs of willingness, so it helps to have an experienced breeder on hand. In fact, you both may have to assist with the mating by holding the animals against each other to ensure the "tie" is not broken, that is, to make certain copulation takes place.

Usually the second day after the discharge changes color is the proper time to mate the bitch, and she may be bred for about three days following this time. For an additional week or so, she may have some discharge and attract other dogs by her odor; but she should not be bred. Once she has been bred, keep her far from all other male dogs, as they have the capacity to impregnate her again and sire some of her puppies. This could prove disastrous with purebred puppies.

THE FEMALE IN WHELP

You can expect the puppies nine weeks from the day of the mating, although sixty-one days is as common as sixty-three. Gestation, that period when the pups are developing inside their mother, varies among individual bitches. During this time the female should receive normal care and exercise. If she was overweight at the start, don't increase her food right away; excess weight at whelping time can be a problem with some dogs. If she is on the thin side, however, supplement her meal or meals with a portion of milk and biscuit at noontime. This will help build her up and put weight on her.

You may want to add a mineral and vitamin supplement to her diet, on the advice of your veterinarian, since she will need an extra supply not only for herself but for the puppies growing inside her. As the mother's appetite increases, feed her more. During the last two weeks of pregnancy, the pups grow enormously and the mother will have little room for food and less of an appetite. She should be tempted with meat, liver, and milk, however.

As the female in whelp grows heavier, cut out violent exercise and jumping from her usual routine. Although a dog used to such activities will often play with the children or run around voluntarily, restrain her for her own sake.

A sign that whelping is imminent is the loss of hair around her breasts. This is nature's way of "clearing a path" so that the puppies will be able to find their source of nourishment. As parturition draws near, the breasts will have swelled with milk and the nipples will have enlarged and darkened to a rosy pink. If the hair in the breast region does not shed for some reason, you can easily cut it short with a pair of scissors or comb it out so that it does not mat and become a hindrance to the suckling pups later on.

PREPARING FOR THE PUPPIES

Prepare a whelping box a few days before the puppies are due, and allow the mother to sleep there overnight or to spend some time in it during the day to become accustomed to it. This way she is less likely to try to have her pups under the front porch or in the middle of your bed. A variety of places will serve, such as the corner of your cellar or garage (provided these

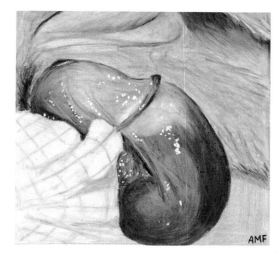

Each puppy is delivered in a separate membranous sac. This sac must be removed by the bitch without delay—if not, the breeder must come immediately to the assistance of the pup.

AMF

places are warm and dry). An unused room, such as a dimly lit spare bedroom, can also serve as the place for delivery. If the weather is warm, a large outdoor dog house will do, as long as it is well protected from rain, drafts, and the cold—and enclosed by fencing or a run. A whelping box serves to separate mother and puppies from visitors and other distractions. The walls should be high enough to restrain the puppies yet low enough to allow the mother to take a short respite from her brood after she has fed them. Four feet square is minimum size (for most dogs) and six-to-eight-inch high walls will keep the pups in until they begin to climb; then side walls should be built up so that the young ones cannot wander away from their nest. As the puppies

grow, they really need more room anyway, so double the space with a very low partition down the middle of the box, and soon you will find them naturally housebreaking themselves. Puppies rarely relieve themselves where they sleep. Layers of newspapers spread over the whole area will make excellent bedding and be absorbent enough to keep the surface warm and dry. These should be removed daily and replaced with another thick layer. An old quilt or washable blanket makes better footing for the nursing puppies than slippery newspaper during the first week; this is also softer for the mother to lie on.

Be prepared for the actual whelping several days in advance. Usually the mother will tear up papers, refuse food, and become restless. These may be false alarms; the real test is her temperature, which will drop to below 100°F (38°C) about twelve hours before whelping. Take her temperature with a rectal thermometer, morning and evening, and usher her to her whelping box when her temperature goes down. Keep a close watch on her and make sure she stays safely indoors (or outdoors in a safe enclosure); if she is let outside, unleashed, or allowed to roam freely, she could wander off and start to go into labor. It is possible that she could whelp anywhere, and this could be unfortunate if she needs your assistance.

WHELPING

Usually little help is needed from you, but it is wise to stay close to be sure that the mother's lack of experience (if this is her first time) does not cause an unnecessary complication. Be ready to help when the first puppy arrives, for it could smother if she does not break the amniotic membrane enclosing it. She should tear open the sac and start licking the puppy, drying and stimulating it. Check to see that all fluids have been cleared from the pup's nostrils and mouth after the mother has licked her youngster clean; otherwise the pup may have difficulty breathing. If the mother fails to tear open the sac and stimulate the newborn's breathing, you can do this yourself by tearing the sack with your hands and then gently rubbing the infant with a soft, rough towel. The afterbirth attached to the puppy by the long umbilical cord, should follow the birth of each puppy. Watch to be sure that each afterbirth is expelled, for the retention of this material can cause infection. In her instinct for cleanliness the mother will probably eat the afterbirth after severing the umbilical cord. One or two meals of this will not hurt her; they stimulate her milk supply, as well as labor, for remaining pups. However, eating too many afterbirths can make her lose appetite for the food she needs to feed her pups and regain her strength. So remove the rest of them, along with the wet newspapers, and keep the box dry and clean.

If the mother does not bite the cord or bites it too close to the puppy's body, take over the job to prevent an umbilical hernia. Tearing is recommended, but you can cut the cord, about two inches from the body, with a sawing motion with scissors that have been sterilized in alcohol. Then dip the end of the cut cord in a shallow dish of iodine; the cord will dry up and fall off in a few days.

The puppies should follow

each other at intervals of not more than half an hour. If more time goes past and you are sure there are still pups to come, taking the mother for a brisk walk outside may start labor again. If she is actively straining without producing a puppy, the youngster may be presented backward, a so-called "breech" birth. Careful assistance with a well-lubricated finger to feel for the puppy or to ease it back may help, but never attempt to pull it out by force. This could cause serious damage, so seek the services of an expert—your veterinarian or an experienced breeder.

Even the best planned breeding can bear unexpected problems and complications. Therefore, do not rely solely on textbook knowledge of breeding and genetics. Experienced breeders and veterinarians will generally lend their words of wisdom—take full advantage of their generosity. Mere trial and error is no basis for any responsible breeding program.

If *anything* seems wrong during labor or parturition, waste no time in calling your veterinarian, who will examine the bitch and, if necessary, give her hormones to stimulate the birth of the remaining puppies. You may want his experience in whelping the litter even if all goes well. He will probably prefer to have the puppies born at his

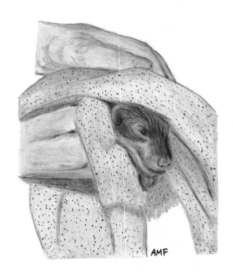

Newborn pups are very susceptible to chills, so the breeder must dry the puppy off thoroughly and place it in a temperature-controlled puppy box.

hospital rather than getting up in the middle of the night to come to your home. The mother would, no doubt, prefer to stay at home; but you can be sure she will get the best of care in a veterinary hospital. If the puppies are born at home, and all goes as it should, watch the mother carefully afterward. Within a day or two of the birth, it is wise to have the veterinarian check her and the pups to ensure that all is well.

Small bowls are helpful in the weaning process. Each pup should have its own bowl so that food intake can be carefully monitored.

Be sure each puppy finds a teat and starts nursing right away, as these first few meals supply colostral antibodies to help him fight disease. As soon as he is dry, hold each puppy to a nipple for a good meal without competition. Then he may join his littermates in the whelping box, out of his mother's way while she continues giving birth. Keep a supply of puppy formula on hand for emergency feedings or later weaning. An alternative formula of evaporated milk, corn syrup, and a little water with egg yolk can be warmed and fed if necessary. A pet nurser kit is also a good thing to have on hand; these are available at local pet shops. A supplementary feeding often helps weak pups

(those that may have difficulty nursing) over the hump. Keep track of birth weights and weekly readings thereafter; this will furnish an accurate record of the pups' growth and health, and the information will be valuable to your veterinarian.

RAISING THE PUPPIES

After all the puppies have been born, take the mother outside for a walk and drink of water, and then return her to take care of her brood. She will probably not want to stay away for more than a minute or two for the first few weeks. Be sure to keep water available at all times and feed her milk or broth frequently, as she needs nourishment to produce milk. Encourage her to eat, with her favorite foods, until she seeks them of her own accord. She will soon develop a ravenous appetite and should have at least two large meals a day, with dry food available in addition. Your veterinarian can guide you on the finer points of nutrition as they apply to nursing dams.

Prepare a warm place to put the puppies after they are born to keep them dry and to help them to a good start in life. An electric heating pad, heat lamp or hot water bottle covered with flannel can be placed in the bottom of a cardboard box and near the mother so that she can see her puppies. She will usually allow you to help her care for the youngsters, but don't take them out of her sight. Let her handle things if your interference seems to make her nervous.

Be sure that all the puppies are getting enough to eat. If the mother sits or stands instead of lying still to nurse, the probable cause is scratching from the puppies' nails. You can remedy this by clipping them, as you would the bitch's, with a pet nail clipper. Manicure scissors also do

furnished with a heating pad and/or heating lamp and some bedding material. Leave half the litter with the mother and the other half in the extra box, changing off at two-hour intervals at first. Later you may exchange them less frequently, leaving them all together except during the day. Try supplementary feedings, too. As soon as their eyes open, at about two weeks, they will lap from a small dish.

"Pooping" the puppies, or rubbing the bowels and genitals to stimulate elimination, may be necessary if the bitch doesn't tend to this herself.

for these tiny claws. Some breeders advise disposing of the smaller or weaker pups in a large litter, as the mother has trouble handling more than six or seven. You can help her out by preparing an extra puppy box or basket

WEANING THE PUPPIES

Normally the puppies should be completely weaned at five weeks, although you can start to feed them at three weeks. They will find it easier to lap semi-solid food than to drink milk at first, so

167

mix baby cereal with whole or evaporated milk, warmed to body temperature, and offer it to the puppies in a saucer. Until they learn to lap it, it is best to feed one or two at a time because they are more likely to walk into it than to eat it. Hold the saucer at their chin level, and let them gather around, keeping paws off the dish. Cleaning with a damp sponge afterward prevents most of the cereal from sticking to the pups if the mother doesn't clean them up. Once they have gotten the idea, broth or babies' meat soup may be alternated with milk, and you can start them on finely chopped meat. At about four weeks, they will eat four meals a day and soon do without their mother entirely. Start them on canned dog food, or leave dry puppy food with them in a dish

for self-feeding. Don't leave the water dish with them all the time; at this age everything is a play toy and they will use it as a wading pool. They can drink all they need if it is offered several times a day, after meals. As the puppies grow up, the mother will go into their "pen" only to nurse them, first sitting up and then standing. To dry up her milk

All puppies are susceptible to worms. Deworming must begin at a very early age with the supervision of a professional.

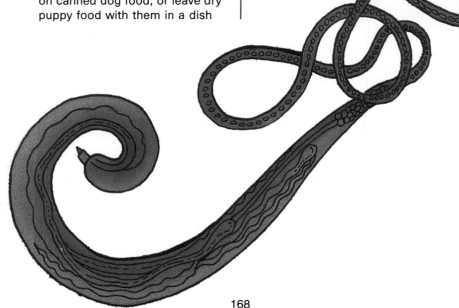

Bottle-feeding may be necessary with particularly large litters or with a bitch who has become overly stressed or neglectful.

supply completely, keep the mother away for longer periods; after a few days of part-time nursing she can stay away for even longer periods, and then permanently. The little milk left will be resorbed by her body.

The puppies may be put outside during the day, unless it is too cold or rainy, as soon as their eyes are open. They will benefit from the sunlight. A rubber mat or newspapers underneath will protect them from cold or dampness. As they mature, the pups can be let out for longer intervals, although you must provide them with a shelter at night or in bad weather. By now, cleaning up after the

matured youngsters is a man-sized job, so put them out at least during the day and make your task easier. If you enclose them in a run or kennel, remember to clean it *daily*, as various parasites and other infectious organisms may be lurking if the quarters are kept dirty.

You can expect the pups to need at least one worming before they are ready to go to new homes. Before the pups are three weeks old, take a stool sample from each to your veterinarian. The vet can determine, by analyzing the stool, if any of the pups have worms—and if so, what kind of worms are present. If one puppy is infected, then all should be wormed as a preventive measure. Follow the veterinarian's advice; this also applies to vaccinations. You will want to vaccinate the pups at the earliest possible age. This way, the pups destined for new homes will be protected against some of the more debilitating canine diseases.

THE DECISION TO SPAY OR NEUTER

If you decide not to use your male or female for breeding, or if you are obligated to have the animal altered based on an agreement made between you and the seller, make the necessary arrangements with your veterinarian as soon as possible. The surgery involved for both males and females is relatively simple and painless: males will be castrated and females will have their ovaries and uterus removed. In both cases, the operation does not alter their personalities; you will, however, notice that males will be less likely to roam, to get into fights with other male dogs, and to mount objects and people.

Your veterinarian can best determine at what age neutering or spaying should be done. With a young female dog, the operation may be somewhat more involved, and as a result be more costly; however, in the long

The breeder must actively partake in cleaning the pup after feedings. Hands-on contact serves as the initial step in socialization—accustoming the pup to his human family.

PUPPY GROWTH AND BREEDER RESPONSIBILITY	
AGE	**REQUIRED CARE/EXPECTED DEVELOPMENT**
WEEKS 1–2	Helpless; dam must provide constant care; owner must ensure warmth and cleanliness; puppy nurses, crawls, needs stimulation for elimination; sleeps 90% of time.
WEEKS 3–4	Owner sustains optimum environment; puppy is alert, laps from bowl, takes first steps; defecates on its own; baby teeth emerge; barks, wags tail.
WEEKS 4–5	Ambles, growls, and bites; play and interaction increase; human contact limited but essential; learning begins.
WEEKS 5–6	Weaning; human socialization vital; pack order apparent; sex play; explores and sleeps less.
WEEKS 6–8	Two to three daily meals; puppy accustomed to human family; breeder initiates housetraining; first veterinary visit; wary of the unknown.

run you will be glad you made the decision to have this done for your pet. After a night or two at the veterinarian's or an animal hospital, your bitch can be safely returned to your home. Her stitches will heal in a short time, and when they are removed, you will hardly notice her souvenir scar of the routine operation. Once she has been spayed, she no longer will be capable of having a litter of puppies.

Check with your city or town or with the local humane society for special programs that are available for pet owners. In many municipalities you can have your pet altered for just a small fee; the low price is meant to encourage pet owners to take advantage of this important means of birth control for their dogs. Pet adoption agencies and other animal welfare organizations can house only so many animals at one time, given the money, space, and other resources they have available. This is why pet owners are urged to have their pets altered, so that puppies resulting from accidental breedings won't end up being put to sleep as so many others have that are lost, stray, unwanted, or abandoned.

Dogs and the Law

BY ANMARIE BARRIE

No matter where you live, there will be laws and ordinances restricting the ownership of pets—exotic and wild animals (such as monkeys, pythons, and ocelots) as well as the more traditionally kept domestics (such as dogs and cats). This chapter purports to investigate with brevity the laws which pertain to the ownership and keeping of the domestic canine. Like all other things, laws change and evolve over time, and vary from locale to locale. The information supplied in this chapter is meant as a general guideline for the dog owner. Every owner is strongly encouraged to contact his local authorities to keep abreast on new laws and amendments to existing laws so that he can be the most responsible owner possible.

BUYING AND SELLING

Certain specific laws apply to the purchasing and peddling of pooches. Laws in these areas grow ever more stringent, so the potential buyer and/or seller is well advised to be aware of the laws pertaining to his transactions where dogs are concerned. Dealers and breeders, in most instances, are treated differently from the average dog owner who is trying to sell his first litter. Regardless, a sales contract is in order, a written agreement outlining the various dimensions of the sale. Sales contracts may indicate the quality of the dog, i.e., the pet-quality, show-quality, breeder-quality; the sex of the dog; and the breed of the dog. In addition to these basic essentials, the specifics, as registered with the national kennel club, should be included, i.e., the names and registration numbers of the sire and dam; the litter registration number; addresses of all involved, etc. Warranties and conditions of the sale should also be expressly stated, and no implications or unexpressed conditions may apply. For instance, the return policy, the guaranteed pedigree of the dog, the health of the dog (including the possibility of congenital defects in later years) should all be addressed. Replacement warranties are also appropriate to include, should something happen to the purchased puppy. Should a given puppy (of intended show-quality) begin to exhibit faults disqualified in the breed standard, the buyer is able to return the dog. Commonly, if the seller is no longer in the business of selling dogs, the buyer is entitled to half of the agreed-upon price.

GENERAL GUIDELINES FOR DOG OWNERS

"Give to God what is God's, give to Caesar what is Caesar's" is a Gospel quote that has been used and manipulated since it was originally uttered two thousand years ago. The concept of paying taxes has never sat well with humans, nor does it sit well with dogs. Licenses are basically taxes on dogs, though as pet owners we need not stew over the unfairness of "yet another tax." The purpose of licensing dogs is a valid and important one. Licenses serve as a positive means of identifying an animal and afford an owner with a fair chance of regaining his dog if lost or stolen. Licenses also provide a dog additional consideration by authorities and even from strangers, who will respect the fact the owner of this dog cares enough to identify it and affix its ID to its collar.

Many owners resist the call to license their dogs on the premise that their dogs are house dogs or yard dogs, or never ever walk off their leashes. Nonetheless, accidents and mishaps occur regularly, and it's better to be safe than sorry (why not be safe and law-abiding!?). The threat of impoundment and the treatment which dogs receive as a matter of course from such authorities should be scare tactic enough to persuade an owner to license his dog.

The cost of licenses varies from place to place as well as from dog to dog. Licenses for assistance dogs, such as Seeing Eye dogs, hearing dogs, or any handicap-assistance dogs, may be substan-

Dogs and the Law

tially less than a regular dog. In some areas, assistance dogs receive their licenses gratis, or are covered by their training agency. Recognizing the growing problem of dog over-population, many towns and cities offer reduced license fees for spayed and neutered dogs.

Vaccinations for dogs deserve special mention. Depending on where you live, the vaccination for rabies may or may not be mandatory. In some places, this vaccination is optional. While the chances of your well-kept canine acquiring rabies today may be minuscule, the cases are not so isolated and unheard of that an owner can rest in ultimate confidence. Generally a vaccinated dog can avoid being

quarantined in the unfortunate event that it should bite a stranger or would-be assailant. The age for vaccination varies, but most usual is six months old. If a puppy is under the age of six months, it is advisable not to permit it to socialize with unknown dogs on the street. Keep in mind that vaccinations need to be kept updated for both rabies and other diseases.

Among the most common-sense concerns of current-day owners are leash laws. Responsible dog owners marvel with dismay over dogs which run the neighborhood without a collar, supervision, or their owner's concern. Caring dog proprietors are grateful for leash laws as it is the protection of the dog, as well as human passers-by, that is concerned. That a dog is under control at all times remains the premise of leash laws. Dogs that are given the "freedom" to wander the neighborhood or city block are likewise given the "right" to be impounded, snatched and/or injured. Fines are often issued against owners who do not abide by the leash laws of their community.

Running hand in hand, or paw in paw, with leash laws are muzzle ordinances. These laws require

that a dog be muzzled at all times when it is in public. Although these laws are less commonplace than leash laws, they do exist in certain communities. Owners are advised to investigate if muzzle laws apply in their area.

Pooper-scooper laws are being enforced in more and more areas these days. "Curb Your Dog" signs have become as common as pedestrian crossings and "Yield signs." For the cleanliness of our communities, these kinds of laws are invented; in order to do our part as responsible dog owners and citizens, we must abide by these clean-up rules. While persons who live in the country have more gripes with these laws, city dwellers fully understand the need to observe these ordinances. Scoops are sold in pet shops, or you can employ simple plastic bags. It is assured that if you are the person walking behind the behind of a 250-pound pooch, you will be grateful for these laws. Some owners use brown paper sheets or newspapers (preferably yesterday's) to assist in the clean-up.

Anti-cruelty laws are geared towards the protection of animals on the whole, sparing dogs from potential, often unintentional, abuse. Laws such as these are sweeping the nations, as an increasing number of people become aware of deleterious situations arising for all animals. While active cruelty to an animal

evokes rage in any human being, there are more subtle displays of cruelty which these laws attempt to pinpoint—cruelty in the form of neglect and careless treatment. Persons who are found in violation of anti-cruelty laws are very often subject to fines. All citizens are encouraged to report any cases of cruelty which they witness or suspect to be happening. Commonly, ordinances prohibit the keeping of a dog in a parked car, which can be a cruel, irresponsible practice in most situations. Dogs have been known to suffer from heat prostration, and worse.

Anti-cruelty laws have also seeped into the world of puppy mills, as more and more of these

175

Dogs and the Law

unethical outfits are being undermined by concerned owners. The cruel treatment of animals in these farms must be combated by increased legislation. Always know the source of your potential new dog. Avoid sellers who cannot give you all the answers you want to know.

As heart-breaking and unimaginable as it seems, our dogs are not permitted in a great number of places. "No Dog" signs are frequently posted in buildings,

parks, restaurants, motels, etc. It seems that dogs are more accepted in Continental countries, where dogs are permitted (even invited) to dine with the family at a fine restaurant. This not being the case in every American state or city of Great Britain, law-abiding citizens must contend with these restrictions.

Ordinances involving the number of dogs which an owner can keep are prevalent in most communities. These laws vary from place to place and from residency to residency. Whether you live in an apartment, condominium, house, or farm, there may be laws regulating the number of pets you are able to keep. Homes that wish to keep more than the maximum number of animals may be forced to apply for a kennel license or be subject to a daily fine and regular inspection.

For sake of neighbors and the general health of your family, it is wise to take these restrictions to heart. No matter how great your love of animals is, it is not humane to the animals involved to subject them to over-crowding and minimal attention. A small suburban apartment can quickly become the haven of 75 stray dogs and cats, should the owner so choose. Laws such as these prohibit these kinds of communes from blossoming all over the nation.

In most well-organized communities, there are organizations that specialize in Lost and Found dogs. For your dog's safety, you must have the dog licensed and vaccinated, as dogs that are protected in this way have a greater chance of finding their way back home, unscathed. If you have lost your dog, do not panic, but do work fast. The more people to whom you speak and angles that you take, the greater your chances of retrieving your lost pet. All local authorities (police, fire company, animal control organizations) and all types of media organizations (radio, newspapers, town crier) should be commissioned to lend a hand, keep out a keen eye and ear for the lost dog. Advertising through posters, newspapers, radio, and community lists will pay off in the end. Written descriptions, accompanied by photographs, can assist in helping people have a better mental image of the dog.

Prevention can never be overstressed. Licensing is a must, and the dog must wear the ID tag. Tattoos are quick becoming very popular. These should be located on the dog's inner thigh, not on its ear, as that appendage can easily be torn off by a thief. Tattoos have

worked for generations on pack dogs, and the same philosophy of identification can work for pet owners too. Often, the dog's kennel club number or other identifying number is tattooed onto the dog.

Impoundment threatens lost dogs and all other dogs running at large, particularly those without collars and licenses. Most animal control authorities maintain the right to impound, sell, and/or destroy any animal that they catch. As an owner's legal property, a dog cannot be impounded or confiscated without the owner's notice. Of course, if the dog is loose and unidentified, the owner is knowingly waiving his rights, and thereby his chances of seeing that the dog has a fair chance to find its way home. A dog that proves itself a nuisance or dangerous to property and people may be confiscated; the owner may be notified ex post facto. An owner may then be invited to court to defend its dog's right to life.

Pounds, as a rule, are required

to keep a dog for a certain period of time before disposing of it in any permanent way. However, this period rarely exceeds four days in length, so owners must act expediently. The fortunate owner who does find his dog at the pound must have the dog vaccinated and licensed (if not done previously), as well as pay a fine. Unclaimed pets are either destroyed humanely or offered for adoption. Many pounds reserve the right to have the owner spay or neuter his unchained canine.

There are also laws that regard the disposal of a dog's remains. Owners must be aware of restrictions in this area. Under certain legislative bodies, a person is not allowed to bury his dog on his own property. In most cases, contacting your family veterinarian or a humane society to handle the details of burial is the most expeditious approach.

DOGS AS PROPERTY

Let there be no doubt about it: a dog is the personal property of its owner. This fact is well substantiated in the various legal codes and statutes under which we all live our daily lives. For dog owners, the dog's legal-property status can be considered a mixed blessing. On the one hand, the dog's legal status as property necessarily guarantees the owner certain rights under the law, the very same rights which pertain to the possession of other property. Homeowners especially should be familiar with some of these rights. On the other hand, the dog's status as legal property places very considerable responsibility on the shoulders of the dog owner, for he will be held legally accountable for the actions of his dog—

just as the homeowner is legally responsible for any injuries that occur on his property and are the result of, for example, negligence resulting from the owner's maintenance of the property.

For the dog owner to be entitled to the rights of a property owner pertinent to his dog, the dog in question must be licensed by the appropriate authorities, usually the local governing body. However, because of the nature of legal systems in most of the free countries, laws may vary from town to town, county to county, and state to state. Thus the owner is strongly encouraged to investigate the necessary requirements for licensing his dog. At the same time, the owner is encouraged to ascertain the exact nature of the rights of a dog owner under the given laws applicable to the given place of residence.

This varying nature of laws makes it impossible for one to offer details on many of the rights and responsibilities of the dog owner. However, regardless of the place of residence, the dog owner is entitled to due process with regard to the taking of the licensed dog. Due process in this regard refers essentially to the necessary notification of the owner before any further action can be taken by the authorities. In

this way, the owner is offered a chance to act on the behalf of his dog, his legal property.

An additional consequence of the legal-property status of the dog is that, as property, the dog cannot be considered a person under the law. One effect of this fact is that the dog therefore cannot be the beneficiary of a will; however, provisions for the care and continued maintenance of the dog can be, and should be, carefully spelled out in the will— just as it would be for the home or any other piece of property.

In summary, the dog is definitely considered property under the law. As such, the dog owner is entitled to given rights and held accountable for given responsibilities. To be granted these rights, the dog owner must license his dog, as well as follow any other guidelines required under the laws of his or her place of residence. Finally, as property, the dog cannot be considered a person, and this fact holds various implications.

Because the dog is the legal property of the dog owner, the dog owner is legally responsible for the behavior of his dog, as well as for the care and maintenance of the animal. However, when the dog is in the possession of a person other than the owner, such as a temporary caretaker, that other person may be held responsible for the dog, depending on the specific circumstances involved

and the specific laws of the jurisdiction in which the action(s) occurs. To offer an example, consider the following scenario: A dog is owned by Mr. Smith, who leaves on vacation and hires an individual to care for his dog. While Mr. Smith is on vacation, the dog caretaker walks the dog without a leash and the dog bites a child. Of course, because the dog is property and not person, someone must be held accountable. Should it be Mr. Smith or the caretaker? In such a case it is likely that the caretaker would be held accountable for the dog's biting of the child, provided of course that Mr. Smith did not leave directions to walk the dog without a leash, etc. As we can

Dogs and the Law

see, many variables can come into play regarding legal responsibility for the dog.

To keep it simple in an attempt to offer the reader as much information as possible without getting weighed down in extraneous details, a few general guidelines will be presented.

First, the dog owner, for all intents and purposes, should raise, train, and keep his dog under the assumption that he is legally responsible for every action and for the entire well-being of his dog, ranging from obeying pooper-scooper laws to anti-cruelty laws to dog-bite statutes. In this way, the owner will act as

responsibly as possible and, in the end, avoid possible law suits. Secondly, whenever leaving the dog in the custody of others, whether for a short time or a prolonged period, the dog owner should leave clear, explicit written directions regarding proper and appropriate care of the dog. These directions can be prepared ahead of time and kept on file by the owner for use whenever the need arises. In so doing, the owner protects himself in the case of a lawsuit. Thirdly, a minor can be held legally responsible for the dog as property, and this fact needs to be considered whenever a youngster is in charge of the

dog. Lastly, the dog owner must familiarize himself with the laws that pertain to him as a dog owner, as a resident of his given community. In no other way can the dog owner act responsibly and thus be protected under the law.

Because the dog owner is legally responsible for his dog, he is liable for all damages and personal injuries that result from the dog. Under strict liability, the owner is liable for any damages or injury caused by the dog, even if they are not the "fault" of the owner. Of course, common law doctrines are the products of court decisions, and thus may vary from place to place. Additionally,

liability may be subject to the same circumstantial variables as those which apply to responsibility in general.

Because the owner is liable for the actions of his dog, he can be taken to court and sued. A person injured by a dog will likely receive reimbursement for all medical expenses, as well as a given sum for pain and suffering, depending on the circumstances. The same conditions apply to damages: a person can receive full reimbursement for the loss or damage of any property that was the product of the dog's actions. In serious cases, e.g., those involving blatant negligence, malice or forethought,

Dogs and the Law

the owner of the dog can be sentenced to prison and/or fined.

The subject of vicious dogs abounds in controversy, in part because of the lack of an all-encompassing definition of viciousness as it pertains to the dog and in part because there is a current trend to label entire breeds of dog as inherently vicious. Because of the controversial nature of the vicious-dog subject, the reader is encouraged to do two things: first, read up on the specific laws pertaining to canine viciousness that apply to his locale; and second, to employ utmost common sense in the execution of his dog-owning responsibilities. The first step is by far the easier of the two, for vicious-dog statutes can be found in most libraries and at many municipal buildings. Beginning with inquiries and following up with research ensures the dog owner expedient acquisition of the applicable laws regarding viciousness and his dog. The second step, regarding the application of common sense to all aspects of canine ownership, requires that the dog owner first obey all laws pertinent to his ownership, e.g., leash laws, proper training, housing, restriction, etc.; second be well aware and understand the nature of his charge and adjust its keeping accordingly; and lastly take all steps necessary to ensure that others who may care for the dog be explicitly instructed on how to execute their caretaker task.

By following the two-step process just described to help you guard against a potential vicious-dog law suit, especially in following the application of common sense to your dog ownership, you to a large degree also work to prevent injury, both to yourself and to others. In so doing, you are also necessarily limiting the possibility that you will find yourself beside your dog in court over your dog's injuring another person.

To assist the dog owner in applying common sense to his dog ownership, the following principles are presented: (1) all dogs, meaning each and every dog, no matter how small or large a dog, young or old a dog, has the potential to injure a person; (2) dogs act largely on instinct and perceive the world much differently than people do, i.e., a dog may see a situation as dangerous and react with fear biting even though a person sees the situation as perfectly non-threatening or even pleasant; (3) not all people are dog fanciers, and some people even delight in provoking and taunting an animal, which can easily lead to their being injured; (4) dogs do not treat all people in the same manner as they treat you, their owner and caretaker.

By considering these principles, obeying the laws of dog ownership (which essentially are designed for the protection of you, your dog, and others), and consis-

tently applying common sense in your daily doggie doings, you by and large prevent injury.

In recent years, insurance companies have offered insurance policies to dog owners. Essentially these policies can be grouped into two general categories: canine life insurance and liability insurance. Of course, many different policies from each category are offered, and the cost of the respective policy varies roughly in accordance with the coverage offered. For example, a "life" insurance policy that covered accidental injury as well as providing a death benefit will typically cost more than a policy that offers only a death benefit, provided of course that the death benefits are of equivalent value.

Canine insurance is not for every dog owner, though every dog owner is encouraged to investigate the various policies offered and for themselves make the determination of whether yea or nay they purchase such insurance. Common consensus offers that canine insurance is best suited for two kinds of dog owners, a splitting that roughly corresponds to the two kinds of canine insurance offered. The first kind of owner is the professional breeder

Dogs and the Law

and/or showperson, who has invested large sums of money in his individual dogs and stands to lose much in the case of accidental injury or death. Such a person is strongly encouraged to investigate the canine life insurance available. In short, he is encouraged to protect his investment. The second type of person is the owner of a guard dog or any dog trained or demonstrating the proclivity to attack a person. For this dog owner, investigation of some type of liability insurance is encouraged.

After all is said and done, after all steps and measures towards responsible lawful ownership have been taken, there may still come a

time when the dog owner finds himself in the midst of a controversy. The cause may be a very simple or insignificant one, or it may be a very complex one. The important point to remember is that a controversy must be managed in a legal and responsible way.

If the controversy is a minor one, it might be best to attempt to resolve the the problem between the two parties, in which case a third party (an objective mediator) often proves helpful. If this fails for any reason, e.g., tempers, then going to the authorities is strongly recommended. In no case should anyone attempt to take matters into their own hands, becoming

judge, jury, and executioner all in one. If the controversy involves a serious matter, you are encouraged to seek legal advice as soon as possible. Remember that you are responsible for the actions of your dog, and therefore you can be held liable for any damages or injuries that your dog may inflict. All controversies should be approached in an objective manner; the dog owner must realize that there are at least two sides to the story and that resolution of the conflict will likely involve at least small compromises from each of the parties involved.

CRUELTY

What determines or defines cruelty to animals often excites great controversy in our society.

Anti-cruelty legislation, nonetheless, continues to make headway, as new laws are being enforced with regularity. Avoiding the inhumane treatment of animals, neglect and abuse should be the target of all caring dog owners. The conditions of a breeding facility or animal shelter, cosmetic alterations of puppies (cropping ears and docking tails), protocol for dealing with an injured animal, and impoundment of lost, vicious or destructive dogs are just some of the topics which anti-cruelty laws address. In the United States, ear cropping and tail docking are not prohibited as they are in Great Britain. Britain has for generations deemed such cosmetic alterations unnecessary and unnecessarily cruel.

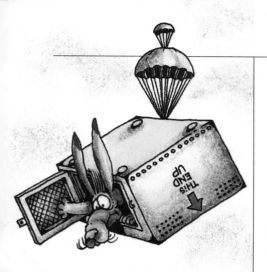

TRAVEL

When traveling with your dog, there are a number of considerations with which to be concerned. The most common method of travel is automobiles, though fewer laws address this mode of transportation. Regarding urban travel, i.e., buses, subways, rails, dogs are usually not permitted on board unless the dog is an assistance dog. Some railways allow dogs to stay in the owner's cabin, while others require that the dog be kept in the baggage compartment (likely there is an area especially equipped for live cargo). Always check with the railway and train station about the regulations regarding your dog. Do this before leaving home! If you intend to travel by sea, less common in today's world of airplanes, it is advised that similar inquiries be made to the ship's station.

Air travel can be a more difficult matter. Airlines most usually allow dogs to fly on their flights. Small dogs can be carried on, while large ones need to be kept in the baggage area. Of course the appropriate crate is required for any dog traveling by air. Mark the crate: "Live Cargo" or "This End Up" for the safety of your canine luggage. Travel agents are usually well informed and will advise you on such decisions.

LANDLORDS AND DOGS

Regardless of how it may seem, there is no *natural* antipathy between landlords and dogs. Dogs in themselves are no more the natural enemy of landlords